GEOGRAPHIES FOR ADVANCED STUDY

EDITED BY PROFESSOR S. H. BEAVER, M.A.

URBAN ESSAYS

STUDIES IN THE GEOGRAPHY OF WALES

GEOGRAPHIES FOR ADVANCED STUDY

Edited by Professor S. H. Beaver, M.A., F.R.G.S.

Human Geography
Geography of Population
Urban Geography
Urban Essays—Studies in the Geography of Wales
Statistical Methods and the Geographer
Geomorphology
Central Europe
Eastern Europe
A Regional Geography of Europe
An Historical Geography of Western Europe before 1800
The Western Mediterranean World
The British Isles—A Geographic and Economic Survey
The Scandinavian World
The Soviet Union
The Polar World
North America
The Tropical World
West Africa
An Historical Geography of South Africa
Malaya, Indonesia, Borneo and the Philippines
Land, People and Economy in Malaya

URBAN ESSAYS

Studies in the Geography of Wales

BY

M. Carter, M.A. AND **W. K. D. Davies, B.Sc., Ph.D.**

*Gregynog Professor of
Human Geography
at the University College of
Wales, Aberystwyth*

*Lecturer in Geography
at University College,
Swansea*

LONGMAN

LONGMAN GROUP LIMITED
LONDON

*Associated companies, branches and representatives
throughout the world*

© LONGMAN GROUP LTD 1970

First published 1970

SBN 582 48153 8

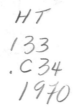
Printed by Spottiswoode, Ballantyne and Co Ltd
London and Colchester

This volume of essays is dedicated to

EMERITUS PROFESSOR E. G. BOWEN
*Gregynog Professor of Geography and Anthropology
at the University College of Wales, Aberystwyth
1946–1968*

with the affection and respect
of all the contributors

PREFACE

Geographers working in Wales have always shown a considerable interest in urban areas. Although H. J. Fleure, the first holder of a Chair of Geography in Wales is best remembered for founding a tradition of work in rural communities, he also published a series of stimulating articles on the comparative morphology of European towns,[1] while W. Fogg was one of the first to deal with urban origins in North Africa[2]. Moreover, the present holder of the Gregynog Chair of Human Geography in Aberystwyth, Professor E. G. Bowen, to whom this volume is respectfully dedicated, recently chose the town of Carmarthen as the topic of his Presidential Address to the Cambrian Archaeological Society (1967). But it is to Harold Carter, however, that all the contributors to this volume owe their greatest debt. For the last seventeen years he has guided, with infinite good humour and patience, hundreds of Aberystwyth students in the preparation of undergraduate and graduate dissertations, while his own studies have borne fruit in his recent book *The Towns of Wales*.[3] In this book Carter aimed at presenting 'an analytical account of the towns of Wales from a geographical standpoint, rather than to derive, from consideration of what can only be a limited number of towns, principles which in themselves will further advance the specialist study of Urban Geography'.[4] It is this alternative objective, the development of the specialist study of Urban Geography that provides the basic motivation for this collection of essays.

Although the contributors to this volume are scattered throughout British universities teaching Urban and Social Geography all, except one, studied for higher degrees at Aberystwyth. But the connecting link provided by their place of study does not mean that the work carried out represents part of a coherent research project on Welsh towns. Each presents an independent piece of work, some derived from graduate dissertations completed during the last four years (Chapters 3, 6, 7, 9 and 10), others representing current research interests. Given the objective of this collection the heterogeneity of topic is, however, inevitable and it would seem rather pointless to try rigidly to integrate these studies. Yet the essays in this book are not as disparate as might be imagined at first, for four broad themes can be distinguished (the study of morphology, social areas, small towns and central places) whilst their relationship to the wider field of Urban Geography is provided by Chapter One.

A more important point of contrast concerns the wide range of technical competence between each essay. Given the time period over which these studies were planned and executed, a period moreover in which Geography experienced a quantitative revolution,[5] this again would seem inevitable. Thus, all of the studies, with the exception of the social area analysis (Chapters 5 and 6) and one of two sections in other chapters, were carried out without the benefit of high speed electronic data processing equipment, and this has limited their range. As the book is not intended to represent a high water mark in quantitative techniques this again is not considered to be too much of a drawback. Instead the book is directed towards a more complete understanding of certain aspects of the Welsh urban scene by the provision of a set of empirical essays.[6] These studies will, it is to be hoped, be of interest to other people, especially planners who are professionally interested in the spatial relationships of urban areas. Thus, at the very least each essay provides a background study of a particular area, though most contributors have attempted to emphasise this potential by briefly sketching in the relevance of the study to certain planning problems. Yet although these essays are all concerned with Welsh towns and therefore have particularistic relevance, it is the generality of these studies that is considered to be of greatest importance; they have a far wider relevance than the Principality. The ideas, techniques, and even the conclusions of the various contributors relate ultimately to the wider field of Urban Geography. Wales simply represents the laboratory[7] in which the various contributors have worked and developed their interests.

One final theme that links together many of the essays in the collection lies in the profound concern with the level of factual information available for Welsh, or for that matter British, towns. Published sources of information are often inadequate as Chapter 3 (Sub-Standard Housing in Wales) in particular, demonstrates. Here a long exploratory investigation into data sources is necessary before the information can be used geographically. In any case most published data is usually aggregated on the basis of administrative units, an artificial partitioning of space that bears little relevance to the present day activities of the majority of people. Hence it is difficult to derive any meaningful conclusions about the real units of society, and a great deal of potentially valuable information is lost. In the last few years, however, census data have been provided for small units and without access to this enumeration district data the social area analysis of Chapters 5 and 6 would not have been possible. But these developments do not go far enough, there is a great need for information to be presented on some more flexible spatial basis, such as the grid co-ordinate system used in Sweden.[8] Advances in the presentation of existing data would, perhaps, lead to more detailed and worthwhile studies, but even this is not enough. Many geographical studies, in particular those concerned with the functional organisation of places (for instance central place studies), require data on the pattern of commercial activities in any area as well as journey to ship movements. At present fieldwork is the only way for geographers to obtain such data, a process of data collection that is both expensive and extremely time consuming. Small wonder that the central place studies in this volume rely on information that is rather dated and is concerned with relatively small areas, for it has been collected by one person. It forces us to rely on surrogates for the statistics we really require and leaves unanswered many of the main problems of our fundamental task, the analysis of the spatial characteristics of our communities.

The duties of editing this collection of essays have been shared with Prof. Harold Carter, M.A., Prof of Geog. at Aberystwyth who is currently Visiting Professor of Geography at the University of Cincinnati, Ohio, U.S.A. Thanks must be extended to him for his invaluable advice and experience, as well as to all the contributors, in particular, Mr. C. Roy Lewis, who have stoically borne my often abrasive and intemperate attitude towards datelines. Finally a word of special appreciation must be given to Mr. Morris Cutler of the University of Nottingham and Mr. G. B. Lewis of the University College of Swansea, who drew the maps in this book, and Mrs C. Everett of Bridgend, who typed many of the Chapters from a set of roughly drafted manuscripts.

W. K. D. DAVIES

Swansea, December 1967

REFERENCES

1. FLEURE, H. J. (*a*) 'Cities of the Po Basin: An introductory study', *Geographical Review*, **14**, 1924, p. 345. (*b*) 'Some types of cities in temperate Europe', *Geographical Review*, **10** 1920, p. 357–374 (*c*) 'The

historic city in western and central Europe', *Bulletin of John Rylands Library*, Manchester, **20** (1936).

2. FOGG, W., 'Villages, tribal markets and towns: Some consideration of urban development in the Spanish and international zones of Morocco', *Sociological Review*, **23**, Nos. 1 & 2, 1940.

3. CARTER, H., *The Towns of Wales*, University of Wales Press, Cardiff, 1965.

4. *Ibid*, p. xvi.

5. A good indication of current work in geography is provided by HAGGETT, P., *Locational Analysis in Human Geography*, Arnold, London, 1965.

6. Several other geographical studies dealing with certain aspects of Welsh towns were not completed in time to be included in this volume. In particular: ROWLEY, G., 'Middle Order Towns in Wales.' Unpublished Ph.D. dissertation, University of Wales (Aberystwyth), 1967. HUMPHREYS, G., Unpublished Ph.D. dissertation, University of Wales (Swansea), 1967
GANT, R. L., 'Low Order Communities on Severnside.' Ph.D. Dissertation (in progress), University of Wales (Aberystwyth), 1968.

7. BUNGE, W., *Theoretical Geography*, Gleerups, Lund, 1962, p. 13.

8. See HÄGERSTRAND T., 'On the Monte Carlo simulation of diffusion' in GARRISON W. and MARBLE D., *Quantitative Geography: Part One Economic and Cultural Topics*, North Western Studies in Geography, Evanston, Illinois, 1967.

CONTENTS

MAPS AND DIAGRAMS

Note

Figure 3.1 is derived from Ordnance Survey 10 miles to 1 inch map of Administrative Areas. Coast outline on Figs. 7.1 and 7.4 from Ordnance Survey as are the outlines and contours on Figs. 7.5 and 7.7.

CHAPTER 1

APPROACHES TO URBAN GEOGRAPHY: AN OVERVIEW

Wayne K. D. Davies

Increasingly the world is urban orientated. No significant aspect of our society, however remote from the physical presence of towns, is untouched by urban life and the organisation and control focused there. Accelerating technological change has also led to wide-spread and still largely uncontrolled changes in the urban settlements themselves, and in doing so has raised considerable problems. In some places, especially the large metropolitan centres, such changes have reached crisis proportions. Newspapers are full of reports of traffic congestion, pollution, blighted areas and ghettos—all of them not remote problems, but characteristic of even the most prosperous of our cities. Elsewhere the changing economic prosperity of regions has left a decaying heritage of towns; a series of settlements struggling to survive in the new organisational and economic environment dominated by large metropolitan centres.

Given the scale and ubiquity of these problems it is not surprising that people have tried to build up an adequate framework of knowledge of urban areas in order to make it easier to control, or even to conquer, these urban problems. At first, interested parties worked within their own academic specialisms, creating distinct fields of interest within the larger body of work. Increasingly, however, the interdisciplinary nature of the field excited interest and led, if not to integrated enquiries, with each specialist contributing his own expertise, at least to formal discussion of the problems involved,[1] as well as to the setting up of urban research institutes. These developments have been particularly well expressed in the United States, where perhaps the crisis of cities is more readily apparent. Practically all major universities now have their own centre for urban studies, whilst most disciplines engaged in the study of the city have attempted to bring together the diverse strands of their enquiries in order to develop a framework for future enquiry.

Geography has not been left out in these developments, for its students have contributed substantially to the general body of knowledge on urban areas. But the role and importance of urban geography transcends the volume of its published literature. Its exponents, by their development of new techniques, their methodological and indeed practical orientation, have been to the fore in revolutionising the whole field of human geography over the past ten years. But not all geographers have accepted the new principles; older attitudes and opinions survive, inevitably creating a considerable degree of confusion to an outsider enquiring as to the aims and purpose of urban geography. Such a situation is not unique to geography, it is also characteristic of other urban specialisms. Thus Lampard observed that 'appropriate boundaries for urban history today are perhaps more difficult to define than those of the city itself',[2] whilst Sjoberg has recently identified eight major schools of thought in urban sociology.[3] It is the object of this chapter to try to clarify some of the confusion that exists in the field of urban geography by demonstrating the common principles that give it a separate identity. Inevitably the scheme developed has some similarities to Foley's[4] scheme for the analysis of metropolitan spatial structure—after all, the concern with spatial differences is basic to both approaches. But it must be stressed that this scheme was developed independently of Foley's analysis, and does seem far broader in scope and comprehensiveness.

The distinctiveness of urban geography from other urban specialisms stems from the spatial viewpoint that is both the hallmark and *raison d'être* of all geography.[5] In dealing with urbanism the urban geographer stresses the spatial arrangements and distributions that he finds, and identifies the spatial organisations and processes that operate in his search for spatial differentiation and spatial integration. Inevitably there is overlap with other disciplines, for they are dealing with the same phenomena, but spatial differences are not the primary motive for study, they are the by-products of some other organisational scheme.

In their studies, urban geographers have utilised both major approaches to description, namely the empirical and the theoretical. Within the empirical side it is customary, and indeed important, to distinguish between the idiographic and nomothetic approach.[6] The former, which has had a long history in geographic research, is devoted towards the characterisation of individual events and situations. Expressed in an urban geographic framework it leads to the belief that urban phenomena, by reason of a uniqueness stemming primarily from a unique location, must be the subject of an individual study. Though not all studies were expressed in such a framework it is probably best seen in the site and situation analyses that were popular forty years ago. The approach survives, and is perpetuated by the mistaken belief of other urban scholars that this is the peculiar 'geographic' contribution to urban studies,[7] as well as by the individualist descriptions of towns given in many regional textbooks. Yet as Lukermann has recently shown,[8] geographers, even in the nineteenth century, attempted to develop more than a catalogue of the individual locational characteristics of urban places and searched for generalisations about the spatial characteristics of towns. In the development of these generalisations, and the elucidation of general principles that may be regarded as social science laws, individual facts were not considered to be important for themselves. They possessed usefulness only in so far as they contributed toward generalisations. It is this nomothetic approach which provides the methodological basis for most urban geography research at the present time.

Although significant generalisations about the spatial characteristics of towns have been developed by the empiricists, this essentially inductive approach was rejected at an early date by a small number of far-sighted geographers. They approached the problem of description of urban phenomena in another way. By theorising about spatial distributions they were able to construct elementary models of the spatial characteristics of urban places that would either be used in a teaching capacity to develop understanding of the system, or would be treated against reality. The most monumental of these works, the central place scheme of Walter Christaller,[9] developed over thirty years ago, was misinterpreted for a long time because the true relevance of a theoretical construction was misunderstood in geographical circles.[10] The rapprochement with the methods and techniques of modern science that has taken place within the last ten years[11] has given Christaller's scheme the credit it deserves, in general method if not in logical construction. Moreover, the stimulus of these theoretical developments has meant that the most important research frontier in urban geography today is concerned with the development and testing of models. The impact of these developments (the theorising, model building and attendant quantification) upon other urban scholars has been quite remarkable. It is, in fact, fast developing into the status of a peculiar contribution to urban studies that is associated primarily with geographers, in the same way that fieldwork and the analysis of site and situation features were considered to be particularly 'geographical' contributions in previous years.

In view of these ranges of methodological orientations, all of them possible within the broad concern for spatial variations, it is not surprising that the published reviews of the field are contradictory or descriptive of seemingly different fields. In part the situation is due to two different methods of review, those dealing with the historical development of the field as a distinct interest,[12] and those dealing with the present content of the study.[13] Moreover, the latter studies can themselves be subdivided into those identifying the major themes of study,[14] those attempting to interlink all aspects of study by means of some diagrammatic classification,[15] and those dealing with the research frontier as presently conceived.[16] Yet whatever organisational basis is used, it must be stressed that all are empirical descriptions of work that has actually been carried out. As all reviewers must be selective, it is inevitable that the material chosen for attention will be affected by the level of perception of the reviewer, and this depends notoriously upon motivation and training.[17] In the light of such considerations, and given the whole range of urban phenomena and methodological orientation, it is not surprising that no clearcut and coherent statement of purpose has been derived.

The attempt to found a satisfactory rationale, or even to weld a complete identity of interest for urban geographers will never, it is believed, be successful if reference is made only to the empirical descriptions of its past and current literature. However unbiased the reviewer, divergent ranges of interest will always stand out in contradiction to his major theme. Only by delving into the theoretical basis of this knowledge, and proceeding one step beyond the development sketched out in the previous paragraphs will a satisfactory statement be obtained. This necessitates the development of a conceptual model for urban geography.

It must be counted as rather surprising that conceptual models have not been the subject of more explicit comment in the geographical literature. Despite the considerable interest in models among urban geographers,[18] and the reference to the basic role of the conceptual model in all organised knowledge by Chorley,[19] few significant attempts to deal with this kind of model have been made by geographers. As the author agrees with McEwan that 'all scientific enquiry requires a conceptual framework for identifying and classifying the relevant observational data which the investigator can use to construct theoretical frameworks of verifiable substantive hypotheses',[20] this lack of interest is considered to be an important omission. Here only a few significant characteristics of these models are emphasised in view of their apparently unfamiliar nature.

Though the conceptual model has priority over the theoretical framework, it must be stressed that it can only be developed after considerable exploratory work in the field has been undertaken. The need for this model is only felt when a considerable body of given facts and regularities has to be explained, and when the original knowledge has to be extended or linked with previously disparate bodies of knowledge. This would seem particularly relevant to urban geography where, in Black's words, 'a need is felt for further scientific mastery of the original domain'.[21]

The model does not need to be constructed, only its components need to be described, for it is only a system of coordinated definitions justified by its fruitfulness in organising data. In other words it is a tentative system of working ideas that can be amended at will. Its usefulness lies in 'so organising the observational data that all channels of inquiry which bear on the problematic situation are kept open'.[22] Hence the difference between a theory and a conceptual model, as Zetterberg[23] has shown, is that the theory, a system of definitions and hypotheses, is capable of empirical verification. A conceptual model is an organisational tool.

The value of conceptual models must not be underestimated, for all research requires such a framework for ordering data into a meaningful system, and for getting to the heart of a problem without starting afresh each time. Thus, as Bonner has observed in the field of social psychology, 'without a conceptual scheme research becomes mere fact grubbing, without any discernible pattern or design'.[24] It is to the detailed elaboration of a conceptual model that can be applied to urban geography that we must now turn. Figure 1.1 represents a

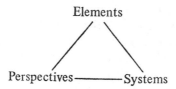

Fig. 1.1. The major components of a conceptual model

simple paradigm of the three major components of this model, the constituent elements, the array of perspectives used to view these elements and the system of urbanism to which these can be applied. Though they are considered separately in the ensuing discussion, and examples of particular geographical investigations are used to illuminate the sections, the essential interlinking of these components should always be kept in mind.

THE ELEMENTS

Every urban system is composed of four basic elements: *environment*, *population, functional activities and morphology*. Though the discussion below shows that each is capable of further subdivision, it makes no claim to be definitive. The object is simply to indicate the range of variation within each type. The classification of elements adopted here is similar to the ecological elements proposed by Duncan[25] and extended by Gist and Fava.[26] Environment and population cover all Duncan's characteristics, but morphology is, rather surprisingly, not considered separately. Duncan treats it only as a manifestation of the organisation of society. In view of the need to consider the physical as well as the social complexity of the city, and the long tradition of geographic research into the morphological characteristics of cities, it achieves the status of a distinct element in our scheme. Also the term 'functional activities' is substituted for organisation. 'Organisation' implies that only the operation of a unit is dealt with, while it tends to get confused with one of the spatial perspectives described below. Finally, Gist and Fava's additional element, 'the social-psychological', is not considered to be distinctive enough to warrant a special category. It is included in the 'population' element, for the preferences and beliefs of the population contribute as much to the differentiation of area as age or sex differences.

Environment

All urban places or urban influences possess a set of locational attributes. It is the composite of these attributes that comprises the 'environmental' element. To the more obvious subdivisions such as relief, climate, natural resources, flora and fauna, must be added the spatial dimensions of the urban place or influence, as well as natural disasters and those geological changes that have had such a profound effect on cities.

Forty years ago, discussion of this group of elements tended to dominate geographical studies. Thus Blanchard, in his classic study of Grenoble, considered 'the basic concept of this study is to explain the origin and development of the town as a function of the physical conditions of its situation',[27] and in his conclusion maintained that 'in spite of human changes nature always asserts its rights, even on an organism as complex as a town'.[28] Inevitably other urban specialists looked on this sort of study as a peculiar 'geographic' contribution to the study of towns. Such untenable environmental explanations have been swept away in geography, though studies of the characteristics, site and situation remain as part of the field of urban geography. However, many of the lines of enquiry into the relationships between towns and their physical environment have been preempted by other specialists. Archaeologists deal with the environmental factors inhibiting or stimulating the initial developments of urbanism,[29] while the study of urban climates remains firmly in the field of climatology.[30]

Population

It is not only the size of population that is considered under this general heading. The composition and characteristics of the population must also be taken into account, ranging from age and sex differences to the whole range of social and economic differences. Special mention must be made of the incorporation of individual and societal preferences into this category. They are as important as any sex or economic category in the differentiation of urban space.

Functional activities[31]

Every person living in an urban area, as well as those outside, indulges in a series of activities, social, economic and political, that have their location in, or have connections with, urban areas. Though the total pattern of these activities may appear chaotic, they are in fact highly organised. A total activity system for the city and the area around emerges from this element, as well as the more traditional internal land use categorisation in terms of residential, recreational, industrial, commercial and institutional uses.

Morphology

This is the structural and visible skeleton of the town, the manmade fibre in which the urban population carry on their activities. Though detailed subdivisions can be made of individual components, it is useful to distinguish between the plan, the two dimensional feature, and the buildings, which provide a third dimension.

Nothing distinctly geographical is claimed for these elements, they are the common property of all urban disciplines. In the past, individual disciplines did concentrate upon particular elements. For instance, the geographer dealt with environmental factors; the study of population was shared by the demographer and the sociologist; economic activity systems were the province of the economist, while morphology was the concern of the architect, planner and the geographer. Today, no such precise relationship exists between the object of study and an academic discipline. Scientists today do not claim distinctiveness for their discipline by the phenomena they study, rather it is by their integrating concepts and perspectives that a particular field of study is carved out,[32] though one phenomenon may well have an overriding significance. Hence, geographers today do not express their concern for particular phenomena but search for the spatial differentiation and spatial integrations of these elements.

THE PERSPECTIVES

Three distinct perspectives on the spatial variation of the elements distinguished above have been employed in geographic research.[33] The first, the study of static structures, is by far the most significant to date in terms of volume of literature. Now, increasing attention is being paid to the other two perspectives, the study of the connectivity of the parts of a system and the study of the dynamic processes that are involved.

Static structure

This is concerned with the distribution of those characteristics that were grouped into four elements in the previous section, whether they be single attributes such as one building type, or any combination of features. The end product of this sort of study is usually some attempt at the regionalisation of space. By dealing with the association of elements in space, distinctive areas can be distinguished. In this way, and at many different levels of technical complexity, uniform social areas, or land use regions or morphological regions have been derived.[34]

If the internal patterning of space is disregarded and the content of space is looked at as a unit, rather than as an area, a different result is achieved. Then the status of each unit can be derived. An example may serve to clarify this distinction. The distribution of individual shop types in any town can be distinguished as well as the distribution of distinctive clusters of shops (shopping areas). Once the total functional composition of these clusters is measured, the functional status of that place will be derived and comparison with other units can be made.[35]

Though the distribution and association of elements remains the primary purpose of this type of analysis, attempts are usually made to account for the spatial variations. Hence explanation rather than description remains the objective.

Connectivity of the parts

The operation and survival of cities cannot be understood without knowledge of their organisational features and the spatial connectivity of their component elements. (In this context connectivity refers not to the causal or casual associations between parts of the system, but to the flow of goods, people, messages and ideas.) These flows can be looked at on a series of organisational levels: from individual activity,[36] whether it be firm, institution, household or person, to individual activity agent; from individual to area; or even from area to area. Many of the flows have a temporal sequence as well as a spatial dimension and this adds to the complexity of analysis. Thus it is difficult to treat journey to shop movements in the same way as journey to work movements. The latter, at least for most individuals, have a fairly regular diurnal pattern and destination, whereas journey to shop movements vary in frequency and in significance in terms of money spent, as well as in direction.

Geographers have been especially aware[37] of the need to study the spheres of influence of cities, and a considerable literature testifies to this.[38] In their search for spatial ordering, a great deal of use has been made of nodal regions.[39] The identity of a nodal region stems not from the formal homogeneity of other regions but from the influence emanating from a central point. As this influence or flow usually declines with distance from the centre the areal coherence is gradually dissipated.

So far the discussion about the connectivity between parts of the urban system has been phrased in terms of two elements, population and functional activities. The other two elements, environment and morphology, do not seem to possess the regular organisational functioning demanded by this perspective, except of course in the plant and animal kingdoms. As they are static at any one point in time, any change represents a change in type. However, the essential backcloth, or even barrier, to the connectivity of population or functional activities provided by these two elements must be stressed. Steep slopes or rivers hinder communication between parts of a city whilst we do not have to look far to see how the morphological pattern of cities designed for a horse and cart age hinders traffic flows based on the car.

Dynamic process

Though the study of temporal changes is a familiar and important line of enquiry in urban geography, the study is not yet sufficiently organised to merit the title of dynamic process. To understand why, we must digress from our general exposition of the differences between these perspectives and show how temporal changes have been described.

Two distinct lines of temporal enquiry appear in the literature. The first consists of the reconstruction at several dates of a set of static structures. Once the differences between these reconstructions are described, inferences are made about the factors conditioning the changes.[40] The alternative approach derives from the work of a group of urban ecologists based in Chicago in the 1920s.[41] A set of ecological principles or processes were developed—concentration, centralisation, segregation, invasion and succession, dominance, and finally interdependence, though routinisation has been added by Breese.[42] These processes describe quite well the result of the spatial direction of change or the organisational trend, and have an important place in geographical literature. But concern with the resultant spatial displacement is not a process in the strict sense of the term, it is merely the spatial result of a process. A true process explanation would require full knowledge of all the variables that affect each element as well as the extent of their interconnection and the forces leading to change. Hence an empirical study attaining the title 'dynamic process' would need the detailed description of the unfolding of the changes that have occurred,[43] together with an explanation phrased in terms of the value systems of society, as well as all the relevant decisions taken. Given such rigorous demands, few works measure up to the standard, and in view of the complexity of the real world this is hardly surprising. Recently, attempts have been made to approximate these developments by means of simulation techniques.[44] A few significant factors are used to construct a probability surface and Monte Carlo methods are used to derive distributions. The object of these techniques is not to imitate rigidly the changes in any spatial pattern; this is considered to be impossible in view of all the isolated chance decisions that have been made. In Morrill's words 'in general, we wish a simulation to be enough like the real world that both could have been produced from the same process'.[45]

THE URBAN SYSTEMS

Now that two of the components of our conceptual model, a set of constituent elements and an array of perspectives, have been isolated, it is necessary to turn to the third and last component. This involves the definition of the urban system in which the elements operate and to which the various perspectives can be applied. Four distinct systems of study can be regarded, though inevitably overlap occurs between them. The first is concerned with the spatial aspects of urbanisation, the second with the city conceived as one unit amongst many units, the third deals with the areal influence of cities (the effect that cities have on the area around them) the fourth with the city as an area. Each of these systems of study are looked at in turn, together with examples of the sort of work that has been, or can be carried out.

Urbanisation as a societal process: spatial aspects

Concern with the role of the city in society has been a major interest throughout recorded history. But since city, state and civilisation were virtually identical concepts throughout much of the period from Ancient Greece to the Renaissance, it is difficult to argue for any distinct urban role as part of a system of society, though Sjoberg's[46] classic comparative study has attempted to deal with this problem in a sociological context, and has provided some geographical generalisations in the process.

The study of the city *vis-à-vis* the society in which it exists, is, however, crucial to the understanding of the other three systems of study, providing an economic, technological, political and even a philosophical[47] frame of reference. This is as true for the geographer as for any other urban specialist, for until the role of the city within society is appreciated, then particular spatial characteristics seem to bear little relevance. One example may serve to clarify this point. If a comparison has to be made between the workplace–residence patterns of cities in different parts of the world and at various times in the past, a spatial analysis would be meaningless until these patterns were related to the changes that occurred between preindustrial and industrial societies. Instead of a close-knit household carrying on all the production and distribution functions under one roof, the specialisation of society led to the spatial separation of these functions and hence the appearance of journey to work as a major diurnal flow within the city.

With one or two exceptions, the work of Berry[48] and Murphey[49] forming notable examples, geographers have not concerned themselves with these problems, though the knowledge of the type of society existing at any place forms an essential backcloth to all investigators. The only sphere in which a great deal of effort and interest has been expended has been in the definition of 'urban' and the study of the degree of urbanisation and the growth of urbanisation in the world.[50] Both aspects have, of course, been dealt with by other scholars. Indeed Lampard[51] has made a special plea for the urban historian to concentrate on the growth and distribution of the urban population in space. Yet this concern with population size and economic or legal definitions, should not obscure the fact that the dominance of urban centres in society is probably only appreciated in terms of functional organisation. The city, as communication specialists like Meier[52] have rightly pointed out, should be regarded as a communication node, not just a settlement pattern.

Of more recent interest than the spatial variation in the accumulation of population into cities has been the attempt by several geographers to study the correlates of urbanism. These range from industrialisation and economic development[53] to the association between invention, innovation and certain large cities.[54] Quite clearly the spatial patterns revealed emphasise the differential roles that cities play in the various countries of the world.

The city as a unit within sets of units

This broad area of study has one coherent theme, the need to identify the character of one city as opposed to all other places. One or several of the component urban elements is measured, and the result is compared with measurements derived from other cities. Hence the spatial variation within centres is ignored, it is the variations between cities that is the dominating feature of this enquiry. The best known lines of this enquiry are those studies that attempt to derive an economic classification of cities,[55] and the central place studies that classify each centre according to its functional size.[56]

The areal influence of cities

In previous centuries the city could be regarded as a separate settlement type with an independent existence of its own. Certainly the surrounding rural areas used the city as a focal place for a variety of purposes, but today cities have a far more intimate relationship with their hinterlands. Not only have the connections between cities and between country and city intensified,[57] but the urban areas have spawned a whole series of structures in the surrounding area[58] ranging from the houses of commuters to cemeteries and waterworks. Moreover, the environmental background of the surrounding area has often been drastically altered.[59] Usually this alteration is regarded as wholly undesirable. In fact the influence of the city can be partially preservationist (note the 'Green Belts' round some British towns) or can improve the economic basis of the hinterland by providing either a market for agricultural goods,[60] or a source of fertiliser in undeveloped lands (e.g. night soil).[61] Again, however, such urban influences are usually dealt with in another field of geography.

Frequently it is difficult to separate this category from the study of the city as a unit. Classification of cities as rural service centres depends on measurement of the areal influence of these cities. In a sense this integration of the two approaches does not matter, though experience has shown it as a useful preliminary to keep the two categories somewhat apart. This avoids confusion between the two issues. Thus attempts have been made to study the rural service function of cities by reference to a direct count of all the functions present in these places, ignoring the fact that many of the functions serve the town population as well.[62]

The city as an area

It is the intra-urban spatial variations that provide the prime focus of this system of study. Individual elements, or any combination of elements are analysed in the search for the internal structure or the internal functioning of urban areas. Although attention is focused upon internal spatial variations, this line of enquiry is not restricted to idiographic analysis. Inductively derived generalisations of the internal pattern of cities, or parts of cities, abound in the literature,[63] whilst theoretically derived models of city structure are also used extensively by geographers, even though the best known of these schemes have considerable limitations.[64]

Critics of the scheme developed in this chapter will point out that the range of material covered is so vast that most of the field of human geography can be accommodated under the four systems of study. This is not a new problem, it is inevitable given the powerful influence of cities in our society. Thus, Aurousseau drew attention to the enormity of the subject matter as far back as 1924 in probably the first review of the field of urban geography.[65] Given the size of the field it might be suggested that there is scope for limitation by differentiating between 'urban geography' and the 'geography of towns'. Under the latter, features such as the climatology of urban areas can be happily accommodated. In other words, any geographical aspect of towns may be considered, whereas 'urban geography' represents the specialist set of studies developed by like-minded scholars whose primary concern is with the town and its spatial characteristics, not with a particular phenomenon, whether it is climate or physiography. Certainly urban geography does seem a distinct field if one looks at the general volume of literature and at the content of its specialist conferences. Thus it is the economic role of cities and their spheres of interest, together with the analysis of internal structures, social, morphological and functional, that have received the most attention. Given the expansion of interest in urban areas, this distinction, tenuous at the best of times because it is affected by the changing attitudes towards themes of study, is likely to become redundant. Hence to restrict the term 'urban geography' to its major current field of operations seems an unwarranted circumscription that would be resented by most scholars.

It is also inevitable, given the great interest in urbanism, that other disciplines impinge on the broad systems of study we have outlined. Since there cannot be any one exclusive disciplinary understanding of urbanism as a phenomenon, these overlaps are to be welcomed. They provide an occasion for the airing of often divergent views, and may increase the understanding of an aspect of towns that is causing a problem to one set of specialists. In any case each individual discipline is likely to become less and less distinctive as time goes on, as one moves from description, which is highly coloured by the disciplinary perspective chosen, towards explanation. Thus the complex of factors that created any urban phenomenon will be the same however one approaches the phenomenon. It is the particular causes that are selected and the stress that is placed on one or the other that lends distinctiveness to particular fields, though it must be stressed that they are dealing with selected aspects of a larger whole. A simple example may serve to clarify this point. Suppose a particular house type in a town was the object of analysis. The sociologist would probably be more concerned with the occupants, but might deal with the type as a symbol of the role of its occupants in society; the economist would be concerned with the prices and land values of the properties; the engineer with their construction problems; the architect would ascribe some aesthetic value to the buildings *per se* and deal with the factors accounting for this particular form; whilst the geographer would be concerned with the regional distribution of the type and the factors that cause this type to vary from surrounding houses. Any complete causal explanation would have to deal with all these aspects of analysis for they are all interlinked, yet each discipline can be seen to deal with different aspects of the whole, particularly when description alone suffices.

Certainly geographers today would not feel themselves bound to studies of site and situation and outlines of the general morphology, the factors that Sir John Summerson[66] would expect them to provide. Most of the causal principles that he mentions in his survey of two suburban areas in London would be dealt with by geographers since they account for the differentiation of space. If these principles were not investigated geography would be merely descriptive. Tunnard[67] has come to a similar conclusion in relation to his own discipline, city planning, for unless motivation is applied to the existing pattern, 'topography alone would suffice'—an equally unattractive role for geographers or city planners. Hence it is inevitable, and proper, that the urban specialisms overlap and perhaps deal with similar causal factors. If they did not, there would really be room for concern. Certainly there is more than enough work to be carried out if we are to understand the complexity that constitutes urban areas and influences.

This review would not be complete without some indication of the way in which the other essays in this book fit into the conceptual model that has been developed. Not only will this provide a working demonstration of the usefulness of the model; it will also provide an introduction to the admittedly heterogeneous set of specific studies that follow and will show how each study relates to the broad field of urban geography.

3

Chapter 2, in more ways than one, provides an introduction to one of the basic features of twentieth-century society, namely the increasing connectivity between the parts of any urban system, and covers the first three systems of urban study. Using two parameters derived from the functional activities of the population, the essay provides two case studies of the interrelationships between the settlements of Wales, and uses the information to suggest a more rational administrative grouping in the Swansea area. One of the same systems of study, namely the relative composition of one unit within a set of units, provides the motivation for Chapter 3. In this case it is the spatial variation in housing quality, an often neglected morphological variable, that provides the object of study. Inevitably, in view of the scale of this study, only a static structure interpretation can be provided, though the description is set against the backcloth of a functional classification of Welsh towns.

Chapter 4 provides another example of a morphological study, but deals specifically with one town. In an attempt to get away from the traditional idiographic description the essay is phrased in decision-making terminology, thereby focusing upon the generality of the process of development rather than the specific morphological characteristics.

Chapters 5 and 6 continue this concern with the 'town as area', but take as their primary element the social characteristics of three Welsh towns. A rather sophisticated classification of the spatial variation in these social characteristics is presented by both essays. However, it must be noted that although both studies represent examples of the static structure perspective, they have rather different objectives. Whilst Chapter 5 attempts to correlate two independent analyses of Cardiff and Swansea, Chapter 6 broadens the social area classification and provides a spatial description of social disorganisation in Barry.

Chapter 7 represents a return to the study of the areal influence of cities and towns, demonstrating, by reference to several variables, the changing nature of small communities around Aberystwyth. The elements used in this study of structural change include aspects of the social and demographic characteristics of communities as well as certain functional activities.

Chapter 8 continues this study of Mid-Wales but looks at the problem from the other way round, dealing with the structural characteristics of Aberaeron, a small town just south of Aberystwyth. In view of the limited number of comparable studies available in the area, it is inevitable that this chapter is largely an idiographic description of certain social and economic characteristics, but it demonstrates the raw material of which generalisations may be built.

Chapters 9 and 10 are both concerned with the classification of the commercial status of a set of settlements in dissimilar areas. However, the need for an integrated approach to the study of central places, incorporating both morphological variables and dealing with the decimal functioning and long term changes in the system provides the basic motivation for Chapter 9. Chapter 10 continues this theme in a problem rural area and provides a useful basis for any future reorganisation of the functional pattern. Finally, Chapter 11 summarises some of the existing urban problems in Wales and stresses the recurrent theme that emerges from these rather dissimilar essays, namely the need to treat the towns of Wales as a network, as an integrated whole. Only in this way will the problems of their parts be satisfactorily solved.

REFERENCES

1. HAUSER, P. M. and SCHNORE, L. F., eds., *The Study of Urbanization*, Wiley, 1965, p. 554.

2. LAMPARD, E. E., 'Urbanization and social change: On broadening the scope and relevance of urban history', in Handlin, O. and Burchard, J., *The Historian and the City*, Cambridge, Mass., M.I.T. Press, 1963, p. 226.

3. SJOBERG, G., 'Theory and research in urban sociology', in Hauser and Schnore, *op. cit.*, Ch. 5, pp. 157–89.

4. FOLEY, D. L., 'An approach to metropolitan spatial structure', in Webber, M. M. *et al.*, *Explorations into Urban Structure*, Univ. of Pennsylvania Press, 1964.

5. (*a*) NATIONAL ACADEMY OF SCIENCES, *The Science of Geography*. Report of *ad hoc* Committee on Geography, Earth Sciences Division, National Research Council, Publ. No. 1277. Washington D.C., 1965; (*b*) BERRY, B. J. L., 'Approaches to regional geography: a synthesis', *Ann. Ass. Am. Geogr.*, **54**, 1964, p. 2.

6. SIDDALL, W. R., 'Two kinds of geography', guest editorial, *Econ. Geogr.* **37**, 1961, p. 188.

7. SUMMERSON, J., 'Urban forms', in Handlin, O., and Burchard, J., *op. cit.*, Ch. 5, p. 165.

8. LUKERMANN, F., 'Empirical expression of nodality and hierarchy in a circulation manifold', *East Lakes Geographer*, 2, 1960, pp. 17–44.

9. CHRISTALLER, W., *Die Zentralen Orte in Suddeutschland*, Jena, 1933.

10. DICKINSON, R. E., *City, Region and Regionalism*, Routledge & Kegan Paul, 1947, pp. 31–2.
Dickinson concentrates upon the empirical evidence for Christaller's scheme and largely ignores the limiting assumptions imposed by the theory.

11. DAVIES, W. K. D., 'Theory, Science and Geography', *Tijdschr. econ. soc. Geogr.*, 57, 1966, pp. 125–31.

12. LUKERMANN, F., *East Lakes Geographer*, 1960, pp. 17–43.

13. CARTER, H., 'Introduction: Urban geography', unpublished discussion paper, University College of Wales, Aberystwyth, 1967.

14. (*a*) DICKINSON, R. E., 'The scope and status of urban geography: an assessment', *Land Econ.*, 24, 1948, pp. 221–38; (*b*) MAYER, H. M., 'A survey of urban geography', in Hauser and Schnore, *op. cit.*, Ch. 3, pp. 81–113.

15. (*a*) THORPE, D., 'The geographer and urban studies', *Department of Geography, University of Durham, Occasional Paper Series No. 8*, 1966; (*b*) CARTER, H., *The Towns of Wales*. Cardiff, University of Wales Press, 1965, p. xvii.

16. BERRY, B. J. L., 'Research frontiers in urban geography', in Hauser and Schnore, *op. cit.*, Ch. 11, p. 399.

17. BERGMAN, G., *Philosophy of Science*. University of Wisconsin Press, 1958, p. 20.

18. (*a*) BERRY, B. J. L., *op. cit.*; (*b*) CHORLEY, R. and HAGGETT, P., *Models in Geography*, E. Arnold, 1967.

19. CHORLEY, R. J., 'Geography and analogue theory', *Ann. Ass. Am. Geogr.*, 54, 1964, pp. 127–37.

20. MCEWAN, W. P., *The Problem of Social-Scientific Knowledge*. Totowa, N.J., Bedminster Press, 1963, p. 134.

21. BLACK, M., *Models and Metaphors*. Cornell University Press, 1962, p. 230.

22. MCEWAN, W. P., *The Problem of Social-Scientific Knowledge*, p. 134.

23. ZETTERBERG, H. L., *On Theory and Verification in Sociology*, 3rd edn., Bedminster Press, 1965.

24. BONNER, H., *Social Psychology: an interdisciplinary approach*, American Book Co., 1953, p. 36.

25. DUNCAN, O. D., 'Human ecology and population studies', in Hauser, P. M. and Duncan, O. D., eds., *The Study of Population*, University of Chicago Press, 1959, p. 681.

26. GIST, N. P. and FAVA, S. F., *Urban Society*, 5th edn, New York, Cromwell Co., 1964, p. 101.

27. BLANCHARD, P., *Grenoble. Étudie de Geographie Urbaine*, Paris, 1911, p. 5.

28. *Ibid.*, p. 159.

29. BRAIDWOOD, R. J. and WILLEY, G. R., *Courses Toward Urban Life*, Edinburgh University Press, 1962.

30. CHANDLER, T. S., *The Climate of London*, London University Press, Hutchinson, 1965.

31. A more extensive typology of these activities is provided by CHAPIN, F. S., *Urban Land Use Planning*, University of Illinois Press, 1965, p. 226.

32. BERRY, B. J. L., *Ann. Ass. Am. Geogr.* 1964, p. 2.

33. *Ibid.*, p. 10.

34. HERBERT, D. T., 'The use of diagnostic variables in the analysis of urban studies', *Tijdschr. econ. soc. Geogr.*, **58**, 1967, pp. 5–10.

35. DAVIES, W. K. D., 'The ranking of service centres: a critical review', *Trans. Inst. Brit. Geogr.* **40**, 1966, pp. 51–65.

36. CHAPIN, F. S., *Urban Land Use Planning*, p. 226.

37. Other urban specialists recognise the importance of the Geographers' contribution to this line of enquiry, c.g. BRIGGS, A., *Victorian Cities*, Odhams Press, 1963, p. 49.

38. (*a*) BERRY, B. J. L. and PRED, A., *Centre Place Studies: a bibliography*; (*b*) BARNUM, H. G., KASPERSON, R. and KIUCHI, S., *Central Place Studies: a supplement to 1964*, Regional Science Research Institute Publications, Bibliography Series No. 1, Philadelphia, U.S.A., 1961 and 1965.

39. BUNGE, W., *Theoretical Geography*, Lund Studies in Geography, Series C, No. 1. Gleerup, Lund, Sweden, 1962, p. 24.

40. Most studies of urban areas use this approach, e.g. CARTER, H., *The Towns of Wales*.

41. PARK, R. E., BURGESS, E. W. and M-KENZIE, R. D., *The City*, University of Chicago Press, 1925.

42. BREESE, G., *Urbanization in Newly Developing Countries*, Prentice Hall, 1966, p. 114.

43. Two examples of the detailed study of the process of change, though without a complete interpretive discussion would be: (*a*) CONZEN, M. R. G., 'The plan analysis of an English city centre', in K. Norberg, ed., *I.G.U. Symposium in Urban Geography*, Lund, 1960, pp. 383–414; (*b*) DAVIES, W. K. D., GIGGS, J. A. and HERBERT, D. T., 'The use of rate books and directories in studies of the commercial structure of towns', *Geography*, **53**, 1968, pp. 41–54.

44. MORRILL, R. L., 'Expansion of the urban fringe: a simulation experiment', *Pap. reg. Sci. Ass.*, **15**, 1965, pp. 185–99.

45. *Ibid.*, p. 197.

46. SJOBERG, G., *The Preindustrial City*, Free Press of Glencoe, 1960.

47. A considerable literature on the idea of the city in intellectual thought has recently developed. This has considerable background value for geographers: (*a*) 'The City in the History of Ideas', in Handlin and Burchard, *The Historian and the City*, pp. 84–132; (*b*) LYNCH, K., *Images of the City*, Harvard University Press, 1960.

48. BERRY, B. J. L., 'Urban growth and economic development of Ashanti', in Pitts, F. R., ed., *Urban Systems and Economic Development*, School of Business Administration, University of Oregon, 1962.

49. MURPHEY, R., 'The city as a centre of change: Western Europe and China', *Ann. Ass. Amer. Geogr.*, **43**, 1954, pp. 349–62.

50. (*a*) DAVIS, K., 'The urbanization of the human population', *Scientific American*, **213**, 1965, pp. 41–53; (*b*) LAW, C. M., 'The growth of urban population in England and Wales 1801–1911', *Trans. Inst Br. Geogr.*, **41**, 1967, pp. 125–44.

51. LAMPARD, E., 'Urbanization and social change' (see note 2), p. 238.

52. MEIER, R. L., *A Communications Theory of Urban Growth*, Massachusetts Institute of Technology Press, 1962.

53. (*a*) GINSBURG, N. S., *Atlas of Economic Development*, University of Chicago Press, 1961; (*b*) BERRY, B. J. L., 'City size distributions and economic development', *Econ. Dev. and Cultural Change*, **9**, 1961, pp. 573–88.

54. PRED, A., 'Some locational relationships between industrial inventions, innovations and urban growth', *East Lakes Geographer*, **2**, 1966, pp. 45–70.

55. SMITH, R. H. T., 'Method and purpose in functional town classifications', *Ann. Ass. Am. Geogr.*, **55**, 1965, pp. 539–48.

56. DAVIES, W. K. D., *Trans. Inst. Br. Geogr.*, 1967.

57. PRED, A., 'The external relations of cities during the industrial revolution', *University of Chicago, Research Papers in Geography*, No. 76, 1962.

58. A general discussion of the transition zone is provided by MURPHY, R. E., *The American City: An Urban Geography*, McGraw-Hill, 1966, pp. 35–49.

59. WHITE, G. F., 'Changes in urban occupance of flood plains in the United States', *University of Chicago Research Papers in Geography, No. 57*, 1958.

60. CHISHOLM, M., *Rural Settlement and Land Use*, Hutchinson's University Library, 1963.

61. JONES, C. F. and DARKENWALD, G. G., *Economic Geography*, rev. edn., McGraw-Hill, 1954.

62. DAVIES, W. K. D., *Trans. Inst. Br. Geogr.*, 1966.

63. MURPHY, R. E. and VANCE, J. E. jnr., 'A comparative study of nine central business districts', *Econ. Geogr.*, **30**, 1954, pp. 301–36.

64. A useful review of these studies is presented by ALONSO, W., 'The historic and the structural theories of urban form', *Land Econ.*, **40**, 1964, pp. 227–31.

65. AUROUSSEAU, M., 'Recent contributions to urban geography: a review', *Geogr. Rev.*, **14**, 1924, p. 444.

66. SUMMERSON, J., in Handlin and Burchard, *The Historian and the City*, p. 165.

67. TUNNARD, C., 'The customary and the characteristic: a note on the pursuit of city planning history,' in Handlin and Burchard, *The Historian and the City*, p. 219.

CHAPTER 2

REGIONAL STRUCTURES IN WALES:
TWO STUDIES OF CONNECTIVITY

Wayne K. D. Davies and C. Roy Lewis

Urban research workers usually consider that the urbanisation process can take place in two ways, either by the creation of more and more urban units, or by the increasing size of the units.[1] Throughout most of recorded history the first of these processes provided the main component of urban growth. Today it is the latter process, the increasing size of urban areas, that dominates the urban growth process, though one must add the qualification that not all urban areas are growing. It is essentially the largest centres, the metropolitan areas that are growing apace and creating problems of urban sprawl.[2]

This interpretation of urban growth is, however, an extremely limited way of assessing the urbanisation process. By dealing only with the physical patterns of growth it grossly underestimates the true role of the large unit in our society. Indeed, it is not only the increasing size of urban areas, remarkable though this is, that is the significant feature of modern economic and social life; rather it is the 'mobility, fluidity, interconnectedness and interpenetration'[3] of many of our activities, characteristics that apply to all movements, whether they are flows of goods, people or information. These movements do not, however, take place in a vacuum, they are focused on the larger urban units. Given this sort of perspective, it is probably more valuable at this point in time to view urbanisation not as a process of settlement, but to adopt Meier's viewpoint[4] and look at urbanisation as a process of communication. This is the process by which more and more people not only live in urban areas, but have increasing contacts with other urban places, and whose life is affected by diurnal pressures and influences emanating from the larger settlements. Once this attitude is adopted it is apparent that a concept such as the rural–urban dichotomy[5] possesses increasingly little relevance for the vast majority of population. Rurality as such has largely vanished, leaving only an occupational heritage. Now the significant partitioning of space lies in the interchanges between places, especially the larger population concentrations. This demonstrates the need for a study of the functional organisation of areas, not just their static structures.[6]

Individual affluence, combined with the increasing mobility of the population, both on an economic and recreational plane, has meant that the frictions imposed by distance have diminished. Operationally this provides increasing opportunity for behavioural spatial anarchy, a situation in which the interconnections between places are characterised by amorphous and chaotic sets of flows. However, most empirical studies of the functional organisation of space have shown that regular patterns can be distinguished, though these patterns are rather different from the ones established in the past.[7] Instead of sets of largely independent towns and areas controlling their immediate environs, with only nominal connections with the larger places, interdependence upon a vast scale has developed. The new mobility has lubricated our social and economic life and reorganised it upon a larger scale with an ever increasing centralisation on the larger cities.[8]

Most of the literature dealing with the geographical structure of Wales has failed to take into account the spatial flows between urban places; it has concentrated on the static structures that exist.[9] Even the extensive literature on the trade areas of towns tends to focus on the patterns of individual towns rather than building up the total pattern of movement of an area into an integrated whole. It is the object of this essay to redress this balance and to use two different parameters to deal with these interchanges. In this way the functional organisation of Wales will be exposed, in the first case by using telephone calls as a measure of the information flow between places, in the second case by using data drawn from a study of shopping habits in the Greater Swansea Area. Conceptually, the studies may be regarded as complementary, though they differ in scale, the first isolating the regional structure of Wales, the other providing a more detailed study of the areal functional organisation around the second largest city in Wales. Operationally, however, a word of warning must be introduced. It is difficult to correlate rigidly the two scales of study, not because of the different parameters used as measurements, but because of the arbitrary areal basis upon which the information on telephones was originally compiled by the General Post Office.

THE NODAL STRUCTURE OF WALES

Urban geographers have developed an extensive body of theory and techniques in their studies of the spheres of influence of towns.[10] Although they were among the first to recognise that the importance of cities transcended the area they occupied, it must be accepted that the majority of these studies have been carried out at the lower end of the urban hierarchy, the data sources and techniques being rarely suitable for the integrated study of large areas or large places.[11]

Accurate and up to date information on the economic and social movements of the Welsh population is hard to obtain. Published sources of information do not exist, except for the journey to work data provided by the decennial census, and as this is compiled on an almost meaningless net of administrative areas it has limited value. Hence workers have used secondary information, or parameters that are the by-product of spatial flows, data such as newspaper circulations[12] or bus services[13] in their search for the important nodal points in our society. The former still provides a useful first approximation for higher order community of interest areas but is subject to all the problems of single element criterion. The bus service index fails to deal with the pattern of more than local connectivity, and inevitably provides a rather dated information source in a period of increasing personal mobility.[14] Ideally, of course, one would like data on the spatial behaviour of the Welsh population, data compiled for a variety of activities in the same way that surveys of the Iowa population were carried out.[15] From such data the whole range of spatial interaction and the degree of dominance of urban places could be ascertained. However, there is little likelihood of this information being available in the foreseeable future. We must depend, for our analyses of functional organisation, on very limited information sources, and inevitably the conclusions we reach are going to be biased by the inadequacy of our data.

The only data source available at present with any degree of reliability, objectivity and accessibility is the number of telephone calls that are made between areas in Wales. As a statistical source illustrating the connectivity in any region telephone call data have been used by many workers in different parts of the world.[16] Certainly there are problems with its use, for the source fails to deal with the 'information content'[17] of calls, and only really covers the transfer of information between the higher paid social groups and certain economic activities.

However, as a measure of 'information exchange' it seems to be the only reliable data source open to us at this point in time.

The actual data input used in the analysis[18] was obtained from a survey of telephone traffic undertaken by the General Post Office in 1958, prior to the introduction of Subscriber Trunk Dialling (S.T.D.). This survey isolated the number of calls from each telephone charging unit to all other units that were not adjacent areas. Hence all 'trunk' or long distance calls were used in the analysis. The local calls that have their origin and destination within the same or adjacent charging unit areas could not be studied because the information was not recorded by the survey. Yet such a restricted data source is not as bad as one might expect. As the majority of calls that are made in any area terminate in the area, restriction of our analysis to trunk calls means that only the long distance flows are analysed. In other words we will be dealing with only the higher order connectivity between places so that our analysis will not be swamped by the multitude of local calls.

A graph theory analytical technique similar to that used by Nystuen and Dacey[19] in their study of Washington State was applied to the data. Flows to and from ninety-nine charging unit areas formed the basic input data, covering all Wales and the Welsh borderland together with the regional capitals outside Wales, namely Liverpool, Manchester, Birmingham, Bristol and London (Fig. 2.1). Although a more detailed areal breakdown would have been more useful,[20] the fact that the pattern of telephone exchange areas is one based primarily on the

TABLE 2.1. *Hypothetical matrix of connectivity* (7 region example)

		To regions A–G						
		A	B	C	D	E	F	G
From regions A–G	A	—	40	7	3	1	3	6
	B	35	—	8	6	2	2	2
	C	2	5	—	20	15	15	18
	D	3	7	30	—	3	3	4
	E	2	6	15	20	—	3	1
	F	4	5	15	19	2	—	3
	G	4	7	25	12	2	3	—
	Total	50	70	100	80	25	29	34
	Rank	4	3	1	2	7	6	5

Numbers in italics represent the largest outflow from each region.

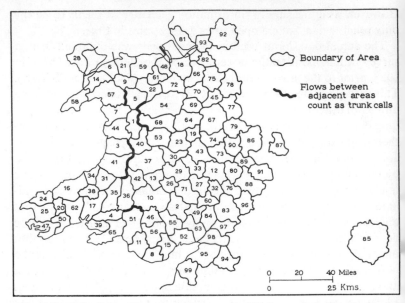

Fig. 2.1. Telephone charging unit areas in Wales and the Borderland.

Index to charging units:

1. Aberangell
2. Abergavenny
3. Aberystwyth
4. Ammanford
5. Bala
6. Bangor
7. Barmouth
8. Barry
9. Betws-y-coed
10. Brecon
11. Bridgend
12. Bromyard
13. Builth Wells
14. Caernarvon
15. Cardiff
16. Cardigan
17. Carmarthen
18. Chester
19. Church Stretton
20. Clynderwen
21. Colwyn Bay
22. Corwen
23. Craven Arms
24. Fishguard
25. Haverfordwest
26. Hay-on-wye
27. Hereford
28. Holyhead
29. Kington
30. Knighton
31. Lampeter
32. Ledbury
33. Leominster
34. Llanarth
35. Llandeilo
36. Llandovery
37. Llandrindod Wells
38. Llandyssul
39. Llanelly
40. Llanidloes
41. Llanon
42. Llanwrtyd Wells
43. Ludlow
44. Machynlleth
45. Market Drayton
46. Merthyr Tydfil
47. Milford Haven
48. Mold
49. Monmouth
50. Narberth
51. Neath
52. Newport
53. Newtown
54. Oswestry
55. Pontypool
56. Pontypridd
57. Portmadoc
58. Pwllheli
59. Rhyl
60. Ross-on-Wye
61. Ruthin
62. St. Clears
63. Shirenewton
64. Shrewsbury
65. Swansea
66. Tarporley
67. Wellington
68. Welshpool
69. Wem
70. Whitchurch
71. Wormbridge
72. Wrexham
73. Bewdley
74. Bridgnorth
75. Crewe
76. Hanley Swan
77. Stafford
78. Stoke on Trent
79. Wolverhampton
80. Worcester
81. Liverpool
82. Northwich
83. Gloucester
84. Lydney
85. London
86. Birmingham
87. Coventry
88. Evesham
89. Redditch
90. Stourbridge
91. Stratford-on-Avon
92. Manchester
93. Warrington
94. Bath
95. Bristol
96. Cheltenham
97. Dursley
98. Rangeworthy
99. Weston-super-Mare

larger places in any area means that the data source provides a crude measure of the flows between urban places and provides us with an approximation to the third type of urbanisation distinguished above. Incorporation of the larger regional capitals outside Wales places the pattern of Welsh connections within their wider spheres of association and avoids any closed system interpretation of connectivity, one of the unrecorded problems of the Nystuen and Dacey analysis.

Table 2.1 provides a simple example of the analytical procedure followed. A 7×7 matrix indicates the connectivity of a hypothetical area, the columns indicating calls received by the charging units, the rows indicating calls transmitted by the centres. Summation of the columns gives the total number of incoming calls for each area and provides a measure of the centrality of the area. The dominant connections between places were isolated by noting the largest outflow from each area. If this connection is to a smaller place, 'small' being determined by the total size of the inflow, the area was considered to be a terminal point on the graph of interconnections. Once these terminal points are mapped, their dependent areas can be linked to them, thereby providing an interpretation of the nodal structure of the area.

It is suggested that this analysis can be taken one stage further by ordering all the units on the basis of their connectivity. All the units are assumed to be first order places, though if any place (e.g. unit B) is the recipient of a flow from at least one other first order place, it is called a second order place. If any place is itself a recipient of a flow from a second order place it is designated a third order place and so on. Figure 2.2b shows the application of these principles to the pattern of connectivity revealed in Fig. 2.2a. A measure of the hierarchical order in any network is derived from this analysis, an order that is similar, but not identical to the patterning of stream order used by Horton.[21] Differences between the two techniques derive from the fact that it is the centres (confluences) that are the object of concern, not the flows (length and number of streams).

Though this simple example demonstrates the logic of the analysis used in isolating the skeleton of regional associations in Wales, it must be stressed that the procedure that was actually followed was more sophisticated. Analysis of the raw data on a 99×99 matrix would only provide information on the direct associations between charging units, whereas it would seem to be important to incorporate those indirect associations that occur, as for instance when telephone calls between places are rerouted through a third centre. In an attempt to incorporate these indirect associations the original 99 × 99 matrix was manipulated by the technique described by Nystuen and Dacey.[22] From the new adjacency matrix, terminal points were isolated and the nodal or dominant flows from each place were mapped. The ordering principle outlined above was applied to the graph of connectivity and the results are shown in Fig. 2.3.

Figure 2.3 confirms that the regional pattern of communication in Wales conforms to a few simple principles. Instead of a series of water-tight functional regions, of the sort derived by Green[23] in his analysis

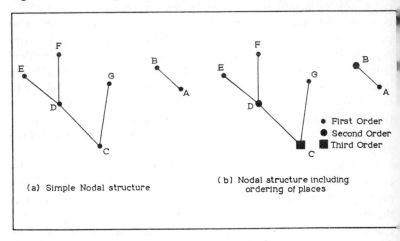

(a) Simple Nodal structure

(b) Nodal structure including ordering of places

Fig. 2.2. The nodal structure of a hypothetical region.

of bus services, an overlapping set of interconnected regions formed the basic regional structure. Although all regions are connected eventually to London the map shows that two major flows exist, one focused on Liverpool in the north, the other focused on Cardiff in the south. In Mid-Wales the pattern is rather more complicated. A considerable area is focused on Aberystwyth, considered to be a terminal point because its dominant connections are with a lower order centre, a finding that demonstrates the isolation of the town. The rest of the area is focused on Shrewsbury and hence Birmingham, or Hereford and then London.

No sign of a uniform hierarchical structure in which regions have their dominant connections with their nearest higher order place is revealed in Fig. 2.3. In part this is due to the limitations of the input data, for flows to adjacent areas are not, except in one or two cases, classed as trunk calls. (This explains anomalies such as the failure of Caernarvon to appear as a second order place, and the presence of Conway and Fishguard in this list of places.) But even where we can discount this factor, the rigid hierarchy is seen to break down and the

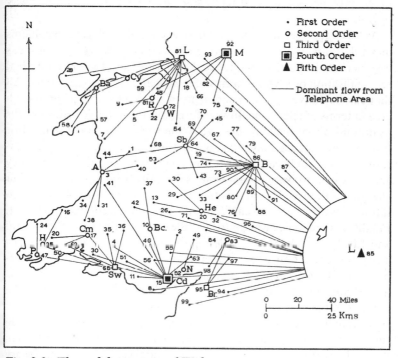

Fig. 2.3. *The nodal structure of Wales.*

Settlements on this figure are indicated as follows:

Ba:	Bangor	A:	Aberystwyth	Cd:	Cardiff
Cy:	Conway	Sb:	Shrewsbury	N:	Newport
L:	Liverpool	B:	Birmingham	Br:	Bristol
M:	Manchester	He:	Hereford	Cm:	Carmarthen
R:	Ruthin	H:	Haverfordwest	L:	London
W:	Wrexham	P:	Pembroke	Sw:	Swansea
		Bc.:	Brecon		

larger places assert their influence. Thus most of Pembrokeshire is orientated directly through Milford Haven and Haverfordwest towards Swansea, not through Carmarthen. Carmarthen is a centre of equivalent rank to Haverfordwest, as Rowley has shown,[24] and is missed out in the pattern of connectivity. Again, Newport is not linked with Cardiff (because of the adjacency problem) but directly to London and not to Bristol. Whether Newport will ever be subjected to the control of Bristol is still a moot point, despite the construction of the Severn Bridge. It may be that the town is large enough to provide a fair range of community services and that people demanding greater range or choice will move directly to London, a mere two hours away by rail.

At this stage it seems important to stress that the adjacency problems mean that it is impossible to group the telephone charging unit areas together on the basis of their nodal structure, and to derive an areal regionalisation of Wales in terms of these patterns of connectivity. All that can be derived is a measurement of the relative ordering of each area in terms of telephone flows. Moreover, this relative ordering tells us nothing about the absolute size of the various orders of place. For instance, Brecon and Newport appear as the same order of communication nodes, not because they are equivalent in size, but because they are equivalent in being nodal centres for calls from at least one other charging unit area. Hence it is the structure of the functional organisation of Wales that is revealed, not the absolute strength of each unit. Finally, a word must be added about the classifications given to Bristol and Liverpool. Their true ordering cannot be ascertained from this analysis because only a few of their dependent trade areas were incorporated into our 99 × 99 matrix. As these places are outside our immediate interest this is not considered to be a drawback to the analysis of the regional structure of Wales.

Although these findings provide an objective justification for those subjective comments made about the pattern of regional connection in Wales, in particular the lack of a single nodal centre,[25] it is necessary to end on a cautionary note. As a data source, telephone flows bias the actual pattern of 'information flows' by dealing essentially with the higher socio-economic groups and all businesses. However, as control of the pattern of movements is vested primarily in these decision-making groups, the index might be said to provide a useful data source on the really significant flows of communication, certainly they are less biased than the bus service analysis. Of more importance to this enquiry, however, is the adjacency problem. Flows to contiguous charging units were not isolated in the G.P.O. survey and this problem is reflected in the regional pattern of nodality shown in Fig. 2.3. Yet used with caution, it does provide a useful first approximation to the problem, and demonstrates the applicability of this sort of analysis to geographical patterns in Wales. Certainly it demonstrates that self-contained watertight nodal areas do not characterise the functional organisation of Wales; there is a considerable degree of interconnection that is characterised by a progressive orientation upon larger and larger units. Although the adjacency problem means that the hierarchical sequence of communication at the lower orders cannot be distinguished, the successive focusing of each place upon even larger places demonstrates that a hierarchical principle of communication to higher order places does operate, revealing not only a considerable degree of uniformity in the regional structure of Wales but also the importance of looking at urbanisation as a communication process.

Now that the nodal structure of Wales has been isolated it is necessary to turn to a detailed study of one area. In view of the sizes of the telephone charging areas, and the adjacency problems outlined above, it is rather pointless to continue to use this information source. Instead information on the functional organisation of the area was derived from a questionnaire survey.

THE GREATER SWANSEA AREA

Functional organisation

Figure 2.4 illustrates the changes that have occurred in the urban pattern of Greater Swansea from 1920 to 1966. Although the detail of this map need not concern us here, it provides a vivid illustration of the fact that it is the increasing size of urban units rather than their duplication that accounts for the accelerating conversion of land to urban uses. Spatially, it is apparent that an imbalance exists in this growth. Indeed, there has been such a concentration upon the coastal belt that the area from Margam to Burry Port is now virtually one continuous urban belt. Hence an east–west orientation is added to the north–south urban corridors established during the Industrial Revolution.[26] As we have seen, the physical coalescence of communities is not the only way in which the urbanisation process operates. One must also consider the scale and scope of economic and social interaction between once separate communities. As it is difficult to establish the degree of change in this interaction, owing to the problem of obtaining information at various times in the past,[27] we must be content with dealing with the present pattern of interaction

A comprehensive survey of the shopping and journey to work habits of all the communities shown in Fig. 2.5 was carried out between 14

4

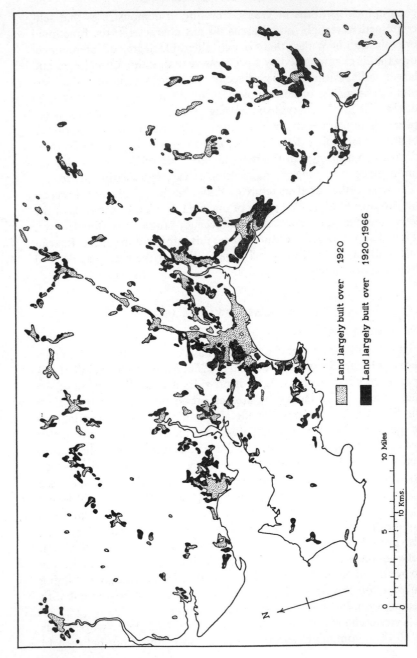

Land largely built over   1920

Land largely built over   1920–1966

Fig. 2.4 Urban growth around Swansea, 1920–1966

TABLE 2.2. *Settlements in survey area*

0. Ferryside	36. Capel Hendre	72. Coelbren
1. Llansaint	37. Tycroes	73. Resolven
2. Kidwelly	38. Ammanford	74. Blaengwrach
3. Trimsarn	39. Llandybie	75. Glyn Neath
4. Pembrey	40. Cwmamman	76. Baglan
5. Burry Port	41. Garnant	77. Port Talbot
6. Pwll	42. Brynamman	78. Margam
7. Llanelli	43. Gwaun-cae-Gurwen	79. Cwmavon
8. Felinfoel	44. Cwmllynfell	80. Pont-rhyd-y-fen
9. Dafen/Cwm	45. Ynyswen	81. Ton Mawr
10. Llwynhendy	46. Abercrave	82. Dyffryn
11. Bynea	47. Upper Cwm Twrch	83. Abercregan
12. Llangennech	48. Lower Cwm Twrch	84. Cymmer
13. Pontardulais	49. Gurnos	85. Glyncorrwg
14. Grovesend	50. Ystradgynlais	86. Abergynfi
15. Pontlliw	51. Ystalyfera	87. Bryn
16. Penllergaer	52. Godre'rgraig	88. Caerau
17. Loughor: Gorseinon	53. Ynysmeudwy	89. Nantffyllon
18. Gowerton	54. Pontardawe	90. Maesteg
19. Porthyrhyd	55. Trebanos	91. Cwmfelin
20. Llanddarog	56. Rhos	92. Llangynyd
21. Crwbin	57. Clydach	93. Pont-rhyd-y-cuff
22. Llangendeirne	58. Glais	94. Pyle and Kenfig Hill
23. Pontantwn	59. Skewen	95. North Cornelly
24. Pontyberem	60. Neath Abbey	96. South Cornelly
25. Pont Henry	61. Rhydding	97. Cefn Cribwr
26. Pont Yates	62. Bryncoch	98. Aberkenfig
27. Five Roads	63. Neath	99. Tondu
28. Llanon	64. Briton Ferry	100. Sarn and Bryncoch
29. Tumble	65. Aberdulais	101. Brynceithin
30. Drefach	66. Tonna	102. Brynmenin
31. Cross Hands	67. Crynant	103. Llangeinor
32. Cefneithin	68. Seven Sisters	104. Bettws
33. Gorslas	69. Tynewydd	105. Pontyrhyl
34. Penygroes	70. Onllwyn	106. Pontycymmer
35. Saron	71. Dyffryn Cellwen	107. Blaengarw

and 17 June 1967. All the settlements from the left bank of the Towy in the west, up to and including the Garw valley in the east were surveyed. The northern boundary of the area ran from just south of Carmarthen and followed the edge of the coalfield towards the east, whilst in the south the western part of the Vale of Glamorgan excluding Porthcawl and Bridgend formed the survey limits. It must be noted that Swansea County Borough and the Gower Peninsula had to be excluded from the survey because of the limited labour force available for this survey.[28]

A total of 3600 questionnaires were completed during the four day survey, giving a coverage of almost 4 per cent of all the households in the area. A cluster sample framework was used to identify the households to be interviewed. In each settlement a central point was chosen (usually the major zone of conflux, the shopping centre) and a set of

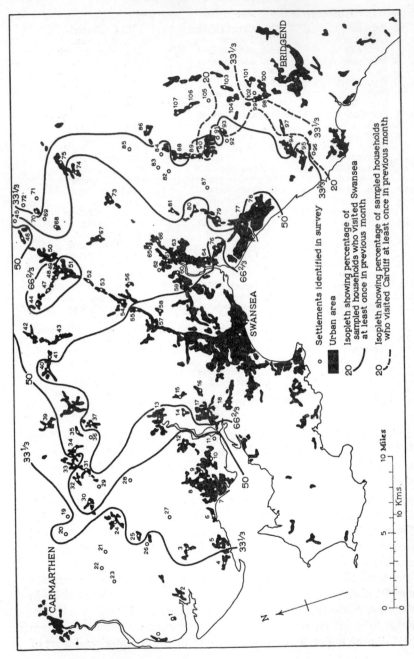

CARMARTHEN

SWANSEA

BRIDGEND

Settlements identified in survey
Urban area
Isopleth showing percentage of
sampled households who visited Swansea
at least once in previous month
Isopleth showing percentage of sampled households
who visited Cardiff at least once in previous month

N

10 Miles
10 Kms.

Fig. 2.5 Settlements around Swansea: frequency of visits to Swansea

randomly located interview points were chosen round this centre. At each point a cluster sample composed of the ten nearest households to this spot was taken. In order to arrive at a uniform coverage for the whole area, the number of cluster samples taken in each settlement varied with the estimated population size. For places with under 100 households at least one cluster sample was normally taken.[29]

The questionnaire was designed to determine the spatial connections of each settlement and the interviewed persons were asked questions about the journey to shop movements of the household.[30] (It was felt that these movements provided the best clue to the community of interest areas.) Despite the difficulty of integrating the different types, intensities and frequency of movements, problems that have been outlined elsewhere,[31] it was decided that the spatial connectivity of each settlement could be determined by calculating the journeys made by the sampled population to the nearest large centres of Swansea, Cardiff, Bristol and London in the previous month, and the journeys made to settlements outside the one they lived in during the two weeks previous to the survey.

Analysis of this data confirmed many of the findings of other surveys. Instead of spatial anarchy in behaviour patterns, a large degree of correspondence existed between the spatial flow of individuals in each settlement. This certainly does not assert that the functional organisation of the survey area, in terms of shopping patterns, was anything like a homogeneous region. Instead, a set of overlapping nodal regions existed, bounded by zones of transition in terms of the direction of spatial flows.

In an attempt to illustrate these connections, in the first instance with reference to Swansea, the percentage number of persons from each settlement who had visited Swansea at least once in the previous month was calculated. A visual portrayal of the variation in these movements is provided by the isopleths in Fig. 2.5. The north–south orientation of the inner zone, in which two-thirds of the sampled population visited Swansea at least once a month, is explained by the presence of large shopping centres to the east and west, namely Port Talbot, Neath and Llanelli. To the north the largest central places such as Ammanford, Ystradgynlais, Ystalyfera and Pontardawe fail to achieve such commercial status and do not act as large alternative magnets. It is this feature, therefore, that accounts for the strong connections between Swansea and the small industrial settlements in the Upper Gwendraeth, Amman, Tawe, Dulais and Neath valleys. In a

British context, it is rather surprising that over half the inhabitants of these settlements travel over fifteen miles to Swansea at least once a month.[32]

To the east the survey area becomes increasingly influenced by Cardiff as the two isopleths showing connections with Cardiff demonstrate (Fig. 2.5). Clearly the zone of overlap between the spheres of influence of Cardiff and Swansea exists in this area, the settlements just north of Bridgend in the lower Llynfi and Ogmore Valleys being more closely connected with Cardiff than Swansea.

The discussion so far has demonstrated the connectivity of each settlement with Cardiff and Swansea. Connections with Bristol (despite the opening of the Severn Bridge) and London proved to be insignificant in this area.[33] Having established these facts the analysis needs to be taken further. Each settlement has connections with other places apart from these four large centres, and it is the extent of these connections that forms the next stage of the discussion.

For each settlement individual travel flows were aggregated, giving the total number of persons who had visited other settlements in the two weeks previous to the survey. Frequency, the number of visits made by each person to the same settlement in the period, was not incorporated into this particular analysis. Once these data were aggregated, the flows from each settlement were ranked according to their size and mapped in Figs. 2.6 and 2.7 as first-, second- and third-ranking flows. In order to eliminate the bias introduced by the size of the sample survey a first- (second) ranking flow was only recognised if there was a difference of 15 per cent from the next largest flow. Otherwise the flow was considered to be shared between the two ranks and mapped accordingly. If a settlement had at least one other settlement dependent on it, it was considered to be a nodal centre. Places shown as probable nodal centres are the places that were the recipients of a shared flow. Finally, a cut-off point of 15 per cent of the total flow was used to eliminate the effects of random movements in the area. Unless a flow from any settlement to another place reached this level it was not mapped.

The close ties between the small settlements on the northern rim of the coalfield and Swansea is again demonstrated in Fig. 2.6. But within the area having close connections with Swansea (Fig. 2.5) it is noticeable that several places act as important nodal centres, namely Llanelli, Ammanford, Neath, Port Talbot and Maesteg, whilst outside the survey area, Carmarthen, Porthcawl and Bridgend also achieve

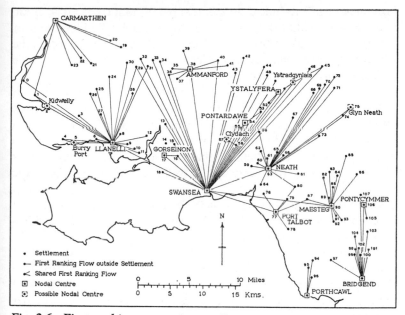

Fig. 2.6. First-ranking connections to Swansea.

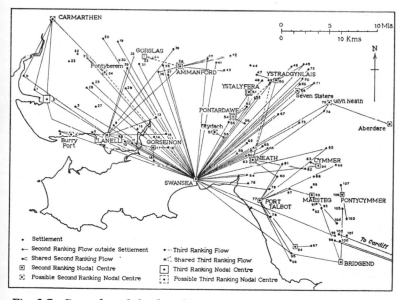

Fig. 2.7. Second- and third-ranking connections in the survey area.

prominence. In a technical sense it is apparent that trade areas of the nodal centres within the survey area 'nest' within the hinterland of the highest order place, Swansea. Moreover, the interdependence of the whole area is demonstrated by the fact that all these nodal places have their first-ranking connections with Swansea.

Figure 2.7 shows the second- and third-ranking connections of each settlement. The most significant feature is the widening influence of Swansea, especially in the west and north-east. To the east this pattern breaks down slightly due to the increasing connectivity of many places with Port Talbot, a settlement that had a very limited first order hinterland, whilst Bridgend and Cardiff increasingly affect the picture.

Given the potential mobility of the population of the area, it must be counted as rather surprising that so few settlements have third-ranking connections. Certainly it must be re-emphasised that the analysis introduced an arbitrary cut-off point. A settlement needs 15 per cent of its interviewed population to make shopping trips to a third place before it would appear in Fig. 2.7. It must be stressed that in the vast majority of cases the third-ranking flow did not attain a size of 5 per cent, the figure 15 per cent was introduced purely to ensure that individual flows from small settlements (in which only one cluster sample was taken) would not distort the general pattern of relationships.

Of the settlements with third-ranking flows the majority are on the fringes of the survey area, precisely in the areas where one would expect an indifference factor to set in. Theoretically, people at the edges of the spheres of influence of cities may be indifferent as to which set of cities they visited.[34] However, although the aggregate pattern gives this impression, the actual process is quite different. Instead of each individual visiting a widely different set of places individuals actually seem to visit one or two places fairly consistently, but there is considerable individual variation in the places visited. Hence it is the differential movement patterns of individuals that contribute to the apparent 'indifference' revealed by the aggregate totals.

Table 2.3 illustrates this point with reference to one of the settlements surveyed, namely North Cornelly, an area that has expanded very rapidly during the last eight years by the building of council and private estates. Here only 25 per cent of the households visited more than one centre, a surprising feature in view of Figs. 2.6 and 2.7. However, it must be noted that it is the differential pattern of movement among the 50 per cent who only visited one place that gives the impression of indifference, once the dominant flow to Porthcawl is excluded from consideration. It may also be noted that the people going to two or more centres apart from Porthcawl seem to have definite orientations in their movements, either they go to Port Talbot and Swansea in the west or to Bridgend and Cardiff in the east. Although the evidence is rather flimsy in view of the numbers involved, the chances of the population visiting Cardiff seems to increase with the

TABLE 2.3. *North Cornelly: places visited by sampled population*

	Total	Swansea	Port Talbot	Porthcawl	Bridgend	Cardiff
a. No visits outside the Cornelly–Pyle area	10					
b. One place visited	20	2	5	10	3	0
c. Two places visited Combinations:	5					
		1			1	
		1		1		
		1	1			
				1	1	
		1		1		
d. Three places visited Combinations:	5					
		1	1			1
		1		1		1
		1	1	1		
				1	1	1
				1	1	1

Source: *Sample Survey*, June 1967.

increasing mobility of individuals. Hence an illustration of the more mobile elements of society focusing upon larger centres is provided.

By partitioning the aggregate spatial movements of the sampled population in this way,[35] order has been introduced into an apparently complicated pattern of connectivity. Each strand in the total movement pattern has been unravelled, and from the specific behaviour patterns of each settlement sufficient unity of behaviour has been established to lead to the conclusion that most of the area forms a functionally integrated area focused upon Swansea, in other words it forms 'a city-region'. Precise boundaries are difficult to establish in view of the overlapping nature of nodal regions, whilst the differential

individual patterns on the edges of the area make the definite allocation of whole settlements to particular regions a difficult task. However, in the next section an attempt will be made to resolve these
problems in the light of the particular task in hand, though it must be
stressed that there is no final solution or answer to what are essentially
zones of transition.[36]

Local government boundary reorganisation

In July 1967 a Government White Paper proposed a reorganisation of
local government areas in Wales.[37] Despite the discussions initiated
by a Royal Commission dealing with changes in the English administrative areas,[38] and in particular with the abundant evidence of the
need for radical reorganisation of areas[39] the White Paper only proposed a regrouping of existing lower tier authorities as the functions
exercised at county district level were outside the terms of reference of
the Commission. As a purely stopgap measure these proposals may be
useful, but in the long term they may be disastrous.

Figure 2.8 shows the existing and proposed regrouping of areas in
the Swansea region. From the evidence presented in Figs. 2.5, 2.6 and
2.7 it is apparent that the existing boundaries are completely irrelevant
to the contemporary patterns of connectivity. If one accepts that local
government should be based on existing community of interest areas,
it is apparent that the proposed regrouping merely compounds existing anomalies. Innumerable examples of this fact could be chosen, but
probably the two most obvious cases concern the Upper Tawe and
Upper Afan areas. In the case of the former area, a settlement such as
Ystradgynlais is to remain in Breconshire, which will be merged into
the new Mid-Wales area (Powys), despite the strength of its connections with, and proximity to Swansea. In the latter case, settlements
such as Cymmer, Glyncorrwg and Abergwynfi are grouped with Port
Talbot despite their orientation upon Maesteg. Clearly, little attention
has been paid to existing community of interest areas, and the boundary juggling in the White Paper was probably dominated by the need
to share out existing rateable value resources.

Sufficient evidence has been accumulated in this essay to propose a
more rational and meaningful reorganisation of local government. As
Swansea forms the primary nodal point in the functional organisation
of the whole area it would seem logical to initiate a county level
administrative unit based on this settlement. To confer such administrative status would merely confirm the existing city-region structure.

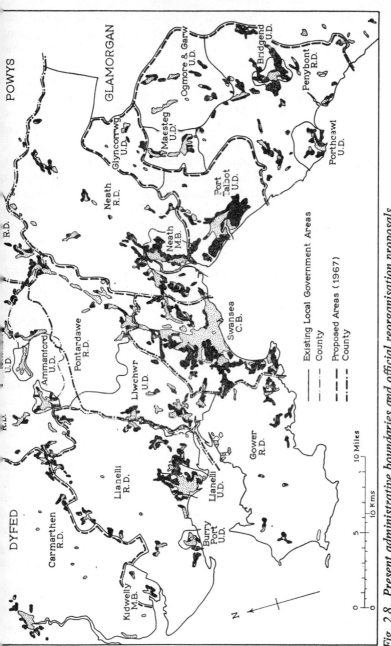

Fig. 2.8. Present administrative boundaries and official reorganisation proposals.

The alternative, the continued split in this functionally integrated area between three new units of Glamorgan, Mid-Wales and Dyfed, seems illogical. At a time when the area is suffering an employment crisis from the manpower run-down in the coal and steel industries[40] a coherent planning policy for the whole area seems to be needed, not a continued administrative partition that would weaken the process of redevelopment and redeployment. Moreover the administrative boost given to the Swansea area by the acquisition of these county functions would provide a valuable stimulus to the economy of the area.

Figure 2.9 shows the boundaries of this proposed unit together with a second tier of seven subareas. The subareas were all derived from the community of interest areas revealed in Figs. 2.5, 2.6 and 2.7, though economic considerations involving the viability and problems of the various settlements were also involved. Despite the partition of this city-region it must be stressed that only minor and delegated functions should remain in the hands of these subunits. All major administrative (especially planning) decisions should be vested in the new unit, together with the powers of rate collection. For far too long have local authorities squabbled over the acquisition of large rate-producing industrial plants for their own area in order to bring financial benefit to their own area at the expense of others.

Problems certainly remain in this administrative reorganisation of the area. Thus, the Glantawe, Amman, Maesteg, Kenfig-Porthcawl areas are comparatively small but seem to form distinct communities of interest that it would be wise to develop. The first three are all alike in their degree of economic depression and neglected environment, and it would seem useful to treat them as coherent subunits in any redevelopment. The Kenfig–Porthcawl area, however, represents something of an anomaly, lying as it does on the fringes of Port Talbot and Bridgend and between the city-region of Swansea and another suggested city-region based on Cardiff. In order to prevent uncoordinated sprawl in the area, in particular the need to prevent the coalescence of Margam and Pyle, it would seem essential to treat it as one unit within the Swansea city-region, though it is true that a case could be made for considering the unit, together with Maesteg, as part of a Greater Bridgend.

A final point needs to be made about the size of the Swansea subunit. The communities on Gower, Gorseinon, Pontardulais and Clydach all have very strong connections with the city, so it seems pointless to subdivide the area just to form a counterbalance to the existing county

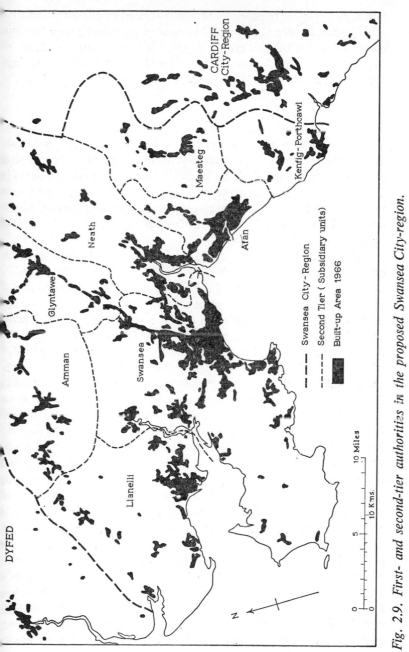

Fig. 2.9. First- and second-tier authorities in the proposed Swansea City-region.

borough. Given the release of Swansea from the present administrative strait-jacket, a more rational and integrated coordination of development in the area with an emphasis upon the preservation of areas of natural beauty would probably be achieved, whilst smaller grouping within the subunits would foster local community development.

CONCLUSION

This essay began with the assertion that the contemporary urbanisation process cannot be understood only by tracing the physical pattern of urban growth. Two studies of the connectivity of areas in Wales have demonstrated the relevance of this statement and have revealed that the flows are not chaotic and amorphous but are highly organised into an overlapping set of nodal regions focused upon the larger urban units.

Although the data source used in the first part of the essay is not as comprehensive as one might have wished, at least the results provide a useful first approximation to the nodal structure of Wales, and is probably the best we can manage at this point in time. The detailed study of the functional patterns of the Swansea area proved more valuable in that a city-region structure was identified. At a time when the city-region concept is being increasingly used, but rarely defined,[4] it is to be hoped that this study provides a useful demonstration of the practicability of the concept. Problems, as we would be the first to admit, certainly exist with boundary definitions, simply because we are dealing with nodal regions and zones of transition. But problems should not be exaggerated, they can certainly be resolved given the purpose for which the regions are to be used.[42] It might of course be asked why we should apply rigid boundaries to what are, after all, regional influences. However, as Senior has pointed out, 'definite non-overlapping areas are essential to physical planning'.[43] Indeed, one can follow his argument and point out that 'our primary purpose in regional planning . . . should be to untrammel and promote the inherent tendency of modern society to organise itself on this [city region] basis'.[44] Hence the new patterns of mobility and developing community organisation will be incorporated into our proposals. Then we shall be able to obtain areas that are derived from, rather than imposed across, existing community of interest areas. For far too long, our planning processes have operated in areas that bear little relevance to the facts of a modern urban society. Given studies of connectivity similar to the examples shown in this chapter, it will be possible to re-plan our communities on a more rational basis in line with existing urbanisation trends, thereby increasing the effectiveness of planning interpretations and decisions.

REFERENCES

1. ELDRIDGE, H. T., 'The process of urbanization', in Spengler, J. J. and Duncan, O. D., eds., *Demographic Analysis*, Free Press of Glencoe, 1956, pp. 338–43.

2. GOTTMAN, J. and HARPER, R. A., eds., *Metropolis on the Move: Geographers Look at Urban Sprawl*. Wiley, 1967.

3. SENIOR, D., *The Regional City*, Longmans, 1966, p. 11.

4. MEIER, R., *A Communications Theory of Urban Growth*, Massachusetts Institute of Technology Press, 1962.

5. HAUSER, P. M. and SCHNORE, L. F., *The Study of Urbanization*, Wiley, 1965, pp. 491–518.

6. BERRY, B. J. L., 'Approaches to regional analysis: a synthesis', *Ann. Ass. Am. Geogr.*, **54**, 1964, pp. 2–11.

7. BERRY, B. J. L., *The Geography of Market Centres and Retail Distribution*, Prentice-Hall, 1967, pp. 123–4.

8. SENIOR, *The Regional City*, pp. 10–36.

9. It may be noted that the most comprehensive geographical text-book on Wales fails to deal at any length with the functional aspects of contemporary human and economic distributions. Even the title reflects this limited content: BOWEN, E. G., ed., *Wales: a physical historical and regional geography*, Methuen, 1957.

10. BERRY, B. J. L. and PRED, A., *Central Place Studies: a bibliography*, Regional Science Research Institute, Philadelphia, 1962.

11. DAVIES, W. K. D., 'The ranking of service centres: a critical review', *Trans. Inst. Br. Geogr.*, **40**, 1966, pp. 51–65.

12. GREEN, H. L., 'Hinterland boundaries of New York City and Boston in southern New England', *Econ. Geogr.*, **31**, 1955, pp. 283–300.

13. GREEN, F. H. W., 'Urban hinterlands in England and Wales: an analysis of bus services', *Geogrl. J.*, **96**, 1950, pp. 64–81.

14. DAVIES, W. K. D., *Trans. Inst. Br. Geogr.*, 1966.

15. In the state of Iowa, comprehensive state-aided surveys were carried out in 1934 and 1961 from which information on shopping

habits have been abstracted by several workers, e.g., (*a*) LASKA, J. A., jnr., 'The development of the pattern of retail trade centres in a selected area of southwestern Iowa', unpublished M.A. Thesis, University of Chicago, 1958; (*b*) RUSHTON, G., *Spatial Pattern of Grocery Purchases by the Iowa Rural Population*, University of Iowa Studies in Business and Economics New Series No. 9, 1966, p. 2.

16. For instance: (*a*) CHRISTALLER, W., (trans. by C. Baskin), *Central Places in Southern Germany*, Prentice Hall, 1966; (*b*) HAGERSTRAND, T., 'On Monte Carlo simulation of diffusion', in Garrison, W. L. and Marble, D. F., eds., *Quantitative Geography Part I. Economic and Cultural Topics*, Northwestern University Studies in Geography Number 13, Evanston, Illinois, 1967, p. 21.

17. WEBBER, M. *et al.*, *Explorations in Urban Structure*, University of Pennsylvania Press, 1964.

18. This analysis was carried out with the assistance of Robert Jones, Dept. of Geography, Queen Mary College, University of London.

19. NYSTUEN, J. D. and DACEY, M. F., 'A graph theory interpretation of nodal regions', *Papers and Proceedings of the Regional Science Association*, 7, 1961, pp. 29–42.

20. The usefulness of a more detailed areal breakdown is revealed by HAGERSTRAND, T., in Garrison and Marble, *Quantitative Geography*, p. 21.

21. For a discussion of this technique see LEOPOLD, L. B., WOLMAN, M. G. and MILLER, J. P., *Fluvial Processes in Geomorphology*, Freeman, 1964, pp. 131–50.

22. NYSTUEN AND DACEY, *Proc. reg. Sci. Assoc.* 1961.

23. GREEN, F. H. W., *Geogrl. J.*, 1950, pp. 64–81.

24. ROWLEY, G., 'Middle Order Towns in Wales', unpublished Ph.D. Dissertation, University of Wales, (Aberystwyth), 1967.

25. THOMAS, J. G., in Bowen, ed., *Wales*, p. 199.

26. For a more detailed account of this growth see MANNERS, G., *South Wales in the Sixties*, Pergamon Press, 1964.

27. Note the surveys carried out in Iowa in the 1930s. See: LASKA, J. A., jnr., unpublished M.A. Thesis, Chicago, 1958.

28. This survey was carried out by the first year geography students at the University College of Swansea in June, 1967, under the direction of W. K. D. Davies. The assistance of Mrs J. Mosely, Mr Adrian Randall, Miss Elizabeth Farrell, Mr Colin Rouse and Dr D. T. Herbert is also gratefully acknowledged.

29. In the small villages of Porthyrhyd (19), Llanddarog (20), Pontantwn (23), Crwbin (21) and Llangendeirne (22) only five households were interviewed.

30. Journey to shop movements seem to identify the major points of conflux in our society and provide a useful parameter in the definition of community of interest areas.

31. DAVIES, W. K. D. and ROBINSON, G. W. S., 'The nodal structure of the Solent area,' *Jl. Town Plann. Inst.*, **54**, 1968, pp. 18–23.

32. Note the discussion dealing with the differences between the mobility of population in Britain and North America in SENIOR, *The Regional City*, 1966.

33. A survey carried out by the planning department in Cardiff showed that even Cardiff probably lost only one per cent of its potential trade to Bristol in 1966, and that this figure failed to account for the increase in trade brought to Cardiff from the Bristol area. Quoted in *Western Mail*, Monday, 20 November, 1967, p. 3.

34. BERRY, *The Geography of Market Centres*, 1967, p. 6.

35. A more detailed partition is given in DAVIES, W. K. D. and ROBINSON, G. W. S., *J. Tn. Plann. Inst.*, **54**, 1968, pp. 18–23.

36. Once it is realised that regional definition is essentially a problem of classification and that different classifications can be devised for different purposes the confusion over the point is resolved. See: GRIGG, D., 'The Logic of Regional Systems', *Ann. Ass. Am. Geogr.*, **55**, 1965, pp. 465–91.

37. *Local Government in Wales*, Cmnd 3340 H.M.S.O., Cardiff, 1967.

38. Minister of Housing and Local Government: statement made at a Press Conference announcing the Royal Commission on Local Government (May 1966), *The Guardian*, 25 May, 1966, p. 6.

39. WELSH, L., *Royal Commission on Local Government. Summaries of the evidence to the Commission and other material*, C. Knight, 1967.

40. *Wales: The Way Ahead*, Cmnd 3334, HMSO, Cardiff, 1967.

41. Despite the interest in city-regions, relatively few studies have successfully defined these areas. Indeed one recent book maintains that the concept is of limited value, 'there seems little doubt that the city-region as commonly described is a product of the imagination with even less visible basis than the formal region.' MINSHULL, R., *Regional Geography: Theory and Practice*, London, 1967, p. 60. Such a view is rejected since the anti-scientific philosophy expressed in this work

5

would condemn geography to a study of the distribution of visible objects.

42. GRIGG, *Ann. Ass. Am. Geogr.*, 1965, pp. 465–91.
43. SENIOR, *The Regional City*, 1966.
44. *Ibid.*, p. 20.

CHAPTER 3

SUBSTANDARD HOUSING IN WELSH TOWNS

D. W. Drakakis-Smith

Most contemporary research frontiers in urban geography are concerned with the functional and sociological characteristics of towns, a feature which is reflected in the contents of this volume. Morphological analysis, on the other hand, despite its promising beginnings, seems to have fallen into some disrepute. Thus Garrison[1] reflected the views of many people at Lund in 1960 when he described morphological studies as being no richer than they were thirty years previously, primarily because of their failure to use adequate measurement devices and to develop theoretical concepts, whilst he might have added that few people have attempted to stress the prescriptive value of the morphological approach. Recently, however, geographers have tried to break out of this impasse and have attempted to place the analysis of interurban and intra-urban morphological variations upon a more vigorous scientific footing,[2] and have begun to explore the prescriptive value of these studies.[3] However, so far, research into the explanation of morphological change, and its prescriptive value has been handicapped by the problem of defining the spatial variation in the morphological variable, and this is especially true where the variable involves some qualitative attribute, as in the case of 'substandard' housing. The decay in the fabric of our towns, combined with our inability to build enough new houses, presents a critical situation. But although concern is often expressed on this issue (for instance, the city planning office in Cardiff recently drew attention to the fact that the percentage of old buildings in Wales is higher than any other region in England and Scotland[4]), the detailed dimensions of the problem are still not known. Thus, even the latest economic policy statement on Wales was forced to admit that 'it is not yet possible to estimate firmly how many of the older houses will need to be replaced as incapable of substantial improvement'.[5] Part of this problem is due to the inadequacy of current methods of definition and it is this issue that is dealt with in the first part of this essay, the second half being concerned with the analysis

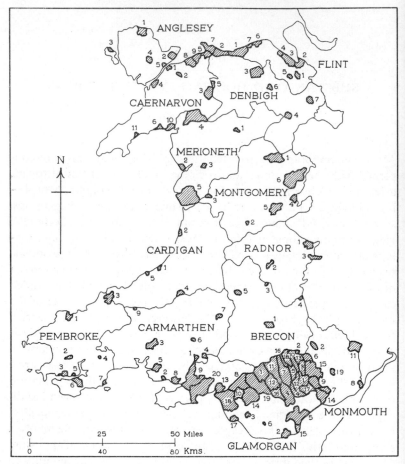

Fig. 3.1. Urban Administrative areas in Wales counties.

1. ANGLESEY
   1. Amlwch
   2. Beumaris
   3. Holyhead
   4. Llangefni
   5. Menai Bridge

2. BRECON
   1. Brecon
   2. Brynmawr
   3. Builth Wells
   4. Hay
   5. Llanwrtyd Wells

3. CAERNARVON
   1. Bangor

2. Bethesda
3. Betws-y-Coed
4. Caernarvon
5. Conway
6. Criccieth
7. Llandudno
8. Llanfairfechan
9. Penmaenmawr
10. Portmadoc
11. Pwllheli

4. CARDIGAN
   1. Aberayron
   2. Aberystwyth
   3. Cardigan

4. Lampeter
5. Newquay

5. CARMARTHEN
   1. Ammanford
   2. Burry Port
   3. Carmarthen
   4. Cwmamman
   5. Kidwelly
   6. Llandeilo
   7. Llandovery
   8. Llanelli
   9. Newcastle Emlyn

6. DENBIGH
   1. Abergele

Fig. 3.1. (cont.)

2. Colwyn Bay
3. Denbigh
4. Llangollen
5. Llanrwst
6. Ruthin
7. Wrexham

7. FLINT
1. Buckley
2. Connah's Quay
3. Flint
4. Holywell
5. Mold
6. Prestatyn
7. Rhyl

8. GLAMORGAN
1. Aberdare
2. Barry
3. Bridgend
4. Caerphilly
5. Cardiff
6. Cowbridge
7. Gelligaer
8. Glyncorrwg
9. Llwchwr
10. Maesteg
11. Merthyr Tydfil
12. Mountain Ash

13. Neath
14. Ogmore & Garw
15. Penarth
16. Pontypridd
17. Porthcawl
18. Port Talbot
19. Rhondda
20. Swansea

9. MERIONETH
1. Bala
2. Barmouth
3. Dolgellau
4. Ffestiniog
5. Towyn

10. MONMOUTH
1. Abercarn
2. Abergavenny
3. Abertillery
4. Bedwas & Machen
5. Bedwellty
6. Blaenavon
7. Caerleon
8. Chepstow
9. Cwmbran
10. Ebbw Vale
11. Monmouth
12. Mynyddislwyn

13. Nantyglo & Blaina
14. Newport
15. Pontypool
16. Rhymney
17. Risca
18. Tredegar
19. Usk

11. MONTGOMERY
1. Llanfyllin
2. Llanidloes
3. Machynlleth
4. Montgomery
5. Newtown
6. Welshpool

12. PEMBROKE
1. Fishguard & Goodwick
2. Haverfordwest
3. Milford Haven
4. Narberth
5. Neyland
6. Pembroke
7. Tenby

13. RADNORSHIRE
1. Knighton
2. Llandrindod Wells
3. Presteigne

of the regional variations and functional correlates of 'substandard-ness' in Wales.

DEFINITIONS

It is essential to define the terms used as clearly as possible. 'Housing' and 'towns' are virtually self-explanatory. Housing is preferred to 'dwelling' because 'dwelling' does not rule out the many households found in those large houses converted into smaller dwelling units without complete structural separation. It is formally described in the 1961 Census: 'a household comprises one person living alone or a group of persons living together, partaking of meals prepared together and benefiting from a common housekeeping.'[6] The definition of 'a town' has long been a controversial issue and the terms adopted have varied greatly both spatially and temporally. However, reliance on the official census for much of the raw material has meant that administrative units providing the framework for these returns must be adhered to. Accordingly all administrative units classified as County Borough, Municipal Borough, Urban District or New Town were incorporated in the study and Rural Districts were omitted (Fig. 3.1). There are obviously many points of dispute arising from such an interpretation, such as the omission of large industrially based settlements in rural areas of which Pontardawe can be cited as an example. Yet given the inadequacies of the British Census in terms of presentation of information, any feasible definition will have its faults. As the availability of reliable recent data is the prime requisite of this study, the use of census administrative units is virtually unavoidable.

Unlike most of the terms used in the census, 'substandard' is not one to which a precise meaning can be attached since its definition involves a set of personal attitudes. Moreover, differing interpretations of the word have existed at various stages in the development of our society, varying with the social conscience of the times. The social background of the observer and the political party to which he belongs have inevitably coloured opinions of what a 'substandard' house actually is, while the incorporation of more and more features of the household unit into the term has increased the difficulty of standardisation.[7]

The changes in the absolute standard to which the term was applied were essentially of a piecemeal character, constant adjustments being added to a basic official framework that remained unchanged for generations. At the present time, there is no precise official definition of 'substandardness' in existence; the contemporary standard of fitness being indicated rather than defined in Section 4 of the Housing Act, 1957. This lists the matters to which reference must be made . . .

(a) Repair.
(b) Stability.
(c) Freedom from damp.
(d) Natural lighting.
(e) Ventilation.
(f) Water supply.
(g) Drainage and sanitary conveniences.
(h) Facilities for storage, preparation and cooking of food and the disposal of waste water.

These considerations are based very largely on the recommendations of the Mitchell Committee in its 1946 report on Standards of Fitness[8] which in turn is based on standards accepted as far back as 1919. The important point to note is that the requirement for the house to be 'reasonably suitable for occupation' leaves a good deal of scope for personal interpretation. Although it is claimed that the present bases for decisions on substandardness give great scope for flexibility, they have nevertheless 'on present evidence, produced an even wider divergence of opinion than ever existed before'.[9] Moreover, the 'flexibility' of this definition has resulted in a wholesale underestimation of the extent of the problem. For instance it has been the practice of some local authorities to calculate the number of unfit houses as being those which they can afford to clear in a given time. 'Local authorities may be reluctant to make estimates beyond the numbers of dwellings, the demolition of which, has been or is about to be confirmed by clearance orders.'[10] In addition there are such misrepresentations as double recording of houses actually cleared,[11] whilst some local authorities exaggerate their housing efforts so as to present housing standards within the town in the best possible light. Hence it follows that local authority estimates of the existing situation should be regarded with a certain amount of scepticism.

It seems inevitable in view of the above discussion that only the worst cases of unfit housing are included in the local authority figures. 'The returns (for unfitness) represent the core of the problem but leave unrecorded the great volume of old substandard houses, not yet slums, which because of their size, design or layout fall far short of present living requirements.'[12] So it would seem that there has been a consistent tendency, since 1945 in particular, to underestimate the extent of substandard housing in Britain; a problem that would be intensified if one amends the abysmally low standards for definitions of 'fitness'.[13] A gross misrepresentation of the actual picture exists, both in terms of totals and distribution. Thus if one accepts that there are three million houses over sixty-five years old in Great Britain and only one million are unfit the other two million must have been exceptionally well built!

Verification of these seemingly severe accusations can be derived from the local authority estimates of unfit housing, which were commissioned in 1954. Of the houses classed as 'fit' (i.e. with an expected life of over fifteen years) Alvin N. Schorr[14] has calculated that (a) over one-third had no hot water at three points; (b) over one-quarter had no wash basin; (c) over 1·5 million lacked all four basic amenities listed in the census.

Additional evidence of variation in local authority interpretations of the 1957 Act is shown by the statistics listed in the Labour Party publication *Plans for Old Homes*, produced in 1963. If one is to believe the statistics presented then Welwyn Garden City has the same proportion of unfit houses as Stoke Newington; and Tonbridge has more than Rhondda.

Despite these absurdities, local authority estimates were again commissioned in 1965 to provide an 'up-to-date' assessment of the situation. It is perhaps sufficient to note of these returns that although virtually no local authority had reached its clearance target[15] and although many more houses had become substandard during the eleven-year period, most of the statistics showed a substantial (and certainly optimistic) decline in numbers, as compared with the 1954 data (Fig. 3.2).

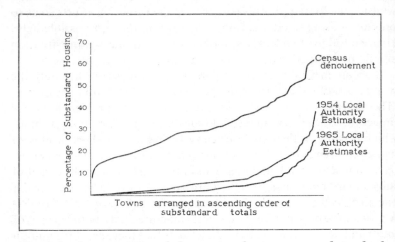

Fig. 3.2. A comparison of three sets of returns on substandard housing totals in Welsh towns.

Recent events have at last begun to indicate the end of the present system. Following a recommendation from a subcommittee of the Central Housing Advisory Committee, a survey was launched in February 1967 to make a more detailed sample survey of old houses in England and Wales than had hitherto been taken. The results of the survey appeared in June 1967 and showed the number of unfit houses to be at least three times as large as was previously recognised (1·8 million as opposed to 0·6 million). As a result the Minister finally and reluctantly admitted the faults of the present system: 'The survey suggests that unfit housing is more prevalent and less concentrated than previous information has suggested.'[16]

All these deficiencies in the present techniques of definition and data collection have long been recognised (in contrast to the official view) by the various investigation teams which have examined housing quality in the past. Several attempts have been made to provide a more suitable means of assessing the real situation. These attempts range from the relatively minor improvements of the Standard Grant standard (making provision for five basic improvements); to the multiple index criteria used by the Welsh Office[17] and by Burnett and Scott.[18] In the Welsh case an attempt was made to determine the housing loss through obsolescence within the next twenty years and was based on a four-fold index, namely: (a) the number of houses built before 1875; (b) the number of houses whose rateable value was below £10 in 1961; (c) the number without fixed baths or water closets; (d) the part likely to be played by improvement grants in prolonging the life of the dwelling. Burnett and Scott's criteria consisted of: (a) dwellings with three rooms or less in 1951; (b) households with no fixed bath in 1951; (c) households with no exclusive use of a W.C. in 1951; (d) dwellings rated at £13 and under in 1958.

Although it is clear that the objectives of these studies vary, one being concerned with the future, the other with the present situation, certain features must be noted that limit their use in this particular study. In the first case arbitrary decisions seem to have been made about the 'cut off' points used to define 'substandard' in the array of rateable values and age of buildings. Moreover some categories, such as age of building, need not bear any relation to housing quality. Yet it must be noted that Burnett and Scott attempted to be consistent, the upper qualities of every array being used to delimit categories. This means that in the case of sanitary facilities only urban areas with over 20 per cent of their houses without the exclusive use of a water closet score on their scale. Although satisfactory for their purpose, this technique is hardly useful here, because all houses without a water closet should be classed as substandard. Secondly, the particular size of house used as an indicator by Burnett and Scott must be questioned, simply because of the number of small houses and flats currently being constructed for the elderly and for young couples.

In some ways these criticisms are rather harsh, because these studies do represent a useful step forward in the survey of housing conditions, particularly as they try to exclude assessments based on personal judgments. However, it is felt that these reports do not go far enough.

Hence another definition of 'substandard' is put forward. As it is considered essential to use reliable, objective and spatially comparable information, census data must be used, and the statistics analysed are those given in Table 23 of the 1961 Census.[19] This lists four basic amenities of the household and all are regarded as essential if a house is going to be classified as fit. These are households without: (a) the exclusive use of a cold water tap; (b) a water closet; (c) a fixed bath; (d) a supply of hot water. In this essay, therefore, the percentage of 'substandard' housing in any urban area is taken as the number of houses without one or more of these essential amenities.

This definition, perhaps, may be regarded as rather extreme, as a house without a fixed bath is regarded as equally substandard as one without a supply of hot water. Certainly some multiple index dealing with the various combinations of these variables could have devised, but in view of the basic nature of these amenities to contemporary living standards it was felt that this was not a particularly worthwhile investigation. In any case the objective of this essay is to define the extent of 'substandardness', not deviation from the average housing conditions, and the index used would seem to provide a useful indicator of the extent of the problem. It might be noted in passing that this measure is the same as the one recently used by Humphrys[20] in Britain, and is similar to the one used by Hook and Hartman[21] in their study of housing quality in the United States. However, a measure of 'dilapidation' is provided by the United States census authorities and this was used by Hook and Hartman as one of their variables. This would certainly be a useful addition to the four indices used in this study, but unfortunately the British census does not incorporate such information, and it proved impossible to obtain any accurate and comparable information dealing with this variable from any other source.

ANALYSIS OF THE SUBSTANDARD TOTALS

In the study of the distribution of housing quality in all administrative areas in Britain, referred to above, Humphrys has shown that Wales has a higher proportion of substandard houses than any other standard region in Great Britain.[22] This conclusion is confirmed by the analysis of the substandard totals for Welsh towns, for 32·07 per cent of all urban households were substandard in 1961. This lends emphasis to the enormity of the existing problem and demonstrates that the situation is more serious than most authorities would seem to admit, for even the Welsh Office survey of South Wales only arrived at a figure of 17·6 per cent of the existing stock.[23]

Figure 3.3 shows the other characteristics of this frequency distribution, in particular the positive skew common to most distributions in the social sciences. At this stage it might be noted that several attempts via logarithmic and arc sin methods were used to try and normalise the data so as to make possible the application of a greater range of sophisticated statistical techniques. However no significant

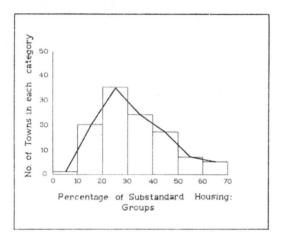

Fig. 3.3. Frequency curve of substandard housing percentages in Welsh towns.

advance in the degree of normality was recorded and so the data were used in their original form in this essay.

Two major hypotheses were tested, the first relating to the relationship between substandardness and town size, the second to substandardness and town function. In the former two different measures of town size were used. The first involved a simple ranking of each town according to the number of households present, while the second used a central place measure of size, in the case, the relative position of each town in Carter's hierarchical table of Welsh Towns.[24] Both rank order correlation coefficients proved insignificant, the degree of association with substandard housing being −0·05 and −0·16 respectively. Moreover an analysis of variance undertaken upon the larger relationship in the former case, that is the actual household numbers, also failed to reveal any significant association.

Pilot investigations dealing with the second of the major hypotheses, using straightforward correlation techniques between substandard housing figures and various types of socio-economic data were at first unrewarding and did not yield significant results. This seemed to indicate that different types and sizes of towns were influenced by different

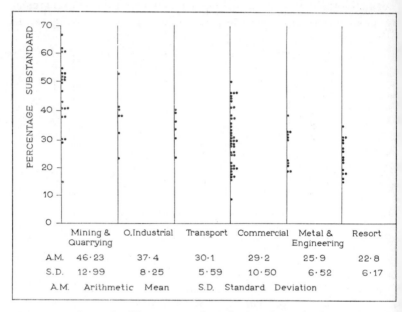

Fig. 3.4. Substandard housing totals and urban functional groupings in Wales.

combinations of socio-economic features. Hence it was decided to group the socio-economic data to derive a classification of towns and then test the association with substandardness. As Carter[25] had recently outlined a functional classification of Welsh towns, this was used in the analysis, though certain modifications had to be incorporated. Of the ten classes listed, four contained numbers which are too few to be analysed statistically. Three of these, comprising a total of five towns, namely the Fishing, Garrison and General categories, were omitted from the investigation, whilst the fourth, Quarrying, was considered to resemble Mining towns so closely that it could safely be included within the latter group. Six functional groups were derived, the types and numbers of towns in each class being as follows: Commercial (42); Mining and quarrying (23); Resort (15); Metal and engineering (11); Other industries (7); Transport (6).

As the functional data are not in a numerical form, non-parametric tests of association had to be applied, the visual correlation of which can be seen in Fig. 3.4.

As the previous tests of association between substandardness and various ranges of socio-economic data had not proved to be significant for the towns of Wales, it was originally postulated that substandard housing totals were independent of functional groups. However the calculated value of X^2 reached 84·9, with twenty-five degrees of freedom, revealing that the initial hypotheses could be substantially rejected (0·01 per cent level). A further test, in this case a variance analysis between the substandard totals in each of the functional groups and the whole set of values confirmed the association (Table 3.1). Hence a significant relationship was established between the functional classes of towns and the degree of substandardness.

TABLE 3.1. *Analysis of variance upon functional data and substandard housing totals*

Source of variance	Sum of squares	Degrees of freedom	Variance estimate
(i) Between groups	6739·6	5	1347·9
(ii) Within groups	9405·7	98	96·0

$$F = \frac{1347·9}{96·0} = 14·04$$

The 0·1 per cent level of variance ratio is $\approx 4·5$; therefore the result is highly significant.

Once this significant association had been established between the functional classification of towns and substandardness it was thought worthwhile to portray the spatial variation in this variable. In order to preserve a rigidly objective basis for the investigation of the substandard totals, the raw figures for each town were first of all converted into standard deviation scores, a technique which clearly shows the degree of departure from the mean figure for Welsh towns. Although this data could be mapped in terms of these standard deviations, it was thought desirable to eliminate mathematical signs and duplication of numbers. Hence the values were rearranged into scores ranging from 0–5. The highest score (5) was given to those towns

having percentages of substandard houses that were more than two
standard deviations above the mean, the lowest score (0) being given
to the towns with the lowest figures, that is to towns that had

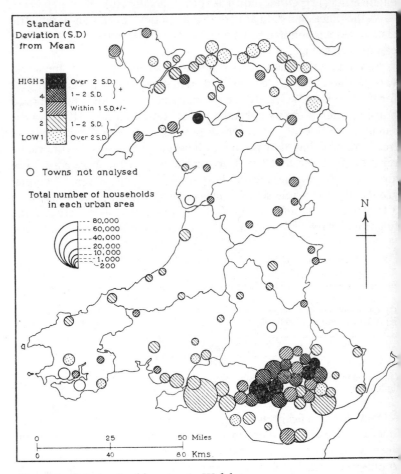

Fig. 3.5. Substandard housing in Welsh towns.

percentages greater than two standard deviations below the mean.
Figure 3.5 shows the spatial distribution of these scores, the size of
each circle denoting the number of households in each town.

The most outstanding characteristic of Fig. 3.5 is the high score
attained by the mining towns in the central and eastern parts of th

South Wales coalfield. Here the substandard values are associated with the group of towns that were heavily dependent upon coalmining. The spectacular decline in the importance of the industry in the last thirty years combined with the failure of the area to attract alternative sources of employment has meant that the area has suffered considerable population loss. Inevitably, the urban fabric has decayed and has not been replaced by major new housing developments.

To the north and south of this central belt substandard totals are slightly lower. In the northern belt the first houses were built before the Public Health Act of 1875, and were associated with the early development of the iron industry. These houses are particularly ill-adapted to modern conditions and have been extensively cleared in the last twenty years. To the south the economic depression of the central belt is not quite so marked. A shift of population associated with the development of new industrial and housing estates on the edge of the coalfield together with the possibility of commuting to the coastal towns has meant that there is far more renewal and replacement of the existing housing stock. This process is currently recognised and is capitalised on by the development control guidelines established by the relevant county planning authorities.[26]

In the west the greater prosperity of the coastal fringe again accounts for the lower proportion of substandard housing, though it might be noted that in this area many of the mining communities are part of rural local government authorities so that equivalent patterns cannot be shown. Elsewhere the decay of other towns that were, or still are, dependent on single industries, whether it be packet functions at Holyhead, or slate quarrying at Bethesda and Ffestiniog, is also to be noted.

In Mid-Wales, in particular, most of the smaller rural service centres also show very high values of substandardness, a feature that is also characteristic of service centres such as Amlwch and Narberth. Clearly the high values are associated with the relative functional decline of these smaller places (see Chapter 10) and the failure of these places to attract alternative employment opportunities and hence renewal potential. The situation is particularly well marked in the Severn valley where towns have never recovered from the decline in the industrial prosperity based on the woollen industry during the last century. Here a decaying stock of older houses dating from this phase of prosperity exacerbates the situation. Moreover it may be noted that the role of many of these communities as retirement centres (see Chapter

8) is another important factor that must be brought into any analysis. Most older people who move into these towns are not particularly prosperous and buy from the existing stock of property rather than contributing to an effective additional demand for new houses. Hence the renewal effort is particularly small, thereby adding to the problem.

By contrast, substandard totals are particularly low along the northern coast of Wales. Here the situation is explained by the fact that the towns act as resort and retirement centres catering for the middle income groups. A similar explanation accounts for the low substandard totals attained by Tenby and Porthcawl, whilst the new town of Cwmbran in Monmouthshire stands out in vivid contrast to the rest of industrial South Wales.

CONCLUSION

Despite the considerable planning implications of any comparative study of urban substandard housing totals, it must be admitted that the field has been remarkably neglected, even though a pioneer work by Hook and Hartman[27] demonstrated the usefulness of such an enquiry over ten years ago. However, before any strictly geographical study of the spatial variations in housing quality can get under way, an adequate definition of substandardness is needed. In this study the official statistics have been shown to be completely unreliable and it was necessary to set up an alternative standard. Certainly problems exist with the definition used in this study, in particular the fact that the index does not distinguish which particular variable accounted for a house being classified as substandard. However, this is not really the point at issue; it is the total substandard stock that is the object of concern, not how any individual house qualified. In the absence of any alternative statistical information, the index seems to provide an accurate, objective and most important of all, a comparative measure of the problem.

From this study it would seem that the overhaul of British statistics concerning housing data involves two main tasks, the modernisation of existing standards and some means of ensuring uniformity in application. With regard to the former it must be stressed that 'the housing standards in any society, and at any point in time, are a product of economic, technological and social factors'.[28] As the basis for present assessments of housing fitness are standards laid down in 1944, and these, moreover, are minimum levels acceptable, not minimum levels desirable, the extent of the problem is revealed. Faults in such a system are obvious. If a minimum fitness standard is operated, it should at least be raised as general standards of living improve. This has not been the case in the past and the absurd condition results whereby 'Katherine Buildings in Stepney, with communal lavatories, 50 per cent of the flats without water taps, and eighty years old were defined as being fit for human habitation',[29] whilst it has been revealed that one-third of all Liverpool's houses do not have enough power points to permit the use of modern heating and other utilities.[30]

These additional examples emphasise that a new set of official housing standards is required, taking into account modern elements of accepted comfort (for example, Parker-Morris space recommendations[31]), and these standards should be reviewed at least every five years. However, any attempt to set new standards whilst the present irregularities exist in the compilation of new data does seem rather pointless. Two remedies would seem to be needed in this direction. Firstly, fewer opportunities should exist for personal judgment in the compilation of statistics, and that means a more objective definition, one based not on derived statistics like the one used here, but on specially collected data. Secondly, local authorities should not be allowed opportunities to underestimate, unintentionally or otherwise, the returns forwarded to the central government. These conditions perhaps point the way towards a system similar to that adopted by the American Public Health Association,[32] but in view of the myriad of vested interests in any local authority, it would seem important not to entrust data collection to bodies who are already overwhelmed with day to day administration. An independent unit such as a regional government body, or a team from interested research institutes would seem to be the obvious candidates.

Finally, it must be emphasised that this analysis is only an introduction to a wider research problem but it does demonstrate some of the complex issues involved. Increasingly it is accepted that morphological investigations must stress the interrelationships between function and form,[33] a point that is especially valid when housing quality is being discussed. But to trace in detail all the multitude of individual variables and decisions[34] that contribute towards variations in the housing quality of towns seems an impossible task. Instead, the general pattern of variation has been described against a background provided by the social and economic characteristics of Welsh towns. Certainly no absolute conformity between towns of similar function has been shown, but

6

enough coexistence has been demonstrated to provide a useful basis for the description of substandardness, and it would certainly seem to point the way towards a more sophisticated analysis of the problem. However, it must be stressed that an historical study of Welsh towns should be a necessary complement to this sort of analysis.[35] This integration, it is to be hoped, would provide a complete coverage to the background of substandard housing in Wales at the present day, and would be essential for any effective attempt to alleviate the existing situation.

REFERENCES

1. GARRISON, W., Comments on a discussion on urban morphology in: K. Norberg, ed., *The I.G.U. Symposium in Urban Geography, Lund, 1960*, Lund, Sweden 1963, p. 463.

2. (a) CARTER, H., Chapter 4 of this volume; (b) JOHNSTON, R. J., 'The location of high status residential areas', *Geogr. Annlr* (Stockholm), **43**, 1966, pp. 23–35; (c) DAVIES, W. K. D., 'The morphology of central places', *Ann. Ass. Am. Geogr.*, **58**, 1968, pp. 91–110.

3. (a) HARTMAN, G. W. and HOOK, J. C., 'Substandard urban housing in United States: a quantitative analysis', *Econ. Geog.*, **32**, 1956, pp. 97–114; (b) BERRY, B. J. L., *Commercial Structure and Commercial Blight*, University of Chicago Research Paper No. 35, 1963.

4. PARKINSON, E., 'Renewal of the urban environment', unpublished paper presented to conference on 'The Planning Needs and Future Development of Wales', Cardiff, 14 April, 1966.

5. *Wales: The Way Ahead*, HMSO, Cardiff, 1967, p. 75.

6. *Census* 1961 (*Housing Tables, Part I*), HMSO, p. x.

7. For a fuller account of changing attitudes towards the slum and substandardness in general, see SMITH, D. W., 'Sub standard Housing in Welsh Towns', Unpublished M.A. dissertation, University of Wales, 1968, Ch. 1.

8. *Standard of Fitness for a Satisfactory House*, HMSO, 1946.

9. CLANCY, J., 'Survey of housing requirements, land resources and programmes to 1971 and 1981', unpublished Research Department Survey, Cardiff, 1961, p. 10.

10. *Ibid.*, p. 11.

11. Since 1960 there have been many instances of both closing orders and demolition orders being received for the same houses, thereby duplicating the numbers actually cleared.

12. BURNETT, F. T. and SCOTT, S. E., 'A survey of housing conditions in the urban areas of England and Wales', *Sociol. Rev.*, **10**, 1962, pp. 35–79.

13. Described in the Association of Public Health Inspectors Programme on Housing (1961) as being worse than 1919. 'Houses without proper heating arrangements, artificial lighting, fuel stores, bathrooms or hot water are still regarded as fit for human habitation.'

14. SCHORR, A. L., *Slums and Social Insecurity*, Nelson, 1964, p. 116.

15. The five-years Plans drawn up in the late 1950s to demolish a total of 21,682 unfit Welsh houses (from a total of 46,947) had achieved only 10,528 by the end of the period specified.

16. *Daily Telegraph*, 27 June, 1967, p. 1.

17. *Wales: The Way Ahead*, p. 24.

18. BURNETT and SCOTT, *Sociol. Rev.*, 1962, pp. 38–9.

19. General Register Office, 1961 Census, County Reports HMSO, p. x.

20. HUMPHRYS, G., 'A map of housing quality in the United Kingdom', *Trans. Inst. Br. Geogr.*, **43**, 1968, pp. 31–6.

21. HARTMAN and HOOK, *Econ. Geog.*, 1956 (footnote 2).

22. HUMPHRYS, *Trans. Inst. Br. Geogr.*, p. 35.

23. Quoted in SMITH, unpublished M.A. Thesis, 1968, p. 16.

24. CARTER, H., *The Towns of Wales*, University of Wales Press, 1965, p. 108.

25. *Ibid.*, pp. 82–5.

26. Glamorgan County Planning Office, *Glamorgan, A Planning Study*, Glamorgan County Council, Cardiff, 1965.

27. HARTMAN and HOOK, *Econ. Geog.*, 1956, pp. 97–114.

28. HOLE, W. V., 'Housing standards and social studies', *Urban Studies*, **11**, 1965, p. 137.

29. SCHORR, *Slums and Social Insecurity*, p. 120.

30. *Ibid.*, p. 120.

31. See: Ministry of Housing and Local Government, *Our Older Homes: a call for action*, HMSO, London, 1966.

32. American Public Health Association, *An Appraisal Method for Measuring the Quality of Housing*, New York, 1946.

33. DAVIES, *Ann. Ass. Am. Geogr.*, **58**, 1968.

34. See CARTER H., Chapter 4 in this volume.

35. CARTER, *The Towns of Wales*, 1965.

A DECISION-MAKING APPROACH TO TOWN PLAN ANALYSIS:

A CASE STUDY OF LLANDUDNO

Harold Carter

One of the most intractable problems in the general field of urban geography has been that of the interpretation of the town plan in any-thing but a local and particular way. Most early efforts, as in geography in general, were descriptive of the observed form and led to an uneasy and barren elaboration of extremely complex systems of plan classifi-cation, a good example of which is that put forward by Tricart in his *L'Habitat urbain*.[1]

The conventional way of avoiding a pointless process of descriptive classification has been to demonstrate the evolution of form in a his-torical context, but although distinctive phases of growth can be identified for an area the whole approach remains idiographic. Conzen has attempted to make an advance by the identification of recurrent phenomena in urban growth as, for example, in his concept of 'fringe belts'.[2] But these too are derivations from the 'phenomenal environ-ment'[3] and, despite the claims made, provide no foundation for theory. It would seem, therefore, that if theory is to be built it must look to what Kirk called 'the behavioural environment',[4] and to the realm where those decisions are made which ultimately determine the urban form.

A parallel development of thought has taken place in the field of planning, for the appraisal of the way in which urban form materialises is of great importance in the development of a coherent planning discipline. In particular the process by which the values of a community become translated into human action (behaviour) and thence into a physical pattern on the earth's surface is a common interest to the traditional academic student of urban morphology and to the prac-tising planner.

F. Stuart Chapin has proposed a conceptual system,[5] based on the 'values–behaviour–consequences' framework which purports to offer a 'basic organising concept for theory development'. Chapin states that,

> in its most basic form, and viewing the components in reverse order, this framework seeks explanation for any man-induced phenomenon being studied (in this instance town plan) in terms of human behaviour (patterns of activity), with behaviour patterns being a function in turn of people's values (or the attitudes held concerning those activities). A fourth element in the framework has to do with control processes (strategies or plans) that influence the interplay among the first three components.[6]

Chapin proceeds to argue that the focus of interest rests on the *decision* as the critical point in the behavioural sequence in location action and he differentiates two groups of decisions. The first he calls 'priming decisions' which are major in scope and concerned, for example, with large-scale layout of an area. The second group are 'secondary decisions' which are triggered off by the priming group and concerned with more detailed matters such as plot purchase and house building.

A similar argument has been set out by Melvin H. Webber,[7] who argues that in order 'to find out what the urban system is, we are beginning to ask how it works, and that it is becoming less common to deal with human settlements as discrete and essentially closed mechanical systems of buildings and roads. Instead, we are finding it helpful to view settlements as but aspects of societal systems.' It follows that 'social organisation and human interaction are replacing density and place as the foci of inquiry and of political strategy'. In that inquiry the clear categorisation of roles becomes difficult, for only rarely is there a simple central command, rather are there 'multitudes of separate groups each pursuing somewhat different bundles of objectives, participating segmentally in decisions that affect their several interests'. Investigators are faced with a difficult situation for 'urban development has been guided, directed, stimulated at some points, redirected or perhaps blocked at other points through a complex and never ending stream of decisions, some of them public and many of them private'.

If these arguments are accepted then it follows that the reinterpretation of any town plan is only possible in terms of the values and decision-making characteristics of the society that gave rise to them, though periodic changes in emphasis and direction can be incorporated into the analysis. It should not be assumed that this represents a fundamentally new orientation in human geography, for in the 1930s Daryll Forde[8] was writing that

> the explanation of the features of a cultural landscape is but part of the explanation of the culture of which those features are manifestations. The cultural features of a landscape are, on the other hand, part of the data for the elucidation of the social conditions of the communities occupying an area, and ultimately for the formulation of sociological principles.

In other words, no explanation of observed phenomena on the earth's surface was possible without an extensive consideration of the social condition which gave rise to them. But whereas these were often seen as particulars they are now looked at for the derivation of common principles.

If we return to the basic argument to which our concern with town plan is related then it will be seen that the more social power (the power of making decisions) is concentrated into the hands of a class or a representative elite, the clearer and more unequivocal will be the consequences and the more uniform the plan, for it is a consequence of one voice and not a multitude. The more dispersed the social power, the less uniform will be the plan because thousands of secondary decisions exert a more potent influence. This throws light on the usual distinction between planned and unplanned towns, so easy to make, so difficult to sustain. What in fact is being considered in this context is the degree of concentration of decision-making. Where this is absolute, an absolute form may follow, whereby not only layout, but build also is directed towards a controlled uniformity. Where there is no central control, in conditions of anarchy, secondary decisions achieve dominance and priming decisions are not present. Between these extremes most actual cases are to be found and 'planned' and 'unplanned' are meaningless terms representing presumably some identified points on the continuum from one extreme to the other sketched above. When Dan Stanislawski[9] outlines the conditions necessary for the emergence of the grid pattern town he is, in fact, describing the degree of authority of the body which makes the primary decisions and thereby making an assessment of the 'societal system'. It would indeed be possible, perhaps desirable, to present the usual study of the development of town plan in this context rather than in the more traditional guise of standard historical periods.

The author has elsewhere attempted to show the basic similarities in form between Caernarfon, a Welsh medieval bastide and Merthyr Tydfil, a creation of the industrial period.[10] This was possible because in the development of the urban system in Wales there were two major phases of genesis, Anglo-Norman, during the medieval period, and Industrial during the late eighteenth and nineteenth centuries, and it was during these times that decision making was most effectively concentrated. Whether the authority be Royal or a Victorian industrialist matters only in so far as the degree of concentration produced variation; the forms which resulted have much in common because of the comparative concentration of authority. Hence the medieval bastide and the company town have many analogous features.

In order to demonstrate the concepts outlined above a brief consideration of the development of one Welsh town, Llandudno, will be undertaken. It is a town which has been completely neglected in the general studies of urban planning in nineteenth-century Britain. Perhaps Llandudno has been ignored because of its westerly location, but the smaller and earlier towns of Tremadoc and Milford appear in most texts. Perhaps its position away from the industrial areas has been responsible. But it has at least a minor role in planning history and its neglect may be partly due to the problem it raises.

Before its development as a resort, Llandudno was a small village strung out on the eastern flank of the Great Orme's Head. The church of St Tudno from which it derives its name was located away from the village on the Great Orme (see Fig. 4.1). A description of the village as it was immediately before the period of development emphasises these features. 'The houses are irregularly built and in the most crowded part stretch across the base of the Orme for about half a mile. They are built of limestone . . . are whitewashed outside. . . . A little plot of garden ground . . . is in the front of most houses. . . .'[11] This straggling village below Llandudno mountain and Great Orme's Head can clearly be seen in Fig. 4.1 where the church built in 1842 and dedicated to St George represented an early stage of development contrasting with the old Llandudno Church on the Orme.

The bulk of the land surrounding the village formed part of the Gloddaeth estate owned by the Mostyn family. The evolution of this estate is outlined in the *Dictionary of Welsh Biography*: 'Gloddaeth, Caerns., came to the family shortly before 1460 through the marriage of Hywel ap Ieuan Fychan (of Mostyn and Pengwern) with Margaret, heiress of Madog Gloddaeth (High Sheriff of Caernarvonshire,

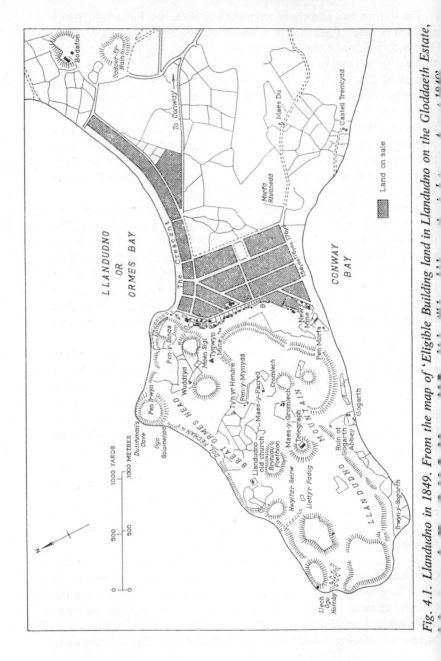

Fig. 4.1. Llandudno in 1849. From the map of 'Eligible Building land in Llandudno on the Gloddaeth Estate,

1325–6).'[12] It was the grandson of this marriage, Thomas, who first took the name Mostyn. Sir Thomas Mostyn (1776–1831), the sixth baronet, died without heir and the estate passed to Sir Edward Pryce Lloyd who was created Baron Mostyn in 1831. He had married Elizabeth, sister and coheir of Sir Thomas, and hence accumulated under his control all the Mostyn estates in North Wales. It was Sir Edward's son, the second baron, who began the development of Llandudno on the Gloddaeth lands. The power of the family and the effective control it exercised is symbolised in the Welsh saying, 'Mae

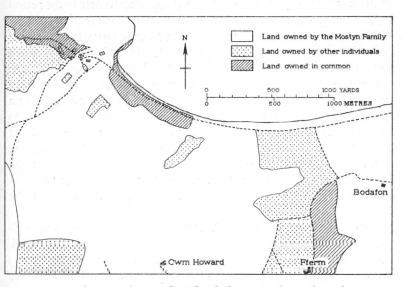

Fig. 4.2. Land ownership in the Llandudno area from the tithe survey (after A. Stuart).

meistr gan Mister Mostyn', which, interpreted rather than translated, means that perhaps somewhere there is someone more powerful than the Mostyns. But the catalyst to development was the effective assemblage of the necessary land. Figure 4.2, in the absence of any estate plans, is derived from the Tithe Map of 1840. It is apparent that the one major problem to development in that part of the land fronting Llandudno Bay was common land.[13] This however, was overcome by enclosure, and of the 950 acres enclosed, 859 went to Edward Mostyn as Lord of the Manor. Already in 1845 he was engaged in draining the marshy lowland at the foot of the Orme.

There are several conflicting versions of the way in which the planning of the resort began.[14] The one usually accepted is that Owen Williams, a surveyor from Liverpool, went to Llandudno to attend a meeting of mine shareholders. While at Llandudno he commented that it was an admirable site for the development of a resort. This was noted by John Williams of Bodafon, the local agent of the Mostyn Estate and later put to Lord Mostyn. The agent is supposed to have sketched the idea 'in a primitive sort of bathing box on the edge of the shore'. This account is derived largely from the letters of Owen Williams and though no chronology is given, seem to date to the period 1843–4. Another account is said to be derived from the remarks of John Williams at the cutting of the first sod for Marine Drive in 1847. He is said to have remembered meeting Lord Mostyn on Llandudno beach and discussing with him 'the bringing-on of Llandudno' and that one of the ideas was to employ a surveyor from Liverpool. A third account makes the link with Liverpool even closer, suggesting that John Smith, the editor of the *Liverpool Mercury*, following a visit to Llandudno, wrote a series of articles on the attractions of the area and advised Lord Mostyn to develop the site. Whatever the immediate stimulus, it is apparent that after his succession to the estate and the acquisition of land by enclosure, Lord Mostyn was concerned with its development and that the opportunity offered was clearly in the building of a resort.

Here is the 'priming decision', although it is a great pity that sufficient evidence is not available to enable the origin to be traced in detail. From what system of values and with what intention the project was derived and begun remains unclear. Also there is no material available from the Mostyn Estate to clarify the early move towards planning, but a volume entitled *The Tourists Guide to the romantic beaches, bays and other objects of interest at the fashionable watering place of Llandudno and the Great Orme's Head*, published at Liverpool in 1849 gives a map of the original sale of land and an abstract of the building regulations which were to apply.

Figure 4.1 shows the intended layout of the town as it was determined by the plots offered for sale. The scheme is conventional, with few original ideas. Like most practical plans it bore little relation to the more ambitious radial concentric schemes which had been mooted. Nor did the planning of the town conceive of it as more than a planned and controlled layout of streets. There was no attempt to endow the new town with appropriate central buildings. The priming decision came from the Mostyn estate but the present urban character is also a consequence of numerous secondary decisions. The plan was dominated by the Crescent which took its form from that of Llandudno Bay and which was backed by a parallel street (now Mostyn Street). The body of the town lay under the Great Orme where drainage of the marsh land had already been undertaken. Here the layout was in a grid form, although two diagonals which led from the old village to the

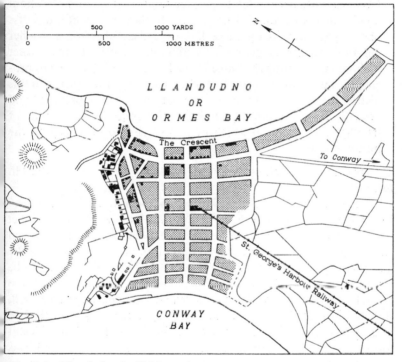

Fig. 4.3. Llandudno in 1856.

new crescent broke across the simple rectangularity of a formal grid. A map of the late 1850s (Fig. 4.3) shows that there were some minor modifications to the intended layout as the result of local actions but the basic pattern was maintained as it is indeed in the town today.

It is in the building regulations given in the *The Tourists Guide*, that some innovation is apparent. These were drawn up in 1849 and subsequently reinforced by the Llandudno Improvement Act of July 1854, which created Town Commissioners to oversee its provisions.

The preamble states that the basic consideration was that 'The "town" that is to be, shall resemble the "country", securing at the same time, in the laying out of the various plots of ground, order and uniformity'. The first part of the last sentence is particularly striking with its virtual identity with the town–country concept that Howard was to popularise very much later. But the regulations according to the 1849 *Guide* went a great deal further:

> Great care has been taken to provide salutory restrictions, without making them exceedingly irksome, and to classify the whole locality, one neighbourhood for large houses and another for a smaller description; thereby giving protection and security to the former without depreciating the value of the latter . . . With a view to provide for the health and comfort of all who may visit or settle in this district the . . . code of building regulations has been prepared and designed to ensure proper ventilation, sewerage and uniformity of frontage and elevation which bestow value upon property to the injury of none.

The structural regulations that were laid down were fairly standard in form.

These regulations are similar in their character to the building bye-laws which many areas were to adopt under the Public Health Act some twenty years later. The original street plan was to be maintained and no haphazard building was to despoil it, 'no new street shall be made without the consent of the vendor'. The new streets were to be strictly controlled for consent 'being obtained it shall not be lawful to form, lay out to any new street unless the same, being a carriage road, shall be at least thirty-six feet wide, and have a clear space for the bed of the street of not less than twenty-four feet in width, with a sufficient footway on each side thereof, of not less than six feet in width'. It was also stipulated that any back street 'may be of a width of not less than eighteen feet'. The height of houses was controlled in relation to the street width while 'no court or courts of houses will be permitted to be erected for habitation'. No cellars were to be let as a separate habitation. In addition, size of room, height of rooms, and size of windows were all given the necessary minimum dimensions. Lastly it was made necessary for duplicate plans to be provided for the town commissioners and 'that the person so lodging the plans and specifications shall not consider them approved of until signed by the vendor or his agent. . . . If such building be begun of, or made without such written consent, the vendor may cause such buildings ... to be demolished'.

The pattern of control over the town can be identified from the discussion above. The priming decision was that of the Mostyn family but the real source of this decision is difficult to identify. It is, however, related to the accumulation of the land necessary for such a venture and the dominant power of the family. The secondary decisions that followed were also in the hands of the Mostyns who served as the first chairmen of the Town Commissioners, and it was only as to minor features that individual decision of the plot purchasers became relevant. This meant that the large-scale of building of Llandudno was preserved to endow it with much of its present character. If this is traced back to the value system from which the planning ideas were derived, it is interesting to note that there seems very little of the Victorian paternalism which was so active a force elsewhere. There was no attempt to endow the town with social facilities; rather there were effective controls to maintain land and property values. It was to this end that overcrowding and congestion were to be avoided and courts and cellars ruled out.

It is often stated that most active planning consists of attempts to move away from contemporary ills rather than towards a clearly conceived goal. Llandudno was built to the specifications of a prosperous Victorian suburb and it is perhaps this quality that results in its failing to appear in planning texts. The phrase 'it shall resemble the country' seems therefore purely fortuitous and there is no evidence that it was the basis of any social or planning theory.

At the outset it was argued that the simple distinction between planned and unplanned towns is misleading. Now that the case of Llandudno has been examined in some detail it is possible to generalise

TABLE 4.1. *Genetic phases* in the morphological development of towns*

Stages of development	Dominant principles in distribution		Morphological trends
Genesis of unifunctional settlements	Separation of nodes	Internal direction	Central control 'Priming decision'
Transition: acquisition of new functions	Interaction: competition between nodes	Transition	Relaxation of central control
'Climax'	Integration of nodes	External direction	Scattered control 'Secondary decision'

* See Note 10 for a consideration of the terms used in this table.

from this example and deal with the relationships between form and function in Welsh towns, not in terms of the period of their development, but in the terms of the dominant principles that influenced their growth. Table 4.1 represents an attempt to categorise these relationships.

The acceptance of these genetic phases involves a rejection of one of the major assumptions of classical central place theory, that towns only come into being to serve rural hinterlands. In most cases they are founded for limited and specific purposes and only subsequently became central places for surrounding territories. As this change to hinterland service takes over it is argued that the focus of interest of the town changes from one which is essentially internally directed to one that is externally directed. This involves the loosening of the control evident at the time of foundation. In the present context it is contended that the period of internal direction usually coincides with a degree of centralised control, with the priming decisions which start the town off. With growth and integration into a system of towns, the outward direction of the town's interest is paralleled by a diminution in central control and the key factor in the morphology becomes the larger number of secondary decisions which are made from time to time by individuals or groups of individuals.

It is clear that the degree of freedom of these secondary decisions is very varied, and modern planning legislation is largely concerned with restoring the efficiency of the primary decision and vesting it in public hands. Compare the many contemporary complaints that are made over controls which are precisely the same as those recorded earlier for Llandudno in the mid-nineteenth century: 'If such a building be begun of, or made without such written consent, the vendor may cause such buildings . . . to be demolished'.

It, must be kept in mind, however, that Table 4.1 is only a partial attempt to generalise the process of development because the only towns considered are those founded under one dominant functional control. It is maintained, however, that it is through this type of approach that insight can be gained into the general controls of town morphology. These are to be sought in the complex realm of the society which gives rise to them, the values held by that society and the nature of the decisions made which affect the town. This poses an extremely difficult task but it also promises rewards in that it might rescue the study of town morphology from the barren outpost of urban geography which it has so long been and, by associating it with the character of urban society, reinvigorate it as a part of the interdisciplinary study of urbanisation. At the same time the study of the past will have intimate association with the present and future, for it is the way which leads from social values through planning action to the realised city area that is the critical path in present planning. The suggestions put forward here, therefore, do not evince a concern with 'the city in history' rather than 'the city in geography', but in reality they demand from both urban historians and urban geographers a more acute awareness of social processes rather than an obsession with the events of history or the 'phenomenal' facts of geography.

REFERENCES

1. TRICART, J., *Cours de Geographie Humaine, Fasc. II. L'Habitat Urbain*, Paris, 1954, pp. 114–19.

2. CONZEN, M. R. G., 'Alnwick, Northumberland. A study in town plan analysis', *Trans. Inst. Br. Geogr.*, **27**, 1960, p. 58.

3. KIRK, W., 'Problems of geography', *Geography*, **48**, 1963, pp. 357–71.

4. *Ibid.*, p. 364.

5. CHAPIN, F. STUART, 'Selected theories of urban growth and structure', *J. Am. Inst. Planners*, **30**, 1964, p. 56; see also:
CHAPIN, F. STUART and WEISS, SHIRLEY F., eds., *Urban Growth Dynamics*, Wiley, 1962, Chs 1 and 14.

6. CHAPIN, *J. Am. Inst. Planners*, 1964, p. 56.

7. WEBBER, M. M., 'The Roles of Intelligence Systems in Urban Systems Planning', *J. Am. Inst. Planners*, **31**, 1956, pp. 289, 293.

8. FORD, C. D., 'Human geography, history and sociology', *Scot. Geogr. Mag.*, **55**, 1939, p. 223.

9. STANISLAWSKI, D., 'The origin and spread of the grid pattern town', *Geogrl. Rev.*, **36**, 1946, p. 105.

10. CARTER, H., 'Urban systems and town morphology', in E. G. Bowen, H. Carter and J. A. Taylor, eds., *Geography at Aberystwyth*, University of Wales Press, 1968.

11. 'Llandudno as it was', *Liverpool Mercury*, 22 May, 1849.

12. *Dictionary of Welsh Biography to 1940*, London, Cymmrodorion Society, 1959.

13. STUART, A., 'The growth and morphology of coastal towns of north east Wales', unpublished M.A. Thesis, University of Wales, 1959.

14. *Ibid.*

ACKNOWLEDGEMENTS

I would like to thank Dr W. K. D. Davies for his critical comments on the original text of this essay and to acknowledge the basic work of analysis on Llandudno carried out by Mr A. Stuart.

CHAPTER 5

PRINCIPAL COMPONENTS ANALYSIS AND URBAN SOCIAL STRUCTURE:

A STUDY OF CARDIFF AND SWANSEA

David T. Herbert

Urbanisation is one of the dominant characteristics of society at the present time, affecting virtually all parts of the world and attaining dimensions and complexities which are unprecedented. The process of urbanisation itself and the urban forms which it is producing are vital areas for research in the social sciences. An appreciation of this need for research and of the increasing complexity which is involved in the analysis of urban areas has produced several repercussions among those social scientists involved. Indicative of these have been moves towards interdisciplinary research, where it is recognised that the formalised skills of one discipline are no longer sufficient and that it is in the transitional areas between disciplines that the most profitable advances can be made. Again, this new complexity in urban areas is recognised as involving many variables and elements, all of which need to be evaluated if a comprehensive understanding is the objective. It is in response to this last feature that techniques of multivariate analysis, made increasingly feasible by the wider availability of computer technology, have been adopted and applied to problems of urban analysis.

Principal Components Analysis is a technique which has considerable application to research work in the social sciences. The technique belongs to the wider field of factor analysis, the utility of which in geographical study is evidenced by its employment.[1] Principal Components Analysis is used here as a preliminary step in the study of aspects of urban social structure in South Wales. The bulk of the study is concerned with Cardiff, the major city in Wales, with a population in 1961 of 256,682, though reference is also made to some results of an application of the technique in Swansea, the second largest town in Wales, with a population of 166,740 in 1961. Some comparative framework for analysis can be obtained from these two case studies. The

7

particular aspects selected for emphasis in this chapter include a■
interpretation of the structure of the components produced by th■
analysis, adoption of the components as a means of identifying urba■
subareas within Cardiff, and a discussion of the contribution of thi■
type of analysis towards the understanding of generalised models o■
urban social structure.

THE TECHNIQUE

The technique of Principal Components Analysis is applied to an in■
put of variables, obtained in this study from the 1961 Census of Popu■
lation. When the emphasis is on studying geographical aspects o■
urban areas, as is the case here, the data are needed in terms of terr■
torial units of a population size which allow a meaningful interpre■
tation of urban structure. The enumeration districts of the Censu■
with a characteristic size of about 250 households, provide thes■
suitable territorial units. These enumeration districts are of such siz■
that they can be assumed to possess the internal homogeneity nece■
sary for this kind of analysis. Where the enumeration districts we■
abnormally small or corresponded with institutions such as hospital■
they were omitted from the analysis; some 334 were included f■
Cardiff and 221 for Swansea.

Principal Components Analysis is an objective and statistical way ■
identifying diagnostic factors or components from any given matr■
of input variables. As with all kinds of analysis the input data is vita■
all results are obtained directly from it and its limitations will be i■
herent in them. The Census provides a unique source of comparative■
comprehensive and relevant information from which the input va■
ables could be selected and derived. The selection of these variabl■
requires care and has been the topic of debate in similar analyses ■
this kind which have been based on Census data.[2] Discussion h■
revolved round such problems as that of obtaining a balance amo■
the variables based on socio-economic, demographic, and househo■
characteristics, the number of variables to be included in the inp■
the use of statistics from the 10 per cent sample tables, and the inco■
poration of non-census statistics. This study was limited to Cens■
information and it was decided to adopt the list of input variab■
which appeared to be the product of the afore-mentioned debate. T■
Centre for Urban Studies, University College, London, itself engag■
in an analysis of Greater London using this technique,[3] had formulat■

a list of twenty-six variables with the suggestion that these might be generally adopted and could form the basis for comparative studies of urban areas in Britain. The list was shorter than had been used in other major studies and included some variables based on the 10 per cent sample. This list of input variables (see Table 5.1) was adopted for both Cardiff and Swansea; this allows direct comparison between these two urban areas and will aid future comparisons with towns in other parts of the country. However, it was found from this application

TABLE 5.1. *Variables used in the analysis of Cardiff and Swansea*

1. Percentage of persons aged 0–4 years.
2. Percentage of persons aged 0–14 years.
3. Percentage of persons aged 65 years and over.
4. Overall sex ratio.
5. Single as percentage adult (15 years and over) population.
6. Percentage of women 20–24 ever married.
7. Percentage of single persons per household.
8. Percentage of households sharing a dwelling.
9. Percentage of households without exclusive use of W.C.
10. Number of persons per room.
11. Percentage of households at occupancy rate of over $1\frac{1}{2}$ persons per room.
12. Percentage of households owning their accommodation.
13. Percentage of housholds renting accommodation from the Council.
14. Percentage of households renting private unfurnished accommodation.
15. Percentage of households renting furnished accommodation.
16. Percentage of people born in British Caribbean Territories.
17. Percentage of people born in British Africa (excepting South Africa).
18. Percentage of people born in India, Pakistan and Ceylon.
19. Percentage of people born in Cyprus.
20. Percentage of people born in Malta.
21. Percentage of people born in Ireland.
22. Percentage of people born outside England and Wales.
23. Percentage of occupied and retired males in professional, managerial, or executive occupations.
24. Percentage of occupied and retired males in manual occupations.
25. Percentage of persons aged 15 years and over with terminal education age under 16 years.
26. Percentage of persons moving into the area within twelve months of the Census date.

that the input variables, based largely on experience in the London area, were less suitable in the analysis of Cardiff and Swansea. The particular point was that the list of input variables contained too many which were concerned with ethnic structure, an irrelevancy in the case of Swansea. Finally, it should be noted that the incorporation of some data derived from the 10 per cent sample meant that small numbers were recorded for a few variables in some enumeration districts. This feature has made the use of 10 per cent sample data a topic of debate,[4] but its advantages were felt to be strong enough to justify its inclusion. (Arguments for the inclusion of 10 per cent sample data include the fact that its errors are no larger in dimensions than many others in the Census, including errors in census-taking, and the fact that this is the only source of vital socio-economic statistics on anything like a comprehensive scale.)

The scores on the chosen list of variables by enumeration districts formed the input data for the analysis. With the two exceptions of persons per room and sex ratio, all the input data was converted to percentage scores for the stated characteristics. Principal Components Analysis uses this data to produce a correlation matrix which measures the relationships between all the possible pairs of variables. Components or factors are derived from the latent vectors of the correlation matrix and each component has a latent root which is equal to the variance of the score derived from it. The analysis extracts each of the roots and vectors in descending order of magnitude so that the first component is that which accounts for the largest part of the total variation over the entire range of input variables. The results of the analysis can be interpreted in such a way that the exact amount of total variability accounted for by each component is known and the structure of each component can be analysed. Each component will be associated with a group of highly intercorrelated variables from the original input data and will be essentially independent of the other components. Hence the specific variables associated with particular components can be identified and the strength of their associations calculated. This main output stage of analysis produces, therefore, a series of components which account for a known amount of the total variability over the original data. Usually the first five components account for about three-quarters of the total variability. The components indicate which of the input variables are the most diagnostic and which can be most profitably used at further stages of the analysis. By using the weighted sums of the initial indices, with the weights proportional to the elements in the latent vectors, the appropriate component score for each enumeration district can be calculated.

RESULTS OF THE ANALYSIS

At an initial level of interpretation of results, the amount of explanation of total variability accounted for by the first five components for Cardiff and Swansea can be stated.

TABLE 5.2. *Percentage total variability accounted for by components*

	One	Two	Three	Four	Five	One to five
Cardiff	27·4	23·5	10·7	6·3	5·0	73·0
Swansea	26·8	14·5	8·7	8·3	4·8	63·2

These results are comparable to those obtained in previous studies: the first five components in Merseyside[5] accounted for 69 per cent of the total variability, those in Sunderland for 77 per cent.[6] The first two components for Cardiff are powerful absorbers of total variability, accounting for over half; the first component for Swansea is of a comparable order but the second is much weaker. The resultant absorption of 41 per cent in Swansea's first two components is much smaller than has been obtained in all the major studies completed so far, with the exception of that in Hampshire.[7]

The components may be analysed in terms of the variables with which they are most closely associated and these relationships are shown in Table 5.3. Thus Component One for Cardiff can almost be described as an index of housing conditions as the most highly correlated single variable is that of persons per room, 82·8 per cent of its variation being accounted for by the component. The other positive high correlations in this component are with proportions of children and of municipal housing. There are high negative correlations with proportions of old people and with single person (adult) households. Component One for Swansea is remarkably similar in composition, four out of the five most highly correlated variables are identical to those stated for Cardiff. Persons per room is again the most highly correlated variable, 73 per cent of its variation being accounted for by this component. A measure of social class, proportion of males in manual-type occupations, appears as the fifth-ranking variable in this component. The first component for each of these urban areas is therefore associated with a rational group of variables which would seem to identify positively a particular type of housing district, with above average density of occupance of buildings, larger households, and municipally rather than privately owned. It must be stressed that the appearance of persons per room as the most significant single variable confirms similar results obtained in Merseyside and Sunderland. These findings are in contrast with those recently obtained in North America where the first component has invariably been a more

TABLE 5.3. *Composition of components*

Variables	Factor loadings	% variability accounted for by component	% variability accounted for by variables over Components One to Five
		CARDIFF	
Component One			
10	+0.91	82.8	24
2	+0·87	75·7	22
13	+0·86	74·0	21
3	−0·85	72·3	21
7	−0·73	53·3	20
Component Two			
22	+0·70	49·0	18
9	+0·69	47·6	18
11	+0·67	44·9	17
14	+0·66	43·6	18
24	+0·66	43·6	20
Component Three			
18	+0·57	32·5	12
22	+0·55	30·3	18
6	−0·49	24·0	8
23	+0·44	19·4	16
25	−0·42	17·6	19

N.B. Some of the ethnic variables with high associations in Component 3 are not included in this Table.

Component Four			
1	−0·63	39·7	13
6	−0·59	34·8	8
5	+0·58	33·6	12
		SWANSEA	
Component One			
10	+0·86	73·3	21
3	−0·85	72·4	20
2	+0·80	64·2	19
13	+0·79	62·7	19
24	+0·71	50·4	18
Component Two			
9	−0·75	57·0	10
14	−0·74	54·5	14
8	−0·62	38·7	9
25	−0.56	31·7	17
23	+0·52	26·9	15
Component Three			
1	+0·74	54·8	10
5	−0·70	48·4	6
26	+0·52	26·8	3
6	+0·51	26·0	6
2	+0·34	11·8	19
Component Four			
22	+0·56	31·9	11
21	+0·54	29·0	7
12	−0·49	23·7	16
15	+0.38	14·2	13
13	+0·37	13·5	19

direct expression of economic status, measured in terms of occupation, income and education.[8]

Component Two for Cardiff also seems more directly associated with housing conditions and only indirectly with social class or economic status. The component has high positive associations with variables which appear to be indicators of poor housing and over-crowding. While no one variable dominates the component, the first five, each positively associated with it, have between 44 and 49 per cent of their variability accounted for by the component. The clearest indicators of poor housing are the proportion with over $1\frac{1}{2}$ persons per room occupancy rate (this being the official index of overcrowding) and the proportion without exclusive use of W.C. There are high positive correlations with the proportions of foreign-born and with the proportions in manual-type occupations. Component Two for Swansea is again of similar composition to that described for Cardiff, excepting the fact that the variables are now negatively associated with the component. Three identical variables are involved, the proportion without exclusive use of W.C., the proportion renting private un-furnished accommodation, and the proportion at over $1\frac{1}{2}$ persons per room. The proportion with a school-leaving age of fifteen years or less also appears in high negative association with this component. Although Component Two can thus be seen to be very similar for the two urban areas, it is appreciably weaker in the case of Swansea, accounting for only 14·5 per cent as opposed to 23·5 per cent of the total variability. Again the cluster of variables seems rational and the high scores on this component in Cardiff could be expected in those districts with the poorest housing conditions.

Component Three for Cardiff proved a complex unit to interpret as it was highly associated with two statistically aligned but empirically disparate clusters of characteristics. The conditions producing this statistical alignment cannot be explained adequately here, but the net effect is that the component has little meaning as a single diagnostic measure. Qualities inherent in the input data which may contribute to the contradictions within the component are the very small values and limited ranges of scores on the ethnic characteristics with which the component is aligned. This is true even of some of the district scores on social class, the data for which is obtained from the 10 per cent sample of the Census. It should also be remembered that this is a much weaker component than the first two obtained for Cardiff, accounting for only 11 per cent of the total variability.

The first cluster of variables involved in Component Three comprises a measure of ethnicity, superficially similar to the segregation index of Shevky and Bell.[9] Four variables associated with the representation of foreign-born population are most highly associated with the component, which accounts for between 25 and 32 per cent of their variability. The second cluster is one associated with high social class, having a high positive association with the proportion in professional or managerial occupations and a negative association with the proportion leaving school at the age of fifteen years or less. The two clusters, internally consistent but mutually incompatible, give the component a duality which appears to be sociologically meaningless. The emergence of ethnic characteristics in Cardiff's Component Three is the product of the fact that the city has traditionally had a more cosmopolitan population structure than most provincial cities. This population has been associated with the city's dock activities and has given a segregated quality to some parts of the urban area. Yet the non-British element has not shown an increase in the postwar period comparable to that experienced by parts of Birmingham and London. Swansea, on the other hand, has not such a large number of foreign-born, either traditionally or more recently acquired and ethnic variables make no appearance in its early components. Thus, Component Three for Swansea is quite different from that for Cardiff. The two variables which dominate the component are the proportion of young children, showing a positive association, and the proportion of single adults, showing a negative association. In other words, the component is a measure of family status, not unlike the Shevky–Bell construct in its composition and high scores on the component could be expected in suburban estates where family life is at a premium.

Cardiff's Component Four is similar in composition to Swansea's Component Three and is again strongly reminiscent of the family status construct of Social Area Analysis. Three variables dominate the component, which accounts for 34 to 40 per cent of their variability. These are the proportions of children and married women which are negatively associated with the component and the proportion of single adults which is positively associated. The low scores on this component may be expected to isolate those parts of suburbia where family life is strongest. Component Four for Swansea is weak in its associations but seems linked with the more transient elements in the population, being positively associated with the foreign-born and Irish and negatively associated with owner-occupiers. This component has, therefore, some resemblance to Cardiff's Component Three.

The first four components for Cardiff and Swansea produce a pattern which, with the exception of Cardiff's Component Three, has a good measure of comparability between these two study areas and with the findings of previous studies. The composition of the first component in each case confirms a British situation which seems to contrast with that observed in North American studies where the first components are invariably measures of social class or economic status. The components become successively weaker and less meaningful after the fourth and it was judged not worth while or necessary in this study to take the interpretation any further.

The discussion so far has shown that the output of components analysis is in such a form that the composition of each component can be analysed. It is also possible to measure the diagnostic power of individual variables by calculating the proportion of the total variability within a component or group of components which is in fact absorbed by a particular variable. The most powerful single variable in Cardiff was that of persons per room which accounted for 22·7 per cent of the total variability in Component One and 24 per cent in Components One to Five. The proportion of children aged 0 to 14 years, accounted for 21 per cent of the total variability in Component One and 22 per cent in Components One to Five. The proportion without exclusive use of W.C. and of foreign-born both account for over 12 per cent of the total variability in Component Two and 18 per cent in Components One to Five. Swansea also shows persons per room as the first-ranking single variable, this accounting for 20 per cent of the total variability in Component One and 21 per cent in Components One to Five.

It is apparent that Principal Components Analysis allows the utility of the individual variables to be measured, statistically and objectively, and those variables which have the greatest discriminating qualities may be selected. This quality of the analysis provides a considerable advantage in statistical validity over systems such as Social Area Analysis, where the discriminating variables are selected from a particular theory, some of the tenets of which may be questionable.[10] An outstanding feature of the results obtained from Principal Components Analysis in this country to date has been the consistency with which some variables, particularly that of persons per room, have emerged as the most discriminating. The need now exists for a new series of empirical tests and allied theoretical reasoning to account for their apparent qualities. This uniformity of findings has also led to the suggestion that Principal Components Analysis need no longer be taken to its full conclusion.[11] A small group of variables have already been identified which may be usefully employed to differentiate urban subareas rather than using the Components themselves. Such an expediency is in fact employed for Swansea in this study and is discussed below.

URBAN SUBAREAS

The scores on each of the first three components were calculated for each enumeration district in Cardiff, using a standardising procedure.[12] Adjacent enumeration districts with identical class scores were grouped to form urban subareas, differentiated in terms of the characteristics from which the relevant components were formed. The scores for the enumeration districts on each of the relevant components were placed into three classes termed High, Medium and Low, based on a threefold

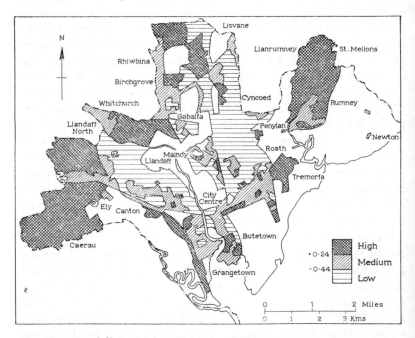

Fig. 5.1. Cardiff. Scores on Component One.

division of the dispersion column, the medium class being centred on the median for the distribution. The numerical scores appropriate to the class boundaries on each of the components are marked in the diagrams, Figs 5.1 to 5.3.

Figure 5.1 provides a subdivision of the residential area of Cardiff, based on the scores obtained on Component One, which accounted for 26·7 per cent of the total variability over the city. The map clearly has a considerable diagnostic quality in terms of Cardiff's urban-social structure. The urban subareas derived from the component scores are characterised by variations in those conditions of housing and associated social class with which the component was most strongly associated. Thus it would be expected that the areas with high scores are typified by comparatively high numbers of persons per room, large numbers of children, and a high proportion of local authority housing. This is in fact the case and the high scores on the component identify the municipal estates of Cardiff, covering such large areas as Ely and Llanrumney, where the main conditions of the component are satisfied. The municipal estates are characterised by large numbers of children, which in turn produces a comparatively high persons per room ratio.[13] The strong negative associations are with old people and single adults. Local authority estates, their boundaries clearly defined, account for the majority of high scores on this component; other areas similarly classed include smaller pockets where redevelopment has taken place and some districts where private housing, being small-size and low-price, possesses qualities similar to those found on municipal estates.

The low scores on Component One isolate housing districts that have the opposite characteristics to those described above. These are the areas of larger, more spacious houses, privately owned and possessing a contrasted set of demographic features. The better-class residential districts in Llandaff, Roath and Cyncoed are identified with low scores on this component. Parts of the older terraced rows district of Canton, Riverside and the inner city part of Roath are also depicted by low scores on this component, as they fail to show the large-family households with which Component One is identified. Thus, Component One makes a clear distinction among the housing districts of Cardiff, emphasising the contrast between publicly and privately owned property, together with their linked characteristics in terms of demographic and social class structure. The contribution of local authority housing to overall urban residential structure is demonstrated by the composition of Component One and the pattern of urban subareas which the component scores by enumeration district produce. It should perhaps be remembered, however, that a study of this kind, based on a local authority area, tends to exaggerate the municipal contribution, as a sizeable proportion of the higher-income owner-occupier group live outside the City boundary.

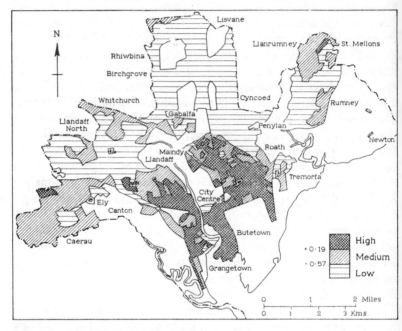

Fig. 5.2. Cardiff. Scores on Component Two.

The scores on Component Two produce a differentiation of Cardiff's residential area unlike that shown in Fig. 5.1, but which nevertheless identifies with the composition of the component and with known aspects of Cardiff's urban structure. The high component scores, shown in Fig. 5.2, are associated with poorer housing conditions and with indicators of overcrowding. Districts possessing high scores on the component are in the older parts of the city; the close-packed terraced rows of the inner urban areas clustered around the city centre, railway stations, and docks. These districts, the products of nineteenth-century urban expansion associated with docks industry and enterprise, now possess high priority as redevelopment areas.

They closely mirror the areas of obsolescence in the city, amounting to some 2130 acres and 2700 dwellings which it has been judged will need slum clearance and redevelopment by the year 2000.[14] The low scores on this component identify the areas of twentieth-century housing, both privately and publicly owned, constructed to new standards of urban design, space and amenity. Practically the whole of the west, north and north-east of the city, comprising districts such as Llandaff, Birchgrove, Cyncoed and Llanrumney, fall within this category. Parts of municipal estates, such as Ely, with higher densities of occupance brought about by family size, obtain medium scores.

It has already been noted that Component Three for Cardiff has a rather heterogeneous structure and it needed careful interpretation when used as a means of defining urban subareas in the city. The two disparate clusters making up the component were of comparable strength, the component accounting for between 25 and 30 per cent of the variability of the ethnic variables and between 17 and 20 per cent of the variability of the high social class variables. Either of these would induce high scores within the component and the separate clusters tend to categorise dissimilar urban subareas into similar classes of scores on Component Three, the weight of one cluster of elements acting to offset the deficiency in the other and giving a similar ranking. The overall result is that Component Three for Cardiff has little or no value as a diagnostic variable for the identification of urban subareas. A map of component scores of the type shown in Figs 5.1 and 5.2 would be meaningless as enumeration districts would be obtaining high scores for strongly contrasting reasons. High score districts occur because of extreme values on either one of the clusters rather than a combination of both. In view of these problems, Fig. 5.3 has been constructed so that the different elements within the component are identified and the contribution of the component towards the analysis of urban structure can be understood. The map is restricted to the delimitation of high score areas on the component, the shaded areas are those attaining high scores. Districts with scores in the upper sextile—the highest scores on the component—are delimited by the denser shading. A distinction is made between those enumeration districts which derive their high scores on this component from the weight of the ethnic variables and those which derive it from the social class variables. Fig. 5.3 distinguishes those districts with a foreign-born population element amounting to 8 per cent or more of the total resident population in the enumeration district (there are twenty-four

enumeration districts qualifying at this level) and those districts with
one-third or more of their resident male population classed as
occupied or retired males in professional, managerial or executive
occupations. These occupations are of course indicators of high social
class or economic status.

The districts qualifying through scores on ethnic variables are
clustered in the inner parts of the city area, Riverside and Butetown.

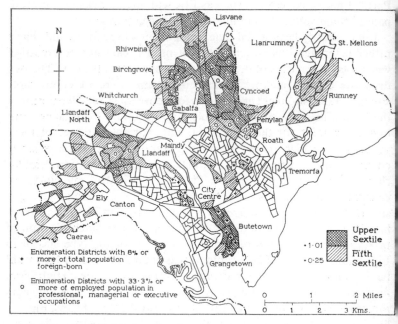

Fig. 5.3. Cardiff. High score districts.

It is the latter district, more widely known as Tiger Bay, which is the
traditional ethnic quarter of Cardiff, and here the average proportion
of foreign-born is well over 20 per cent per enumeration district. The
highest proportions of all, occasionally over 40 per cent, occur in those
districts falling within the upper sextile of component scores. As those
districts have only small proportions of their population in high status
occupations, it is clearly the ethnic variables which account for their
high scores on the component. The districts qualifying for high component scores through the weight of the social class variables are in the
north and west of the city area, comprising parts of Fairwater, Llan-

daff, Birchgrove and Cyncoed. The districts obtaining upper sextile scores in these parts of Cardiff are those with high proportions of their populations in high status occupations. Only small proportions of the populations of these districts are classed as foreign-born. Thus the two clusters of variables account for the high scores on Component Three for Cardiff, particularly when analysis is limited to the highest class of component scores, those of the upper sextile.

A small number of anomalies remain in Fig. 5.3. They are principally those enumeration districts obtaining high scores on the components where neither cluster of variables offers an adequate explanation. Two points may be made with reference to these. First, one other variable, the proportion of women aged twenty to twenty-four years ever married,[15] shows a strong negative association with this component (see Table 5.2). The upper sextile score districts not explained by ethnicity or high social class, such as the two districts in Ely, all have abnormally low scores on this variable. Secondly, there are many districts of Cardiff, qualifying for high scores on the component (though not of the upper sextile) where medium scores on the social class cluster combine with medium scores on the ethnic variables to produce a high component score. Several factors may have served to produce this effect, heterogeneity of house type within the enumeration district, and the presence of overseas students boarding in residential areas, are among those which could be put forward.

In order to take the comparison with Swansea a little further, it was thought desirable to give one example of a pattern of urban subareas obtained from the mapping of Swansea data. Fig. 5.4 shows the urban subareas of Swansea obtained by mapping high, medium and low scores for the single variable of persons per room. This variable proved, as has been previously seen, the most discriminating, 74 per cent of its variability being accounted for by Swansea's Component One, while the variable itself accounted for 20 per cent of the total variability contained within this first component. Mapping scores by the variable is therefore 74 per cent as efficient as mapping scores by Component One for Swansea.

The local authority estates, such as Fforestfach, Penlan, and Mynyddbach, are identified by high scores in Fig. 5.4 in much the same way that Component One identified these for Cardiff. The positive associations of this variable with publicly owned housing, large numbers of children and comparatively few old people are clear. Some districts of older terraced row housing, such as the distinctive communities of St Thomas and Pentrechwyth, also obtain high scores on this variable. Low scores on the variable correspond with areas of private housing development which are predominantly in the west of the Borough. The appropriate sections of Sketty, Killay

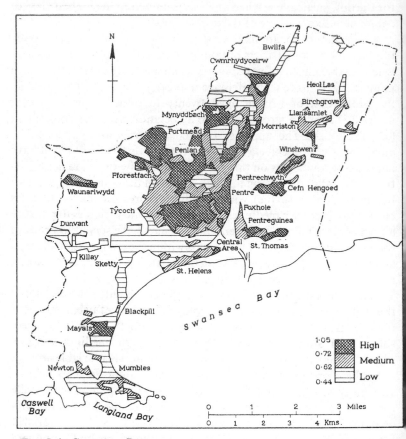

Fig. 5.4. Swansea. Persons per room.

and Langland Bay, with their established local reputations as middle-class suburbia, are examples of the identified areas. Thus, the single variable of persons per room identifies a pattern of urban subareas for Swansea possessing a measurable amount of diagnostic value, and which could justifiably be used as a basis for further analysis. Inevit-ably, however, some qualities are lost by using the single most highly associated variable rather than the component of which it forms part. Judged in terms of its value as a discriminating technique, the component itself remains the most desirable medium in this kind of analysis of urban subareas. Calculation of component scores for enumeration districts in Swansea is in fact still proceeding and maps based on these scores have not yet been produced.

GENERAL IMPLICATIONS OF THE ANALYSIS

A frequently stated objective in this type of research is the formulation of generalised, empirically derived models of urban social structure. The so-called 'classical' models, falling into the three types of concentric zones, sectors, and multiple nuclei, can be tested by comparing them with the 'shapes' or 'patterns' produced by the mapping of broad categories of component scores. The processing of mass statistical data by comparatively sophisticated techniques, of which Principal Components Analysis forms an example, can be likened to the activities of the 1920s when the development of the ecological models of the Chicago school were preceded by the mapping of similar data, obtained from field survey and observation. The Chicago ecologists intended their models as bases from which more detailed community studies should proceed, and this again has its counterparts in the stated objectives of contemporary analysts.[16] The last potential analogy is one which should perhaps be avoided. The major criticisms of the classical ecologists were aimed at the theoretical frameworks which they erected to explain their generalised models, theories which are now thought to be inapplicable.[17] A temptation certainly exists to formulate new concepts in order to explain patterns which the mapping of the component scores produces, but it is perhaps fair to say that the research knowledge of the processes influencing spatial patterns is insufficient to attempt this. Urban areas become increasingly complex, their dynamism becomes increasingly apparent and new factors emerge as influential. Alonso, describing his structural theory of urban growth, states that the new structural forces are dependent on tastes which are difficult to evaluate.[18] Others have spoken of the need for a fuller investigation of psychological motivations in urban society.[19] The suggestion is that there is little value in approximating patterns found in individual study areas to the traditional model forms; the need is first for a deeper knowledge and appreciation of the spatial forces and processes contemporarily active in urban societies. Yet

8

even with these reservations in mind, there are certain generalised statements which can be made with respect to the urban pattern identified in Cardiff from the mapping of scores on Components One and Two.

The results of this analysis confirm previous British studies in identifying Component One as a measure of housing characteristics. This forms a contrast, as stated earlier, with North American studies which have tended to endorse economic status, the main construct of Social Area Analysis, as the first-ranking measure. Social class or economic status is of course associated with the housing characteristics identified in British studies but does not exert as much direct influence on the components as is suggested by American experience. One of the main conclusions derived from consideration of Component One for Cardiff lies in the need to differentiate between publicly and privately owned housing. The index of persons per room provides a measure of this and the variable expressing the proportion of local authority housing is highly associated with the component. This points to an important difference between North American and British housing, namely the relative contributions of the public sector in urban development. The outstanding feature of British housing since the 1920s has been the increasing contribution of the local authority. Just under a quarter of the total dwellings in England and Wales in 1961 were rented from the local authority;[20] furthermore, 44 per cent of dwellings completed in England and Wales in 1966 were in the public sector.[21] The scale of this operation has no comparison in North America where the public sector is a considerably less active contributor to overall residential development. The activity of the local authority and its ability to subsidise housing and acquire land on a large scale means that the generalised ecological laws with their connotations of economic competition, basic to the 'classical models' are no longer applicable. The old set of rules no longer apply and any new set can only be formulated in terms of the availability of space and municipal policy. The limitations placed on the local authorities are the borough boundaries beyond which their powers are not effective except where they may enter into agreements with other local authorities as in town development schemes, but within the borough development can be implemented on peripheral land and on more central land which has been cleared.

Figure 5.1, therefore, faces these difficulties of generalisation. The most valid statement would seem to be one which links the crude form of sectors to the type of sociocultural factors outlined originally by Firey.[22] The high-class residential districts within the city remain sectors of land, resistant to change and persistent in character. These districts, such as Llandaff North and Cyncoed, are typified by low scores on Component One and are established high status residential areas comparatively unaffected by the normal processes of ecological change. A statement of this kind appears to be the limit of generalisation, though even this sector pattern must be tempered by the realisation that the public sector can appear in the path of any extending sector where the local authority powers are in existence. Some parts of North Cardiff, such as Llanishen, provide examples of interruptions of this kind. Again, this offers grounds for comparison with North American experience which suggests that Component One, based on economic status, assumes a sectoral form.[23] Sectoral growth in North American cities is less liable to interruptions from activity in the public sector, but the spread of low-cost housing may have similar effects. It is an observable fact that in cities like Toronto peripheral residential development is by no means restricted to high-cost housing. The ubiquity of private motor transport and the comparatively low cost of land away from central city areas are only two of the factors involved.

Component Two, again associated with housing conditions, provides a clear, generalised division of Cardiff into inner and outer urban areas. The inner urban area of Riverside, Grangetown, Butetown, Roath and Splottlands, forms a distinctive zone, identified by poorer housing conditions and some measure of overcrowding. At this level of generalisation the resemblance to a concentric pattern is obvious, but some qualification is again necessary. The map (Fig. 5.2) simply discriminates between old and new residential districts in terms of the higher standards of space and amenity associated with modern housing. The planned process of urban renewal could upset any simple zonal pattern which appears to exist by scheduling redevelopment for inner city areas. Such redevelopment is of course common to many major British cities and over the next few decades could re-form the structure of inner city areas.

Study of the generalised patterns produced by the mapping of scores on Components One and Two for Cardiff allows, with the qualifications discussed above, some statement in which the areas derived from Component One show some sector arrangement, while those derived from Component Two resemble zones. There is some ground for comparison here with North American studies which have identified more than one spatial pattern, each associated with a particular cluster of characteristics.[24] Zonal patterns, for example, have been found to be associated with the cluster of variables identifying family status. Cardiff's Component Four could be identified as that possessing these family status associations but the pattern produced by mapping the scores, not shown here, bears little resemblance to a zonal form. Perhaps the lesson to be gleaned from discussion of this kind is that intervention and redevelopment in British urban form by planning authorities is so great as to render the simple spatial associations produced by ecological forces almost redundant and the generalised models derived from those forces have considerably less universal applicability than was formerly held. It may still be possible to argue in relation to some British cities that planning interventions are isolated anomalies and do not detract from the generalised pattern, but the increasing scale of planning action is such that this argument becomes less tenable.

CONCLUSION

This study has illustrated the way in which a comparatively advanced technique, Principal Components Analysis, can be used to study urban social structure. It provides a means of identifying diagnostic variables among the characteristics of urban society, without reference to any particular theory of growth, and shows how these may be used to differentiate subareas within cities. The basic results of this analysis provide, for the two specific urban areas studied, essential guidelines for further analyses and constitute a 'data bank' which has relevance to many aspects of empirical town planning. It is relevant to state here that these are results recently obtained and form part of a continuing study project in South Wales. Seen in a more general context the application must be related to previous studies and to the wider field of analysis of which it forms part. The limitations of the technique must be recognised, particularly in terms of the availability and quality of input variables. The need for comparability among various applications has been stressed and this aspect is one which is receiving a considerable amount of attention in Britain.[25] This type of analysis provides the kind of objective empirical basis which is an essential preliminary for the fuller understanding of urban processes and which must be the point of reference for any future theory of urban structure.

REFERENCES

1. (a) KING, C. A. M., 'An introduction to factor analysis with a geographical example from northern England', *Nottingham Univ. Bull. of Quantitative Data for Geographers*, **6**, 1966. (b) RODER, W. and BERRY, B. J. L., 'Association between expected flood damages and the characteristics of urban flood plains: a factorial analysis', in *Papers on Flood Problems*, G. F. White, ed., University of Chicago, Department of Geography Research Paper, No. 70, Chicago, 1961, pp. 46–61.

2. The Census Tract Committee is an interdisciplinary group which is now concerned with coordinating research work using Census material by enumeration districts. The Committee, of which the author is a member, has met at irregular intervals over a number of years and the discussions referred at various points in this paper took place during these meetings, though they were largely undocumented.

3. NORMAN, P. C., 'A new typology of London's districts', *Proceedings of the Symposium on Quantitative Ecological Analysis in the Social Sciences*, Evian, France, 1966. Publication in preparation.

4. Census Tract Committee.

5. GITTUS, E., 'The structure of urban areas', *Town Planning Rev.* **35**, 1964, pp. 5–20; and 'An experiment in the definition of urban subareas', *Trans. of the Bartlett Society*, 1964.

6. ROBSON, B. T., 'Multivariate analysis of urban areas', *Proc. Inst. Br. Geogr. Study Group in Urban Geography*, '*The Social Structure of Cities*', 1966, pp. 1–14.

7. BROADY, M., 'The Hampshire census project', *J. Tn Plann. Inst.*, **51**, 1965, pp. 300–2.

8. MURDIE, R. A., 'Some aspects of ecological structure and change in metropolitan Toronto', Unpublished paper, presented to Canadian Association of Geographers, Ottawa, 1967.

9. SHEVKY, E. and BELL, W., *Social Area Analysis*, Stanford University Press, 1955.

10. HERBERT, D. T., 'Social area analysis: a British study', *Urban Studies*, **4**, 1967, pp. 41–60.

11. Census Tract Committee.

12. Dr B. T. Robson, Department of Geography, University of Cambridge, kindly provided advice on this standardising procedure.

13. Most local authorities will in fact use the number of children in a

family as a favourable weighting factor in the allocation of municipal housing.

14. BUCHANAN, C. and Partners, *Cardiff: Probe Study Report*, Development and Transportation Study, 1966.

15. This term 'ever married' is a Census definition.

16. ROBSON, B. T., *I.B.G.* Study Group Report 1966.

17. THEODORSON, G. A., ed., *Studies in Human Ecology*, Row, Peterson and Company, 1961.

18. ALONSO, W., 'The historic and structural theories of urban form', *Land Econ.*, **40**, 1964, pp, 227–31.

19. Census Tract Committee.

20. *Housing Tables, Census of England and Wales*, 1961, HMSO, 1965.

21. *Local Housing Statistics, England and Wales*, Number 1, HMSO, 1967.

22. FIREY, W., 'Sentiment and symbolism as ecological variables', *Am. sociol. Rev.*, **10**, 1945, pp. 140–8.

23. MURDIE, R. A., unpublished paper.

24. DUNCAN, B., 'Variables in urban morphology', in Burgess E. W. and Bogue, D. J., eds., *Contributions to Urban Sociology*, University of Chicago Press, 1967, pp. 17–30.

25. Census Tract Committee.

ACKNOWLEDGEMENTS

I should like to acknowledge the help and advice given by Mr R. Startup, Department of Sociology and Anthropology, University College, Swansea and also his permission to use some of the Swansea data. Mr E. Parkinson, Cardiff City Planning Officer, kindly allowed me access to Census data and other material held in his Department. Other members of the Cardiff City Planning Department, particularly Mr G. Steeley, have given freely of their advice and assistance.

CHAPTER 6

SOCIALLY DISORGANISED AREAS IN BARRY:

A MULTIVARIATE ANALYSIS

John A. Giggs

During the last twenty years all the social sciences have been character-ised by a growing methodological debate on their scope and methods.[1] Thus in two recent, independent, reviews of postwar trends in 'social' and 'human' geography, Pahl[2] and Brookfield[3] traced the extension in the scope of the subject from Febvre's idea that 'geographers start from soil, not from society' to the wider view that it is concerned with 'processes and patterns involved in an understanding of socially de-fined populations in their spatial setting'. They concluded that an increasing amount of attention will in future be devoted to the importance of human decisions and that geographers have much to learn from sociology and related disciplines. In 1967 Gould,[4] in a preliminary enquiry into the mental images that men have of geographic space, affirmed that 'As human geographers reach out across traditional disciplinary boundaries, it is increasingly apparent that the truly satisfying explanation they seek is going to come from emphasising the *human* as much as the *geography*. We may, perhaps, define our subject as essentially that which tries to understand the spatial aspects of man's behaviour.'

One of the results of this debate has been the realisation that many of the traditional disciplinary boundaries are artificial, and that despite varying professional orientations scholars have remarkably similar preoccupations and techniques. This situation is especially true of studies of intra-urban structure, a field in which geographers, sociologists, economists and psychologists have all been interested.[5] Although a few rather limited theories or schematic descriptions of spatial structure emerged at a very early period—schemes associated with the names of Burgess, Hoyt, Harris and Ullman[6]—all of them fail to offer a coherent and universal explanation of city structure.[7] Rather it is true to say that aspects of all three schemes may be found in individual cities.[8] Hence, it has become increasingly apparent that intra-urban patterns have a complex nature and that any explanations must be of a multifactor nature. Fortunately the current development and refinement of multivariate statistical techniques competent to deal with organised complexity make analysis of the evolving spatial structure of the urban community a more manageable task.[9] Now urban researchers have begun to make more precise statements concerning the true regularities and uniformity of the internal spatial patterning of towns and cities, and need not be constrained by theories dealing with only one or two variables.

Of many aspects of urban community structure under review few have attracted a greater amount of attention than social problems. At both national and local government levels planners are concerned with the tasks of providing better services and environments for the burgeoning urban segments of their populations. For these authorities, problems such as ill-health, crime and financial delinquency affect many phases of the social economic and political lives of their communities and it is important to look at these problems from as many different perspectives as possible.[10] Certainly it has long been recognised that urban communities are not homogeneous with respect to the internal distribution of social problems. There is a spatial basis to the incidence of social defects, a basis that has been the subject of many enquiries both in Europe[11] and the United States. Much of the stimulus to this kind of research was provided by Burgess and his associates working at the University of Chicago in the 1920s.[12] Although the theoretical basis laid down by Burgess has been shown to represent only a limited view of reality it is still useful as a standard against which empirical results can be more easily compared. The deviation from this simple spatial pattern will then be more obvious.

Although these many and varied studies have added considerably to our store of knowledge it is generally agreed that the work has barely begun.[13] The case for further research is therefore strong and scarcely requires justification. This study seeks to test three basic assumptions of the two Burgess schemes, with particular reference to social problems:

1. During the 1920s and 1930s the members of the Chicago school formulated, elaborated and tested (by descriptive means) the 'social pathology' or 'social disorganisation' approach to the study of urban social problems.[14] Social disorganisation was identified as a state

which would develop in a community when social solidarity and social controls were weakened. The condition would have many manifestations, for example physical and mental illness, family disorganisation, high rates of criminal residence and commission, juvenile delinquency and varied financial problems (economic hardship and poverty). The degree of social disorganisation would vary among different parts of the community, since the population of different areas (identified by census tracts) would be socialised to varying degrees. Further, it was postulated that the distribution of social defects was not haphazard, but that the community was highly structured with respect to the incidence of social problems. Characteristically the rates would vary in a way which confirmed the Burgess Zonal and Gradient hypotheses, that is the community would be characterised by a set of concentric zones, each distinguished by a distinct range of defect rates. The rates would be highest in the innermost zones and fall off through successive zones to lowest rates at the periphery. Schmid's findings in a multivariate analysis of twenty different crime categories in Seattle accorded with these principles: 'Characteristically the central area of the city shows the highest concentrations, with contrastingly low rates in peripheral residential sections.'[15]

2. The concentric zone hypothesis presents a model of a highly structured community in which the relationships between physical and social space are very close. Thus the central parts of the city (Zones 1 and 2) are distinguished by heterogeneous land use patterns (i.e. a close association between commercial, industrial and residential uses), decaying, retrogressing neighbourhoods, and the highest concentrations of social disorganisation. In succeeding zones better quality residences assume a progressively larger proportion of the land use and the rates of social disorganisation steadily decline.

3. Explicitly or implicitly social disorganisation was regarded as a side effect of social change, effected primarily by mobility, and something that would tend to diminish as social reorganisation (effected by accommodation and assimilation) progressed. The incidence of social problems was therefore closely related to the degree of mobility. In a study of the relationship of delinquency to mobility in Omaha, Sullenger stated: 'Where the mobility is large the delinquency is also large; and where there is little mobility, there is little delinquency.'[16] The incidence of social disorganisation was thus found to be highest in Zone 2—the Zone in Transition—for there the proportions of unstable residences were greatest (unassimilated first-generation immigrant

colonies, transient residence, for example rooming-house districts and homeless-men areas, and accelerating rates of population loss to outlying zones). In outlying zones, residential stability, assimilation and accommodation result in low rates of social disorganisation.

Two problems now present themselves: the selection of a suitable town and of appropriate data. The choice of the study area was dictated by two considerations. First, the store of knowledge concerning the spatial patterning of social problems in British urban communities is small compared with that existing in other countries, notably the U.S.A. Additional research is required to increase this store so that viable cross-cultural comparisons will eventually be feasible. Secondly, a general characteristic of extant studies in this field of research is that they have related to medium-sized or large cities. Smaller communities have been virtually ignored. Consequently we have a series of tentative generalisations about the nature, extent and distribution of social problems in settlements in a limited segment of the urban hierarchy. The analysis of social problems of small urban communities, therefore, forms an essential prerequisite to the formulation of general hypotheses or theories.

This study focuses upon the social problems of Barry, a medium-sized town (population 42,084 in 1961), with port, resort, service and mixed industrial functions. The borough is a late nineteenth-century creation and might therefore be expected to have characteristics similar to those found in Chicago and other fast-growing industrial American cities. To test these three concepts, the spatial distribution of social defects is determined and the characteristics of disorganised areas identified and described. Two sets of variables, the first comprising thirteen measurements of social defect characteristics, the second forty-three other urban characteristics, were selected for analysis. (They are shown in detail in an Appendix, p. 134.) The choice of these particular variables was dictated partly by the fact that previous investigations point to their pertinence with regard to the field of study. In some cases they are not, theoretically speaking, the best or most desirable indices, but they appear to be the best of those currently available for the borough. Thus tuberculosis is not a behavioural social defect in the strict sense like, for example, venereal diseases. It is an infectious disease which thrives in areas where there are frequent inter-personal contacts, for example in overcrowded terraced houses. Undoubtedly many important cultural factors, such as values and attitudes, affect the results. It is felt that the variables employed in this study provide at least partial indicators of these important but less tangible factors.

Although the number of variables is large, the coverage is by no means complete. The most important gaps are the lack of adequate data pertaining to changes over time, e.g. in population size, structure and mobility. With the publication of more statistical information on the enumeration district (E.D.) scale in future censuses, these gaps can be filled[17] and the study repeated, so that the results, at different points

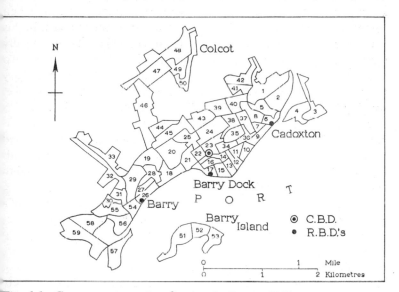

Fig. 6.1. Census enumeration districts in Barry, 1961.
C.B.D. = Central Business District.
R.B.D. = Retail Business District.

n time, can be compared. Several variables are indirect measures of these important dimensions, that is 2, 6, 19, 20, 36–40, 45–46, 54–55.

Since this study is concerned with the internal structure of the town, the 56 variables have been calculated as rates or other suitable measures for the 59 E.D.s identified in the 1961 census (Fig. 6.1). Despite several limitations, the value of census tracts and census tract data has been conclusively demonstrated by many students of intra-urban spatial variation, chiefly in the U.S.A. and more recently, in Britain.[18] In an attempt to determine the basic factors in the distribution of social defects, and to describe more precisely the specific attributes of disorganised areas, the defect indices are then related to a large number of significant intra-urban attributes. The two sets of data are analysed by Principal Components Analysis (the 'principal axes' solution) and a grouping algorithm.[19] The results are presented and discussed below.

The necessity for applying rigorous statistical techniques to the problems of analysing urban social areas and of deriving valid regions is clear. The traditional methods of preparing maps for each variable and of comparing them to determine causal relationships and delineate geographical regions become very complex to handle visually when combinations of more than three or four variables are involved. In this particular study effective visual comparison would be practically impossible. To view all possible combinations of the two sets of thirteen and fifty-six maps it would be necessary to consider 2^{13} and 2^{56} or 10^4 and 10^{17} combinations (i.e. roughly 10,000 and 100,000,000,000,000,000 ways). In addition, it is now recognised that a subjective element creeps into visual comparisons of distributions. McCarty and Salisbury[20] have demonstrated that students produced varying, often inaccurate, conclusions in reading isopleth maps because they produced results that they expected to see rather than correlations that existed.

Principal Component Analysis is currently the most widely used of a wide range of multivariate techniques chiefly because no hypotheses need be made about the variables. There is only the assumption 'that a variety of phenomena within a domain are related and that they are determined at least in part by a smaller number of functional units or factors. . . . In the more fundamental factorial problem the object is to discover whether the variables can be made to exhibit some underlying order that may throw light on the process that produces the individua differences shown in all the variables.'[21]

The importance of both the Principal Components Analysis and the linkage procedure is that they are analytic. 'Decisions on the part o the investigator between preparation of a data matrix and formation o the groups are eliminated, for the entire process may be accomplishec as a two or three phase run on an electronic computer.'[22]

ANALYSIS OF DIFFERENTIAL DEFECT RATES

Aggregate structural relationships

The thirteen variables selected as a meaningful characterisation o social defects in the town were subjected to Principal Component

Analysis. Table 6.1 reveals that, collectively, the five components extracted[23] account for 79·6 per cent of the total variance of the thirteen variables measured over the 59 E.D.s.

TABLE 6.1. *Social defects: major dimensions of variation*

Component	Eigen values	% of total variance	Cumulative %
I	5 74	44 2	44·2
II	1·46	11·2	55·4
III	1·24	9·5	64·9
IV	1·01	7·8	72·7
V	0·90	6·9	79·6

The correlation between each of the original variables and the new components is measured by a 'loading' value. The loading of a variable on a component is measured by a value on the scale from 0 to 1 in either a positive or a negative direction. The value indicates the strength of the contribution of the variable to the component and the sign indicates the direction in which the variable is related to it. The significance levels established for the variables on the 59 E.D.s[24] are also applicable to the loadings, since they are correlations between the variables and the component vectors. The most important variables on any components can thus be identified as those having the highest loadings. Only those variables having loadings in excess of the 0·05 level of confidence (i.e. ± 0.25) are considered here.

TABLE 6.2. *Social defects: significant loadings for the five principal components*

Variables	Components				
	I	II	III	IV	V
1. Percentage with T.B.	−0.81				
2. Percentage distribution T.B.	−0·70	−0·59			
3. Percentage credit delinquents	−0·83		0·32		
4. Percentage rate delinquents	−0·35	−0·53		0·44	−0·47
5. Percentage rent delinquents		0·82			0·43
6. Percentage distribution rent delinquents		−0·69	0·53	0·31	
7. Residence: adult offenders	−0·67	0·41			0·27
8. Residence: juvenile offenders	−0·73			−0·43	−0·31
9. Residence: offenders to persons	−0·85				
10. Residence: offenders to property	−0·67	−0·53			
11. Commission: offences to persons	−0·78				
12. Commission: offences to property	−0·52		0·48		0·29
13. Percentage divorces	−0·48			0·57	0·37

Empirical interpretation suggests that the statistical relationships revealed by the five component structures are genuine. The first principal component would seem to provide clear justification for the hypothesis that social disorganisation is a basic factor, of which these variables are equally manifestations. This single dimension accounts for 44·2 per cent of the total variance. Although four of the variables are partially interdependent (i.e. variables 7–10), and their covariation would therefore be expected to be strong, Table 6.2 shows that Component I incorporates eleven of the original thirteen variables. Further, all eleven have very strong, uniformly negative loadings, with values in excess of the 0·01 level of confidence (i.e. $\pm 0·33$) and nine have values exceeding the 0·001 level (i.e. $\pm 0·56$). The component is clearly the most important single dimension of variance among the thirteen social defects in the 59 E.D.s and may be empirically labelled as the 'social disorganisation' component. The remaining four components account for significant but progressively smaller shares of the residual total variance. They reveal smaller sets of variables loading less strongly and in varying directions on each dimension and are less easily explained empirically. The variables that constitute the second component emphasise a dimension in which tuberculosis, recidivist rent delinquents and adult offenders (residence) figure prominently in a negative (or inverse) relationship with 'all other' offenders (residence) and recidivist rate delinquents. Component III, which represents the third most important dimension of variation, is associated with variables relating to financial delinquency—rate delinquents, per cent distribution of rent delinquents and credit delinquents—and commission of 'other' criminal offences.

Component IV is characterised by only three significant variables. Divorce loads more heavily on this component than any other and is the chief diagnostic variable. Rate delinquents also load positively with divorce at a significance level in excess of 99 per cent. Juvenile offenders (residence) forms the weakest member of the group, loading negatively in relation to the leading variables.

Component V is the weakest of the set abstracted for examination, accounting for only 6·9 per cent of the total variance. The significance levels of all the variables loading on Component V are relatively low, with three ranging between 95 and 99 per cent. Rate delinquents and juvenile offenders (residence) figure most prominently on the negative scale, with rent delinquents, divorced persons and adult offenders (residence) loading positively.

Spatial variations

Once the basic dimensions have been identified for the borough as a whole it is possible to ascertain how they are related to specific areas within the town. One of the most useful outcomes of component analysis for the geographer is the reappearance of the observations (the 59 E.D.s in this case) assessed not on the verdict of the thirteen separate variables but on scales of scores for each of the derived components. The scores allow the E.D.s to be analysed first with respect to the contribution of each component to their character. This procedure gives a set of gross characterisations which may be followed by more rigorous grouping analysis.

Table 6.3 shows that the E.D.s exhibit considerable diversity within the confines of the original thirteen variables, i.e. there is a wide range of scores on all five components. The town is not a homogeneous community with respect to social disorganisation, therefore, but is composed of subareas which have distinct levels and diverse kinds of social defects.

The degree of diversity exhibited by the E.D.s on all five components makes it possible to distinguish relatively homogeneous regions within

TABLE 6.3 *Social defects: extreme scores for Components I–V*

Components				
I	II	III	IV	V
8·52	3·31	4·34	2·59	1·85
−20·49	−6·12	−2·39	−3·59	−2·40

the town on the basis of their score characteristics. A map was prepared for each of the five components showing the distribution of socially defective regions as revealed by quartile divisions of the ranked scores. Only one map (for Component I—'Social Disorganisation') is presented here for illustrative purposes, because of space restrictions. The advantages of such a set of maps is clear, however, for the bewildering detail shown on thirteen individual maps of the original variables can be effectively collapsed to five basic dimensions, which collectively account for the major part of the total variance among the fifty-nine E.D.s.

Figure 6.2. portrays the socially defective areas, as identified by the E.D. scores on Component I. The dimension was identified with pronounced negative loadings on eleven of the thirteen original variables

(Table 6.2), consequently all the communities in E.D.s with extreme negative scores are seriously disorganised. Conversely, E.D.s with extreme positive scores are not disorganised. The figure shows, however, that although the E.D.s in the four quartile divisions possess a fair degree of regional contiguity, the pattern is by no means a simple one. The highly defective (lowest quartile) and moderately defective (lower interquartile) areas are located chiefly in the central and eastern parts of the town, but they are found in both inner and peripheral locations. E.D.s in the weakly defective range (upper interquartile)

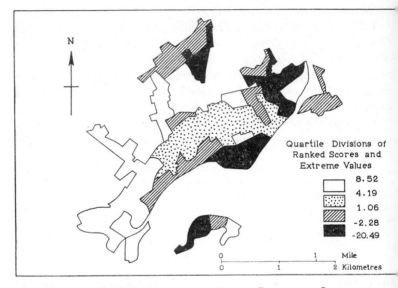

Fig. 6.2. Socially defective areas in Barry: Component I.

form a single large continuous region in Barry Dock and Cadoxton which includes inner, intermediate and suburban areas. The non defective areas (extreme positive quartile) are strongly segregated fo ten of the fifteen E.D.s form a continuous region at the western end o the town. Significant outliers are found on the outskirts of the town in Colcot, Cadoxton and Barry Island (E.D.s 46, 39 and 53). Two E.D. with very low defect rates on this component (E.D.s 1 and 34) abu directly against areas with extreme defect scores.

The degree of diversity among the E.D.s with respect to socia defects has been demonstrated briefly by reference to their scores on th five individual dimensions (Table 6.3) and an examination of their spatial distribution on a single component. The arbitrary assignment of E.D.s to quartile divisions on each component, however, while essential for comparisons between dimensions, does insufficient justice to the complexity of the situation.

Recently attention has been focused on the problem of how the objects of classification may be grouped in the *total* dimensional space of the system under review, in preference to the *partial* solution provided by locating the relative positions of objects on the different dimensional scales. The most promising solution to this problem would appear to be the grouping algorithm discussed by Ward and Berry.[25] This procedure produces a multivariate classification which provides a much better impression of reality than earlier, univariate, classifications. The area of human decision is reduced to the minimum—the selection of the appropriate variables at the beginning of the analysis.

The technique involves utilising the scores derived from the component analysis and grouping the observations (the fifty-nine E.D.s here) together on the basis of their total scoring on all the five extracted components. Since the components extracted in this study are orthogonally disposed and hence uncorrelated, the distances between E.D. points in the five-dimensional space may be regarded as measures of their similarities. The distances between the individual score-profiles (each consisting of five values—for example E.D. 17's scores on components 1–5 were −20·49, 0·57, 0·39, 2·39 and 2·39 respectively) are computed. These distances form a multifactor similarity matrix which is used in a stepped grouping of the E.D.s. The matrix is progressively broken down (i.e. Stage 1, 59 × 59, Stage 2, 58 × 58 . . .) by a process of computing the mean of the profiles of the two most similar E.D.s at each stage of the grouping procedure. The process is terminated when the whole of the town forms a single region.

The process is summarised in Fig. 6.3. It is apparent that the analysis results in the progressive pairwise grouping of the E.D.s until the final pair of groups is linked into the entire population of observations. A complete 'linkage-tree' results, proceeding from fifty-nine outermost branches (the fifty-nine E.D.s) to the final grouping at the single main trunk (the whole town). At each stage of the grouping process the loss of detail is recorded (Within-Group Distance squared) and the percentage loss of detail is measurable. The weighted ratio of increment to total distance (R) characteristically decreases in the grouping process to a minimum value and then increases again. Table 6.4 shows

9

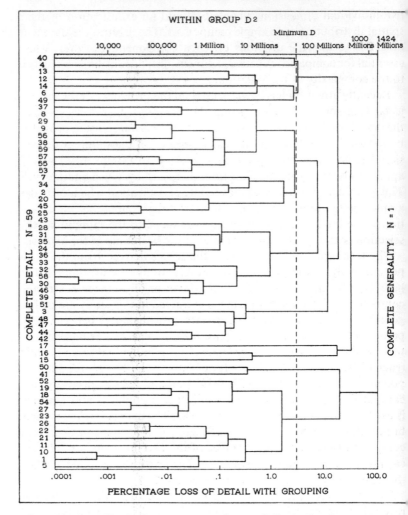

Fig. 6.3. Socially defective areas in Barry: linkage tree.

that in this example the minimum value of R appears when the nine-group solution is reached. Beyond this point the value increases again.

The resulting set of E.D. groups is presented in Table 6.5. These nine groups form the most homogeneous sub-sets of the fifty-nine E.D.s in terms of the original variables employed. At succeeding stages in the grouping process the E.D.s form fewer, larger, but more

TABLE 6.4. *Ratio of weighted increase (R) to total*

No. of groups formed	W.G.D. squared	Loss of detail	R	
58	3	—	1·0000	Complete
30	1·969	0·1	0·0027	detail
20	5·459	0·3	0·0058	
10	37·532	2·5	0·0031	
9	37·910	2·6	0·0003	
8	41·520	2·9	0·0087	
2	418·612	29·4	0·0260	Complete
1	1,423·842	100·0	0·0706	generality

heterogeneous groups. The percentage loss of detail rises until complete generality is obtained, with 100 per cent loss in detail.

An inspection of the scores on the five components for the E.D.s composing each group revealed that their profiles were consistently uniform. The score-profiles for two small groups are presented in Table 6.6 for illustrative purposes. Group 1, consisting of one member, E.D. 17, is identified by a massive negative score on Component I (i.e. eleven social defects—see Table 6.2) and two moderately high positive scores on Components IV and V (variables 4, 6 and 13; and variables 5, 7, 12 and 13). Group 4, consisting of two members, is distinguished

TABLE 6.5. *Social defects: optimum E.D. groupings*

	Groups 1	2	3	4	5	6	7	8	9
Individual	17	15	6	41	3	4	1	2	24
enumeration		16	12	50	42	40	5	7	28
districts			13		44		10	8	30
			14		47		11	9	31
			49		48		18	20	32
					51		19	25	33
							21	29	35
							22	34	36
							23	37	39
							26	38	43
							27	45	46
							52	53	58
							54	55	
								56	
								57	
								59	
Total number of members	1	2	5	2	6	2	13	16	12

by high negative scores on Components I and II (i.e. eleven defects on Component I, and variables 2, 4, 6 and 10 on Component II) and moderately high negative scores on Component V (i.e. variables 4 and 8).

TABLE 6.6. *Component scores for two selected E.D. groups*

		Component scores				
Group	*E.D.s*	I	II	III	IV	V
1	17	−20·49	0·57	0·39	2·39	2·39
4	41	−5·82	−3·33	1·43	2·34	−2·40
	50	−4·82	−3·12	0·77	1·42	−2.20

Although the groups are identified by five sets of scores it is apparen that they are primarily distinguished by their scores on Component I This is to be expected since both the proportion of total variance and the range of scores on the dimension are, respectively, four and three times those on the next highest dimension (i.e. Component II—see Tables 6.2 and 6.3). The nine groups have consequently been ranked according to their degrees of defectiveness as revealed by their score profiles on the chief diagnostic item (Table 6.7).

TABLE 6.7. *Social defects: ranked multifactor groups*

Group	Score profile	
1	−20·49	Highly defective
2	−15·78	−15·89
3	−5·99	−9·37
4	−4·82	−5·82
5	−0·05	−4·71
6	−0·28	−1·48
7	+1·71	−3·96
8	+0·60	+5·60
9	+2·54	+8·52	Non-defective

Discussion

Figure 6.4 shows that these statistically derived groups have a high degree of regional contiguity, since the E.D.s in each group cluster fairly strongly into distinct areas in the town. The community is clearly highly structured with respect to both degree and type of social defectiveness, if we accept Besher's definition of social structure as a set of persistent patterned social relationships among persons or positions'.[26] The relatively seriously disorganised areas are markedly segregated and it would appear that they form what Shaw termed 'delinquency areas',[27] in which deviance of varying sorts forms an important pattern of behaviour (active or permissive) among a fairly large proportion of their inhabitants.

If the pattern of incidence of social defectiveness revealed here is compared with that produced in similar studies of North American

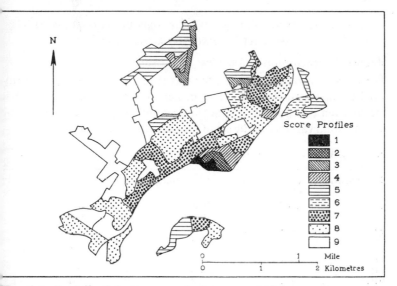

N

Score Profiles

1
2
3
4
5
6
7
8
9

0 ——————————— 1 Mile
0 ——————————— 1 ——————————— 2 Kilometres

Fig. 6.4. Socially defective areas in Barry: multifactor regions.

cities, it becomes apparent that substantial differences exist. The findings in most American studies of large cities confirm the concentric zone and gradient hypotheses of Burgess. Schmid, for example, in his study of the crime areas of Seattle, concluded that 'There is a tendency for most crimes to decline more or less in direct proportion to the distance from the centre of the city.'[28] Fig. 6.4 shows that although the centre of the town shows the highest concentrations (groups 1–3), many of the highest defect rates are to be found in the outer suburbs (groups 3–5). Conversely, regions with very low rates (Groups 7–9) are found not only on the outskirts of the town, but in inner residential areas, often abutting against extensively defective regions.

Thus, although it has been shown that the town is composed of several regions and hence exhibits considerable spatial variation in the degree of social disorganisation, it is apparent that the patterns so formed do not substantiate either of the Burgess schemes. The interpretation and explanation of the derived patterns and the appraisal of the reasons for the divergence between these specific empirical findings and the hypothetical constructs depends upon investigating the reciprocal causal relationships between the original variables and the wider set of urban characteristics.

ANALYSIS OF SOCIAL DEFECTS AND THEIR RELATIONSHIPS TO SELECTED URBAN CHARACTERISTICS

Aggregate structural relationships

The fifty-six variables selected for this study were subjected to Principal Components Analysis. The 'principal axes' solution reveals that the first ten components extracted account for 79·9 per cent of the original total variance in the set of fifty-six variables (Table 6.8).

TABLE 6.8. *Major dimensions of variation*

Components	Eigen values	% of total variance	Cumulative %
I	16·6	29·6	29·6
II	11·2	19·9	49·5
III	3·8	6·8	56·3
IV	3·1	5·6	61·9
V	2·2	3·9	65·8
VI	1·9	3·4	69·2
VII	1·7	3·0	72·2
VIII	1·6	2·8	75·0
IX	1·4	2·6	77·6
X	1·3	2·3	79·9

Empirical interpretation of most of the components is feasible through an examination of the variables loading significantly upon them (Table 6.9).

The first principal component clearly constitutes the most important single dimension in the system. It has the largest cluster of variables with significant loadings: forty-three have values which exceed the 0·05 level, and twenty-five have loadings exceeding the 0·001 level. The variables that constitute Component I emphasise both high social class and massive social defectiveness. The social class dimension is distinguished by pronounced positive loadings on seventeen variables

TABLE 6.9. *Urban dimensions: factor loadings**

Variables	Components									
	I	II	III	IV	V	VI	VII	VIII	IX	X
1. Percentage with T.B.	68	30	36							
2. Percentage distribution, T.B.	75	34								
3. Credit delinquents	75	36								
4. Rate delinquents			43	29					*33*	
5. Rent delinquents		*36*			*32*			*36*		
6. Percentage distribution rent delinquents	83									
7. Residence: adult offenders	42	44	44							
8. Residence: juvenile offenders	51		35				*51*			
9. Residence: offenders to persons	63		43				*29*			
10. Residence: offenders to property	40	47	39							43
11. Commission: offences to persons	67	39	25	27						
12. Commission: offences to property	42		46						*33*	
13. Percentage persons divorced	39		*34*				37		29	
14. Percentage aged 0–14		94								
15. Percentage over retiring age	33	83								
16. Average age	30	87								
17. Females/100 males	49	47						34		
18. Fertility ratio	46		28		*33*		25			
19. Percentage foreign-born	44		*51*				33			
20. Percentage distribution L.A. tenants	76									
21. Percentage 1 person households		76								
22. Percentage 1–2 person households		86	25							
23. Percentage 5+ person households		*83*								
24. Percentage 1–3 room dwellings	54	40	36							
25. Persons/room		90								
26. Percentage households > 1 person/room	68	25		29	33	36				
27. Percentage households > 1·5 persons/room	65	26			37					
28. Persons/acre	73		31							
29. Percentage shared dwellings	69	28		29	32	34				
30. Percentage shared kitchen	73	28		34	27					
31. Percentage shared W.C.	75	39				27				
32. Percentage substandard houses	72	34								
33. Rateable value	78		34							
34. Percentage households owner-occupied	35	65		48						
35. Percentage households L.A.—Rented		*80*		47						
36. Housing: % L.A. 1914–45				82						
37. Housing: % L.A. 1945–64		87								

* Italic numerals indicate negative values.

TABLE 6.9.—*Continued*

Variables	Components									
	I	II	III	IV	V	VI	VII	VIII	IX	X
38. Housing: % built < 1914	66	57	26							
39. Housing: % built 1914–45	59		37	54		27				
40. Housing: % built 1945–64	33	79		26						
41. Land use: % commercial, etc.	56	33	28	28					25	35
42. Land use: % institutional			36				31	52	40	
43. Land use: % open space	29	28				41				69
44. Land use: % residential	29			40		38	48	34		
45. Fare to C.B.D.	46	42						40		
46. Distance to R.B.D.	45	36			29			37		32
47. Average altitude	64	35								28
48. Average amplitude		25			45			45	25	
49. Percentage population occupied				42	36	52				
50. Percentage women occupied	70					38			31	
51. Percentage unemployed persons	70		37		28		27			
52. Percentage in social classes I and II	88									
53. Percentage in social classes IV and V	73	28		35						
54. Percentage households with telephone	79		38		27					
55. Percentage households with car	76		31		38					
56. Percentage T.E.A. > 15	84	27								

which reveal an older, preponderantly female population dominated by social classes I and II, with high educational status, and numerous cars and telephones. A large proportion of the population lives in modern, expensive, owner-occupied houses located in elevated suburban areas. Housing and public open space comprise the dominant land uses. The sole social defect (10) loading positive on this component ranks only thirty-fifth in the table of loadings. The remaining twenty-six variables load negatively and relate to high rates for ten of the thirteen social defects, together with a cluster of variables with expected high values which identify populations with large proportions of foreign-born persons, high fertility ratios, low economic, social and family cohesion (i.e. unemployed persons, social classes IV and V, occupied women and divorced persons). These populations live in old, substandard, overcrowded, multifamily dwellings with shared use of amenities. Commerce and industry comprise the dominant land uses. In terms of the present data, therefore, this constellation represents the social defect dimension *par excellence*.

The second component has thirty-four variables loading with values in excess of the 0·05 level and twelve of these exceed the 0·001 level. Component II loads highest on variables that emphasise high social defects and low social-economic status. The chief diagnostic variables load negatively and distinguish large young families living in postwar, predominantly municipal housing. The houses are slightly over-crowded, peripherally located and associated with substantial areas of public open space. Of the seventeen variables loading negatively, six relate to social defects and isolate areas of criminal residence, credit and rent delinquents, T.B. cases and commission of violent acts and sex offences. The seventeen variables which load positively indicate older populations living in small family units. The houses are generally owner-occupied but a large proportion are shared, old, and in poor condition. They are located adjacent to the major business districts and consequently the land use pattern is dominated by commercial and industrial functions. Only one social defect (2) loads *positively* on this dimension.

The third component is less easily interpreted. It is indexed by modest loadings on variables which reveal a high degree of social defectiveness and low family cohesion. Significant negative loadings indicate an association between foreign-born persons, unemployed persons, small households, high population densities, interwar housing and commercial and industrial land uses. The 'social defects' cluster is represented by eight variables, with the criminal residence and commission subset accounting for five of these. The areas affected are not uniformly poor, because high educational status and highly rated houses, with private telephones and cars, also load negatively on this dimension. Low family cohesion can be inferred from positive loadings on variables indicating a high proportion of occupied persons, divorced persons, rate delinquency and small old dwellings.

The cluster of variables loading negatively on Component IV represent the interwar residential areas *par excellence* (e.g. the highest loading shows −0·82 for per cent interwar local authority housing). Significantly, not one social defect loads negatively on this dimension. The weak positive loadings reveal an association between postwar owner-occupied housing, commercial land use, rate delinquency and commission of offences to persons.

Component V is rather ambiguous, since only five of the twelve variables loading on it have confidence levels in excess of 0·01. The nine negatively loaded variables characterise the dimension as one with mixed economic status and few social defects. Component VI indicates a significant association between fairly low economic and residential status (positive loadings on five variables). Three variables load negatively, identifying predominantly residential land use with moderately low residential status.

Component VII shows relatively high negative loadings for residential areas typified by high proportions of juvenile delinquents, offenders against the person, and unemployed persons. The positively loaded variables reveal a significant association between divorced and foreign-born persons, high fertility ratios and institutional land use. The variables that constitute Component VIII emphasise a dimension in which positive loadings on intermediate residential areas (identified by variables 43–46 and 48) figure prominently in an inverse relationship with moderately defective peripheral estates.

Weakly defective residential areas and a propinquity between commercial and industrial land uses and offences against property are indexed by Component IX. The final Component is readily identifiable as a land-use/physical dimension. Public open space and distance to R.B.D.s are inversely related to commercial land use and average altitude.

Spatial variation

The loadings on Table 6.9 allow for fairly detailed interpretations of the ten components for the town as a whole. The corresponding component scores for each E.D. (Table 6.10) confirm that considerable internal variations exist on each dimension. A map was produced for each of the ten components using quartile divisions. Because of space restrictions, only those for components I and II are presented here. These two maps collectively account for 49·5 per cent of the total variance in the set of fifty-six variables, and forty-six of these load more heavily on these two components than on any of the remaining eight originally abstracted for analysis.

TABLE 6.10. *Intra-urban dimensions: extreme scores for Components I–X*

Components I	II	III	IV	V	VI	VII	VIII	IX	X
33·16	16·62	8·07	4·36	4·75	5·32	4·07	3·57	5·40	3·16
−48·88	−38·74	−11·47	−10·58	−5·08	−3·42	−6·07	−3·29	−3·41	−3·39

Figure 6.5 shows that the E.D.s outside the interquartile range on Component I are strongly segregated. Those with high negative scores (i.e. the highly defective areas) are all old inner residential neighbourhoods located adjacent to the port. These areas are most continuous and extensive in Barry Dock and Cadoxton. A gradient is clearly discernible, as values fall successively away through the negative and positive segments of the interquartile range, in Cadoxton and Barry Dock. The northern and western sides of the town are characterised by massive, almost continuously high, positive values (i.e. they are very

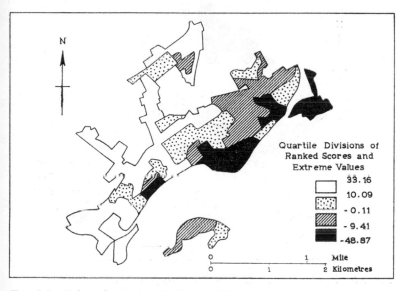

Quartile Divisions of
Ranked Scores and
Extreme Values

33.16
10.09
- 0.11
- 9.41
-48.87

Fig. 6.5. Urban dimensions in Barry: Component I.

weakly defective). The three peripheral E.D.s with negative values (i.e. 49, 51 and 52) have mixed physical and social characteristics and their defective populations are sufficiently large to place them just within the defective interquartile range.

Figure 6.6 shows Component II. This time the E.D.s with extreme scores are less highly segregated than on Component I. The fifteen E.D.s with extreme negative (i.e. defective) scores form three distinct groups. The largest subset consists of nine E.D.s located on the periphery of the town in Colcot, Cadoxton and Barry Island. They are readily identified as regions dominated by large postwar municipal

estates. The second subset consists of a continuous arc, composed of
five E.D.s, linking Barry and Barry Dock. The region contains five
small postwar municipal estates, built on formerly neglected, steeply
sloping, elevated sites, close to the C.B.D. E.D. 17 is the sole member
of the third, innermost, subset. Significantly, the E.D. has the highest
negative score on Component I and clearly represents the hard core of
the largest socially defective area in the borough. The E.D.s in both
negative and positive interquartile ranges form relatively compact

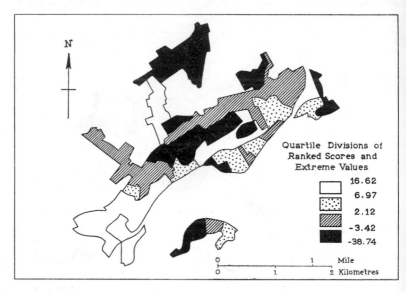

Fig. 6.6. Urban dimensions in Barry: Component II.

regions—the former in peripheral locations, the latter in older, inner
residential areas—particularly in Cadoxton and Barry Dock. The
fifteen E.D.s with high positive scores (i.e. weakly defective on Component II) form two large compact regions, one in Barry, the other in
Barry Dock, with a single outlier (E.D. 46) in Colcot.

The foregoing analysis of the distribution of the fifty-nine E.D.s on
the score-profile for Components I–II gives a gross characterisation.
The relative location of the E.D.s to one another in the total 'intra-
urban dimensions' space can now be examined. For the purpose of this
analysis the ten components extracted earlier, accounting for 79·9 per
cent of the total variance, are considered to form the basis of this space.

The step-wise groupings of the fifty-nine E.D.s were computed using the grouping algorithm employed above (Table 6.4) and the minimum value of R appeared when the 9-group solution was reached. (Table 6.11).

TABLE 6.11. *Ratio of weighted increase (R) to total*

No. of groups formed	W.G. D^2	% loss of detail	R	
58	14	—	1·0000	Complete
40	1·031	0·1	0·0131	detail
20	8·173	0·6	0·0121	
10	39·490	2·3	0·0009	
9	47·929	2·8	0·0002	
8	68·779	4·0	0·0303	
3	1,336·222	78·5	0·0633	
2	1,425·979	83·7	0·0063	Complete
1	1,701·215	100·0	0·0162	generality

The results of the grouping analysis are summarised in Table 6.12.

TABLE 6.12. *Intra-urban dimensions: optimum E.D. groupings*

	E.D. groups								
	1	2	3	4	5	6	7	8	9
Individual	6	5	1	49	47	9	19	32	32
enumeration	16	7	3		48	20	29	18	33
districts	17	8	4		50	25	43	21	46
		14	10			28	44	23	55
		15	11			35	45	24	56
		37	12			39		30	57
			13			41		31	58
			22			42		36	59
			26			51		53	
			27					54	
			34						
			38						
			40						
			52						
Total number of members	3	6	14	1	3	9	5	10	8

Inspection of the ten sets of score profiles for the nine groups (not presented here because of space restrictions) revealed that they were principally identified by their scores on Components I and II. The nine groups have accordingly been classified and ranked according to their degrees of defectiveness on these two principal dimensions. Three subsets emerge from this procedure (Table 6.13).

TABLE 6.13. *Ranked multifactor groups*

Groups	Component score profiles I		II		Subsets
1	−34·35	−48·88	−3·42	+5·24	Defective
2	−7·18	−25·17	+2·09	+6·97	on
3	−2·44	−16·05	−8·67	+11·95	Component I
4	−0·30			−38·74	Defective
5	+5.30	+10·41	−21·39	−26·03	on
6	−5·83	+8·94	−1·31	−27·66	Component II
7	+4·83	+18·29	+0·09	−4·79	
8	−4·44	+9·06	−3·54	+13·48	Only slightly
9	+20·60	+30·60	−0·18	+16·62	defective

Figure 6.7 shows that these complex groups possess a high degree of regional contiguity. The pattern of multifactor regions is multinuclear in character. Regions with high defect scores on Component I are located adjacent to the port entrances in Cadoxton, Barry Dock, Barry and on Barry Island. An east–west gradation is clearly discernible, with the largest and most intensely defective areas (i.e. groups 5, 6 and 7) located on Cadoxton and the smallest least defective areas (i.e. Group 7) in Barry and on Barry Island. In both Cadoxton and Barry Dock the E.D.s adjacent to the port entrances have the highest defect scores, and progressively lower values are found further (but not uniformly so) from these areas.

The regions with high defect scores on Component II are located chiefly in peripheral locations. The two groups which form the 'hard core' of this set (i.e. 8 and 3) are situated in Colcot, at the northern extremity of the town. Moderately defective areas (group 4) occupy peripheral, intermediate and inner locations, primarily in Cadoxton and Barry Island. They are thus widely separated and abut against regions with high defect scores on Component I and regions with low scores on both components alike. The least defective region in this subset (i.e. 7) occupies a peripheral location, linking Barry and Barry Dock.

The third subset consists of two regions which are only slightly defective on Components I or II (i.e. only five scores out of a total of thirty-six had negative signs). Figure 6.7 shows that the least defective regions (i.e. group 9-A) are strongly segregated on the western side of

Barry and to the north of Barry Dock. The E.D.s forming group 8 (B) occupy a wide variety of locations in peripheral, intermediate and inner residential areas. A strong central and western tendency is apparent, for only two E.D.s in this group are located outside Barry and Barry Dock (E.D. 2 in Cadoxton and E.D. 53 on Barry Island).

Discussion

It is apparent that the statistical measures employed in the present study have yielded findings which do not substantiate the Burgess

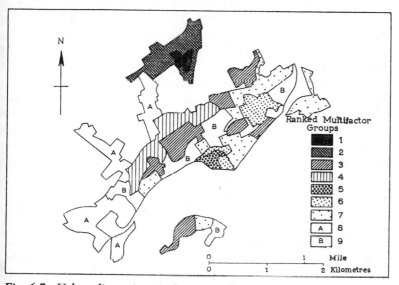

Fig. 6.7. Urban dimensions in Barry: multifactor regions.

formulations *vis-à-vis* the relations between land use variates and social defect variates. The dimensions produced by the component analysis of the fifty-six variables reveal that there are no consistent systematic relations between social defects and land uses of specific types, age, quality or location. Certainly, high defect rates are associated with areas characterised by commercial and industrial uses and substandard housing in both central and peripheral locations but high defect rates are also found in areas characterised exclusively by postwar municipal housing estates in peripheral and intermediate locations. Furthermore, in the period under review, Barry's 'Zones in Transition' contained areas where the defect rate was close to zero. The incidence of social disorganisation was also low in areas characterised by interwar municipal housing estates. The results of the analysis confirm the conclusion reached by Feldman and Tilly that 'the relationship between physical and social space, and by inference mobility, eludes easy and excessively broad generalisation'.[29] The descriptive constructs devised primarily in the 1920s overstate the extent to which order in physical space reflects order in human behaviour.

Similar inconsistencies are apparent in the relationship between the incidence of mobility and that of social disorganisation. There is no general tendency for rates of mobility and of social disorganisation to diminish together inversely with distance from the town centre. Mobility rates are also high in both intermediate and peripheral locations and there are wide variations in defect rates in different parts of these recently settled areas.

The generalised descriptive models of Burgess and his associates, based on one or two variables, thus bear little resemblance to those produced by the rigorous statistical procedures employed in this study. These hypotheses, therefore, are of little use as analytic devices by means of which the patterns of distribution of social defects discovered in Barry can be explained. The second principal component solution has, however, produced dimensions and maps which, if analysed with care, may suggest some plausible alternative answers to the thorny problems of explaining the causal basis of the differential defect rate.

The large body of extant research has demonstrated that social disorganisation is a complex problem and that many factors contribute to it—environmental, social and personal.[30] We are not concerned here with disorganisation as an individual phenomenon but as a social problem, in a spatial setting. With the exception of the two variables relating to ill-health the defects selected for analysis represent common aberrant behavioural traits. The explanation of the distribution of social defects in Barry and the more general problem of explaining the causes of social disorganisation are thus clearly primarily dependent upon achieving an understanding of the motivation of human behaviour. This is clearly outside the realm of this study which is only concerned with establishing the spatial framework of deviant characteristics, though some tentative interpretation may be attempted.

Most of the existing hypotheses relating to the problem of social disorganisation are characterised by conflicting assumptions and nebulous definitions, and all contain a measure of empirical plausibility.[31] Many sociologists allocate the central and basic role in the understanding of the differential defect rate to the concept of *anomie*. Durkheim[32] suggested that a differential crime rate was a reflection of different degrees of social cohesion and the corresponding social controls. Anomie, or 'normlessness' implies the breakdown of the regulatory structure of society in a population subgroup or an area, with the result that social disorganisation develops. Lander's research led him to conclude that the level of delinquency in an area was a function of the degree of anomie. Mobility would create the conditions of instability and anonymity in an area necessary to reduce social controls and to generate delinquent mores. 'Unstable community conditions and the consequent weakening of social controls that are congruent with the dominant culture provide fertile ground for the emergence of variant norms and group standards.'[33]

Freedman, however, in a detailed study of mobility in Chicago during the period 1935–40, concluded that mobility *per se* was not a 'cause' of social disorganisation. In highly urbanised societies 'the population consists largely of persons accustomed to urban life to whom mobility itself is routine and less likely to be disorganising'.[34] He identified two types of zone of migrant residence; one in which the population was adapted to persistent mobility and where the incidence of social disorganisation was consequently low; the other where there were concentrations of people who were unaccustomed to mobility or unable to adapt to it. In conclusion he advanced the hypothesis that 'it is not the *amount* of mobility alone which distinguishes disorganised from normal urban areas, but also the extent to which the population is *mentally mobile*—the extent to which it is *adapted* to mobility, and an established part of its culture'.[35]

In 1938 Merton[36] elaborated and refined the concept of anomie still further by adding a socio-economic dimension. Clinard, commenting on Merton's restatement, summarised his view thus:

Deviant behaviour . . . is a result of anomie, or the clash between institutional means and cultural goals in access to the success goals of a society by legitimate means. Modern urban societies emphasise such status goals of competitive success as material gain and higher education, but provide limited means for everyone to achieve these goals legitimately, because of differentials in racial and ethnic status, and particularly social class. The greatest pressure for

10

deviation arises among the lower socio-economic groups, where opportunities to acquire material goods are fewer and the level of education is lower.[37]

Moreover, several investigations have shown that formal social participation is inversely associated with social class.[38] The poorer members of the community, lacking financial resources, advanced education and useful social contacts, are daily made aware of the disparity between their condition and that of their favoured neighbours by mass media. Many wives attempt to overcome the handicap by taking part-time or full-time jobs. Family ties tend to break down as the material replaces the social as the dominant social value. As a result of these trends it is suggested that extensive emotional deprivation currently exists among the lower social classes, a deprivation that exists in the economic sphere as well, judging by recent reports[39] revealing the existence of poverty on hitherto unsuspected scales. Thus there may be a growing temptation for socially and economically disadvantaged people to reject the mores of the larger community which make it impossible for them to obtain success-goals by legal means.[40]

An inspection of the dimensions yielded by the second component analysis (Table 6.9) reveals that many of the high correlations between social defects and other variables produced in earlier studies are adventitious.[41] Component analysis demonstrates that the statistical associations are in many cases inconsistent. Thus the association between social defects and commercial and industrial land uses is shown to be very strong on Component I but inverse on Component II. If the defects in Barry's social structure are hypothesised as aspects of an anomic factor, then the apparent irregularities are explained. The appearance of the factor on several dimensions suggests that the specific distribution pattern of social disorganisation in Barry during the period of study is related to the age of the town and its pattern of physical development. It is to these patterns that we must now turn.

Barry is a comparatively modern phenomenon. The transformation from a rural to an urban landscape began when the construction of the port and railway system commenced in 1885.[42] Between 1885 and 1913 the population rose from 500 to 34,535. Since the majority of the working population was employed at the port[43] the four dock entrances exerted a powerful 'gravitational pull' over the location of the earliest residential development. The form assumed by the expanding residential area was of four distinct germinal subtowns located adjacent to the dock entrances at Barry Island, Barry, Barry Dock and Cadoxton (Fig. 6.8). Residential segregation was marked even in the first twenty-five years of uncontrolled growth. Commercial residential areas (hotels and boarding houses) were located immediately adjacent to the dock entrances, principally in Cadoxton and Barry Dock. Beyond these the serried ranks of small brick and stone terraces of the dock labourers and railwaymen occupied the lower valley slopes. The large terraced houses and villas of the wealthier families occupied the higher slopes, principally on the north and west sides of Barry and Barry Dock.[44]

The areas of transient residence in Cadoxton and Barry Dock quickly acquired unenviable reputations. Mobility[45] and delinquency[46] rates among their cosmopolitan populations were extremely high and stable interpersonal relationships consequently stunted. The communities in these areas have never become fully stabilised or adjusted to mobility. Since 1920 their populations have steadily declined as residents have moved outwards. The persistence of delinquent subcultures is evidenced by the fact that, at the present time, the rates of social disorganisation are the highest in the town. The principal diagnostic variables are a set of eleven social defects loading negatively on Component I. These inner areas have the highest negative scores on this, the principal dimension of variance. Further, the high loadings for areas of adult and juvenile criminal residence $(-0.43 + -0.51$ respectively) suggest that the subcultures persist through the transmission of delinquent mores from one generation to another. These anomic variables are associated with an unstable population (variables 2, 6, 19, 20) characterised by low and uncertain earning power (variables 51 and 53), low educational achievement and family cohesion (social defect variable 13 and variable 50).

The high positive loadings on Component II depict equally old inner residential areas which are *not* socially defective. They have, in common with the defective areas, high proportions of substandard shared dwellings. Commercial and industrial areas occupy large proportions of the total land use. Despite these physical and social similarities, only one defect variable (variable 2, percentage distribution, T.B.) loads positively in these areas. Their communities appear to be stable, however, for none of the set of mobility variables loading on Component I are to be found here. The evidence would appear to

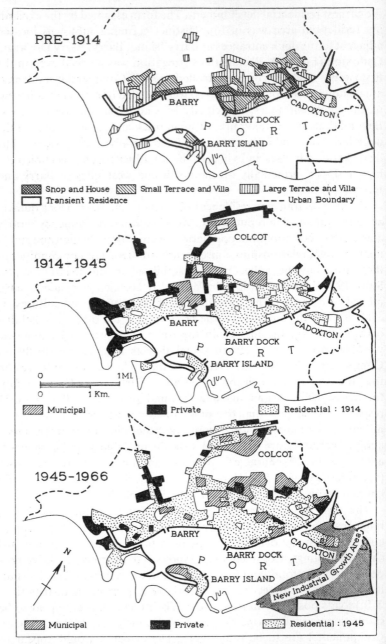

Fig. 6.8. Barry: selected residential growth phases. 1885–1966.

suggest the presence of stable communities and the absence of anomically orientated subcultures.

Since 1914 the three mainland subtowns have been linked and backed by an expanding surround of low density housing as people have moved out to live motor transport orientated suburban lives. Despite the substantial reduction of social differentials in the present century this outward sprawl has not been undifferentiated. The clear distinctions between the location of middle- and lower-class housing, which emerged in the late nineteenth century, have persisted to the present day. The distinctions have generally been intensified rather than reduced by the enforcement of local government land use zoning and planning principles. The price orientation of twentieth-century housing is thus reflected in the continued expansion of homogeneous new private estates on the western and northern sides of the town and of municipal estates to the north and east.

The negative loadings and scores on Component III identify areas of interwar private housing, fringing and interpenetrating the inner, disorganised areas. Their transitional character is revealed by loadings which indicate both high social status (variables 33, 54, 55, 56) and low environmental status (variable 41). Mobility and uncertain employment are indexed by variables 19 and 51. These unstable regions are characterised by a set of eight social defects. The entire criminal residence and commission subset (variables 7–11) account for six of these anomic traits.

Although earning power is invariably low (variable 53) in the interwar municipal estates (identified by negative loadings on Component IV), social disorganisation is completely absent. The resident populations are stable, since none of the variables indexing mobility load negatively on this dimension. In addition, they are farther advanced along the life cycle. The average age is relative high and families are small because most of the dependent children have grown up. The financial burdens are correspondingly diminished.

The populations of the postwar private and municipal estates (the former identified by positive loadings on Component I, the latter by negative loadings on Component II) have had relatively little time in which to develop stable social relationships comparable with those existing in older residential areas. In addition, the lack of adequate commercial, industrial and institutional facilities in these estates (variables 41 and 42) combined with their remoteness (variables 45 and 46) from the central areas where these functions are located, imposes a financial burden of frequent and expensive horizontal mobility on their residents. These dimensions show, however, that the responses of the two populations to these unfamiliar conditions have been very different. The communities living in new private estates are relatively law-abiding, those in municipal estates are more disorganised.

These findings support the evidence presented by Freedman in Chicago and of Sullenger[47] in Omaha. Thus mobility can be both a stabilising and a disrupting influence on social relationships. Horizontal mobility, accompanied by vertical (i.e. social) mobility yields low rates of social disorganisation. Conversely, areas with high horizontal mobility rates and low vertical mobility are characterised by extensive social disorganisation. The populations living in the peripheral private estates possess many integrative traits—high earning power (indexed by variables 33, 34, 52, 54, 55) and high educational status (variable 56). The residents of the municipal estates, in contrast, have low earning power (variables 35, 37, 53), large dependent families (variables 14, 23) and low family cohesion (variables 13 and 50). In the more remote areas the rates of social disorganisation are very high, particularly on the variables relating to financial problems (variables 3, 5). It may, perhaps, be inferred that the sharp increase in the financial burden of poorer families, living in relatively more expensive accommodation, combined with increased travelling expenses to places of work, education, worship and shopping, and to visit relatives, account in part for the intense concentration of social defects in these areas.

CONCLUSIONS AND IMPLICATIONS OF THE FINDINGS

The principal purpose of the study was to determine the spatial distribution of social defects in Barry and to relate the findings to a wide variety of spatial and non-spatial attributes. The principal components model provided an effective, objective means of determining the basic regularities in two universes of complex data and of reducing them to a few, comprehensible, dimensions. The sets of scores produced by the two runs formed useful summaries of the simultaneous variation among the clusters of variables for the 59 E.D.s. The grouping procedure yielded two sets of multifactor groups which, when mapped, were found to form distinct regional patterns.

The empirical results were found to bear little consistent resemblance to three of the major formulations built into the Burgess Concentric and Zonal Hypotheses. It was suggested that the sociological concept of anomie seems to provide a more plausible explanation of the existence of disorganisation in the town's social structure. Patterns were found to be related to the age of the settlement and its mode of physical expansion.

The empirical results of the analysis suggest that the development of a satisfactory formal theory of the structure and distribution of social disorganisation in urban areas lies a long way in the future. This study has been concerned with *social* disorganisation, with correlations between properties of *groups*. The results provide a framework for the more intensive study of disorganisation among *individuals*. A fuller understanding of the differential defect rate will also come from examining in greater detail than that attempted here the ways in which urban community instability is dynamically related to the differential behaviour of population subgroups.

At the outset attention was drawn to the fact that social disorganisation is of interest to planners. It is clear that the results of this and related studies contribute to the existing store of knowledge about the way in which towns develop and provide additional guides for town planners. The results suggest that disorganisation is generally a transitory phenomenon, persisting for a generation as adjustments to change and the development of mature interpersonal relationships develop in newly established estates.

The evidence suggests, however, that both inner and peripheral socially disorganised areas are partially the result of the general lack of effective and implemented planning in the past. Far too often planning has been associated with the problems of buildings rather than those of the people living in them. The inner residential areas of our towns have been allowed to run down after they have been assigned lives of ten, twenty or so years. Authorised decay and eventual drastic 'comprehensive' renewal have been the familiar modes of treatment. At the same time the burgeoning municipal estates by reason of their remote locations and unbalanced development have produced fertile breeding grounds for disaffection and disorganisation. Large, low density estates, often visually uninspiring and depressing, minimise face-to-face contacts between new neighbours and increase the costs of travelling to visit relatives and old friends. In most cases nothing has been done to ameliorate the shock of moving to new and unfamiliar areas. Invariably, essential amenities such as shops, social and institutional centres and play space (which encourage and hasten the development of a sense of belonging to a neighbourhood) are provided long after the houses go up.

Clearly the responsibility for this past unbalanced development lies ultimately with successive governments, whose primary concern has been with economic rather than social costs. Local authorities have been limited, financially and legally, to minor pieces of social engineering such as providing playing space and home improvement grants in decaying neighbourhoods, and better housing for special health cases. All the evidence points to the necessity for providing the financial and legal framework for encouraging a greater degree of involvement in planning, and in employing specialists in human relations in what is, or should be, at least as much a problem of social as of physical engineering.

Appendix

SET 1: SOCIAL DEFECTS

Health defects

1. Percentage of the population with T.B. 1965.[1]
2. Percentage distribution of T.B. cases.[1]

The cases listed under variable 1 were assigned to their former addresses (if in the borough) where the condition was first diagnosed. The figures were then aggregated for each E.D. and expressed as a percentage of the total for the borough.

Financial problems

3. Percentage credit delinquents summoned, 1965.[2]
4. Percentage recidivist rate delinquents (private tenants) summoned, 1959–64.[3]
5. Percentage recidivist rent delinquents (municipal tenants) summoned, 1959–64.[3]

Persons summoned (variable 4) or served with 'Notices to quit' on two or more occasions during the study period were defined as recidivists and included in the analysis.

6. Percentage distribution of recidivist rent delinquents.[3] The cases listed under variable 5 were assigned to their former addresses (if in the borough). The figures were then aggregated for each E.D. and expressed as a percentage of the total for the borough. Comparable data were not available for delinquents in the private housing sector (variable 4).

Criminal offences[4]

7. Residence: adult offenders.
8. Residence: juvenile offenders.
9. Residence: offenders against the person.
10. Residence: offenders against property.
11. Commission: offences to persons.
12. Commission: offences to property.

Mean annual rates were calculated for variables 7–12 for the period 1960–64. Distinctions between the sexes were ignored, since the porportion of female offenders (2·8 per cent) was too small to warrant separate treatment.

Marital disorganisation

13. Percentage persons divorced of ever married, 1961.[5]

SET 2: OTHER INTRA-URBAN CHARACTERISTICS

Population structure[5]

14. Percentage of population aged 0–14, 1961.
15. Percentage of population over retiring age, 1961.
16. Average age of the population, 1961.
17. Females per 1000 males, 1961.
18. Fertility ratio, 1961.
19. Percentage of the population 'foreign-born', 1961.

Mobility

20. Percentage distribution of L.A. tenants, 1965.[6]

The tenants living in postwar municipal estates were assigned to their former addresses (if in the borough). The figures were then aggregated for each E.D. and expressed as a percentage of the total for the borough. Comparable data were not available for residents of the postwar private housing sector.

Accommodation and household composition[5]

21. Percentage households with one person, 1961.
22. Percentage households with one or two persons, 1961.
23. Percentage households with five or more persons, 1961.
24. Percentage of dwellings, occupied or vacant, with 1–3 rooms, 1961.
25. Average number of persons per room, 1961.
26. Percentage households with over one person per room, 1961.

27. Percentage households with over 1·5 persons per room, 1961.
28. Average number of persons per acre, 1961.[5, 7]

The area to which the density relates is the net area of each E.D., that is, residential area of E.D. ÷ resident population of E.D.

Housing characteristics

29. Percentage households living in shared dwellings, 1961.[5]
30. Percentage households with shared use of kitchens, 1961.[5]
31. Percentage households with shared use of W.C., 1961.[5]
32. Percentage dwellings in substandard condition, 1949–1965.[8]

Very few dwellings in Barry are old enough and/or in a sufficiently advanced state of disrepair to warrant demolition. Many houses built before 1945, however, require major repairs or lack certain amenities (e.g. bath, shower, washhand basin, indoor W.C., hot water supply and a food store). Since 1949, several Housing Acts have empowered local authorities to make standard and discretionary grants for owners to make improvements to houses built before 1945. In addition the 1957 Housing Act enables private tenants to appeal to their local authority for a reduction in rents until their landlords make good certain improvements or major structural defects. The record of the combined distribution of these varied improvements constitutes the only accessible objective measure of dwellings which have been in a substandard condition at some time during the period 1949–65.

Household tenure

33. Mean gross rateable value 1961.[9]
34. Percentage households owned by occupier, 1961.[5]
35. Percentage households rented from Local Authority, 1961.[5]

Age of housing[10]

36. Local Authority dwellings built 1914–45.
37. Local authority dwellings built 1945–64.
38. Dwellings built before 1914.
39. Dwellings built 1914–45.
40. Dwellings built 1945–64.

The rates for variables 36–40 have been calculated as percentages of the total stock of houses in the Borough in 1964.

Land use[7]

41. Commercial/Industrial as percentage of total land use, 1961.
42. Institutional as percentage of total land use, 1961.

43. Public open space as percentage of total land use, 1961.
44. Residential as percentage of total land use, 1961.

Distance

45. Cost distance: Average single bus fare to C.B.D., 1961.[11]
46. Distance to R.B.D.s, 1961.[7]
   Measurement of distance in ecological studies traditionally involves calculation from the original nucleus of the settlement, or the C.B.D. (often synonymous). Since Barry has 4 distinct regional centres, each E.D. has been assigned to its nearest R.B.D.

Physical traits[12]

47. Average altitude.
48. Average amplitude of relief.

Economic Character[13]

49. Occupied population as a percentage of total resident population aged fifteen or over, 1961.
50. Women as percentage of the total occupied population, 1961.
51. Unemployed as percentage of the economically active population, 1961.

Social class

52. Percentage of occupied and retired males in social classes 1 or 2, 1961.[13]
53. Percentage of occupied and retired males in social classes 4 or 5, 1961.[13]
   The social classes consist of amalgamated socio-economic groups listed in the *Classification of Occupations, 1960*. Classes 1 and 2 are composed of groups 3 and 4; 1, 2 and 13: Classes 4 and 5 of groups 7, 10 and 15; 11, 16 and 17.
54. Percentage of households with private telephone, 1961.[14]
55. Percentage of households with private car, 1961.[15]

Education

56. Percentage persons with terminal education age over 15, 1961.[5]

Sources

1. Public Health Dept., *Special Health Housing List*, Barry Borough Council.

2. County Court Records Department, Barry.

3. Rating Dept., *Delinquent Register*, Barry Borough Council.

4. Barry Central Police Station, Records Department.

5. General Register Office, *Census*, 1961, *Barry*, *Special Tabulation*, *Scale B*.

6. Housing Dept., *L.A. Housing Records*, 1945–1965, Barry Borough Council.

7. Statistics based on calculations taken from relevant 1:2500 O.S. Maps.

8. Public Health Dept., *Housing Improvements Record*, 1949–1965, Barry Borough Council.

9. Rating Dept., *L.A. Valuation List*, *1961*, Barry Borough Council.

10. Rating Dept., *General Rate Books for 1914*, *1945 and 1964*, Barry Borough Council.

11. Western Welsh Omnibus Co., Ltd., *Fare Lists*, *1961–62*, Barry Offices.

12. Statistics based on calculations taken from relevant 1:10560 O.S. Maps.

13. General Register Office, *Census 1961*, *Barry*, *Special Tabulation*, *Scale D*. Expanded uncorrected 10 per cent sample.

14. G.P.O. Telephone Directory, South Wales East, 1961.

15. Vehicle Taxation Dept., County Council Offices, Cardiff, 1961.

REFERENCES

1. RUDNER, R. S., *Philosophy of Social Sciences*, Prentice-Hall, 1966.

2. PAHL, R. E., 'Trends in social geography', in Chorley, R. J. and Haggett, P., eds., *Frontiers in Geographical Teaching*, Methuen, 1965, pp. 81–100.

3. BROOKFIELD, H. C., 'Questions on the human frontiers of geography', *Econ. Geog.*, **40**, 1964, pp. 283–303.

4. GOULD, P., 'On mental maps', Discussion Paper No. 9, Michigan Inter-University Community of Mathematical Geographers, Michigan, 1967.

5. PAHL, 'Trends in social geography'; also SCHNORE, L. F., 'On the spatial structure of cities in the two Americas', in Hauser, P. M. and

Schnore, L. F., eds., *The Study of Urbanization*, Wiley, 1965, pp. 347–98.

6. HARRIS, C. D., ULLMAN, E. L., 'The nature of cities', in Hatt, P. K., and Reiss, R. J., eds., *Cities and Society*, 2nd edn., Collier-Macmillan, 1957, for an excellent synthetic discussion of these generalisations.

7. SIMMONS, J., 'Descriptive models of urban land use', *Canadian Geogr.*, **9**, 1965, pp. 170–4.

8. DUNCAN, B., 'Variables in urban morphology', *Contributions to Urban Sociology*, Chicago, 1964.

9. DUNCAN, O. D., *et al.*, *Statistical Geography*, Free Press of Glencoe, 1961; also TIMMS, D., 'Quantitative Techniques in Urban Social Geography', in Chorley and Haggett, *Frontiers in Geographical Teaching*, pp. 239–65.

10. ROBINS, N. L., 'Social Problems Associated with Urban Minorities', in Hirsch, W. Z., ed., *Urban Life and Form*, Holt, Rinehart & Winston, 1963, pp. 201–18; BURGESS, E. W., and BOGUE, D. J., eds., *Contributions to Urban Sociology*, University of Chicago Press, 1964, esp. Part IV; WOLFGANG, M. E., *et al.*, *The Sociology of Crime and Delinquency*, Wiley, 1962.

11. MAYHEW, H., *London Labour and the London Poor*, London, 1861, for an excellent summary of nineteenth- and early twentieth-century ecological research with specific reference to criminology, see Morris, T., *The Criminal Area*, Routledge, 1958, esp. pp. 37–106.

12. BURGESS, E. W., *The Determination of Gradients in the Growth of the City*, Publications of the American Sociological Society, **21**, 1927; and 'Urban areas', in Smith, T. V. and White, L. D., eds., *Chicago: An Experiment in Social Science Research*, Chicago, 1929, pp. 114–23.
The most comprehensive and objective examples of this kind of research are those of: SHAW, C. R. and McKAY, H. D., *Juvenile Delinquency and Urban Areas*, Univ. of Chicago Press, 1942; LANDER, B. *Towards an Understanding of Juvenile Delinquency*, Columbia U.P., 1953; SCHMID, C. F., 'Urban Crime Areas: Parts I and II', *Am. Sociol. Rev.*, **25**, 1960, pp. 527–42, 655–78.

13. SCHNORE, 'Spatial structure of cities in the two Americas', p. 389.

14. BURGESS and BOGUE, eds., *Contributions to Urban Sociology*, pp. 488–9.

15. SCHMID, *Amer. sociol. Rev.*, 1960, p. 531.

16. SULLENGER, T. E., *Social Determinants in Juvenile Delinquency* Wiley, 1936, pp. 179–180.

17. The 10 per cent sample census taken in 1966 included question relating to mobility: interviewees were required to state whether they had moved to their existing address in (*a*) the previous year or (*b*) the previous five years.

18. Several workers have demonstrated that the analysis of aggregate information for small areal units has certain specific limitations, see for example: ROBINSON, W. S., 'Ecological correlations and the behavio of individuals', *Amer. sociol. Rev.*, **15**, pp. 351–7; ROBINSON, A. H. 'The necessity of weighting values on ecological analysis of areal data' *Ann. Assoc. Am. Geogr.*, **46**, 1956, pp. 233–6; DUNCAN, O. D., *et al. Statistical Geography*, Free press of Glencoe, 1961; MABRY, J. H. 'Census tract variation in urban residential areas', *Amer. sociol. Rev.* **23**, 1958; CASETTI, E., 'Analysis of spatial association by trigonometri polynomials', *Canadian Geogr.*, **10**, 1966, pp, 199–204.

Examples of American work in the field of intra-urban variatio have already been cited (see footnote 12). Recent examples of Britis research are: GITTUS, E., 'An experiment in the definition of urban sub areas', *Trans. Bartlett Society*, Nov. 1964; ROBSON, B. T., 'An ecologica analysis of the evolution of residential areas in Sunderland', *Urba Studies*, **3**, 1966, pp. 120–42; ROBSON, B. T., 'Multivariate analysis o urban areas', in *The Social Geography of Urban Areas*, I.B.G. Stud Group in Urban Geography, Liverpool, Sept. 1966.

19. The 'principal axes' method makes it possible to maximise th variance between factors and provides the smallest possible residuals For a full outline and appraisal of the methods and advantages o factor analysis, see the preceding chapter. The grouping algorithm i discussed in WARD, J. H., 'Hierarchical grouping to optimise an objec tive function', *J. Am. statist. Ass.*, **58**, 1963, pp. 236–44. See als BERRY, B. J. L., 'A method for deriving multi-factor uniform regions' *Polish Geogr. Rev.*, **33**, 1961, pp. 263–79.

20. MCCARTY, H. M. and SALISBURY, N. E., *Visual Comparison of Iso pleth Maps as a Means of Determining Correlations between Spatiall Distributed Phenomena*, Dept. of Geography, State University c Iowa, No. 3, 1961.

21. THURSTONE, L. L., *Multiple Factor Analysis*, Univ. of Chicag Press, 1947, pp. 60–1.

22. BERRY, B. J. L. and RAY, M., 'Multi-variate socio-economic regionalisation: a pilot study in central Canada', paper presented at the Canadian Political Science Association Conference on Statistics, Charlottetown, June 13–14, 1964.

23. All the components are required to reproduce the correlations between the variables exactly. In practice, however, only those components with high eigen values (i.e. *c.* 1·00 or more) are generally used for summarising data, since the method has the property of extracting the latent roots in descending order of magnitude. Consequently, in this study, the programme was terminated after five components had been extracted on the first run and ten from the second, larger, set of variables (3.1). In both cases the remaining components have been ignored since they account both individually and collectively, for insignificant proportions of the residual common variance. Further, interpretation becomes increasingly difficult, since the proportions of specific and error variance tend to rise sharply. A useful outline of factor analysis is presented by KING, C. A. M., 'An introduction to factor analysis with a geomorphological example from northern England', *Bull. Quant. Data for Geographers*, 6, Geog. Dept., Nottingham University, 1966.

24. For a sample of 59 E.D.s the lowest significance-levels at the 0·05, 0·01 and 0·001 levels of confidence are respectively ±0·25, ±0·33 and ±0·56.

25. See note 19.

26. BESHERS, J. M., *Urban Social Structure*, Free Press of Glencoe, 1962, p. 35.

27. SHAW, *Juvenile Delinquency and Urban Areas*, 1942.

28. SCHMID, *Am. sociol. Rev.*, 1960, p. 666.

29. FELDMAN, A. S. and TILLY, C., 'The interaction of social and physical space', *Am. sociol. Rev.*, 25, 1960, p. 884.

30. WOLFGANG, *The Sociology of Crime and Delinquency*, 1962.

31. For a critical review of the major hypotheses, see WOOTTON, B., *Social Science and Social Pathology*, Allen & Unwin, 1959.

32. DURKHEIM, E., *On the Division of Labor in Society*, trans. Simpson, G., Macmillan of New York, 1933, pp. 297–301.

33. LANDER, *Towards an Understanding of Juvenile Delinquency*, 1954, p. 90.

34. FREEDMAN, R., 'Cityward migration, urban ecology and social theory', pp. 178–200 in Burgess and Bogue, eds., *Contributions to Urban Sociology*, 1962, p. 198.

35. *Ibid.*, p. 198.

36. MERTON, R. K., 'Social structure and anomie', reprinted in *Social Theory and Social Structure*, rev. ed., Collier-Macmillan, 1957, pp. 131–60.

37. CLINARD, M. B., ed., *Anomie and Deviant Behaviour*, Free Press of Glencoe, p. v. Recent evidence suggests that there is a growing tendency in the U.S.A. and U.K. for social status to be associated with material possessions. See JONES, H., *Crime in a Changing Society*, Penguin, 1967, Ch. 2, 4, 12 and associated references; also U.K. Government, *Social Changes in Britain: A Government Survey*, reprinted in *New Society*, 27 Dec., 1962.

38. MIZRUCHI, E. H., 'Social structure and anomie in a small city', *Am. sociol. Rev.*, **25**, 1960, pp. 645–54.

39. HARRINGTON, M., *The Other America*, Collier-Macmillan, 1962; also ABEL-SMITH, B., and TOWNSEND, B., *The Poor and the Poorest*, G. Bell, 1965.

40. CLOWARD, R. A., 'Illegitimate means, anomie, and deviant behavior', *Am. sociol. Rev.*, **24**, 1959, pp. 164–76.

41. Most of the early studies of social disorganisation involved the use of limited statistical methods. Product-moment correlations often yielded results which suggested significant associations between variables at the town or city level. Higher-order statistical techniques have shown, however, that the results produced by simpler analyses are largely spurious.

42. For a detailed account of the growth of Barry see GIGGS, J. A. 'Barry: an urban and social geography, 1885–1966', unpublished Ph.D., Univ. of Wales, 1967.

43. The precise importance of the port and railway in employment terms cannot be measured, since the Censuses for 1901 and 1911 only provide information concerning occupational distribution. Consequently the importance of these industries tends to be understated. Nevertheless, two classes of occupation—Conveyance of men, goods etc. (Class 6) and Manufacture of metals, machines, etc. (Class 10) together accounted for 47 and 53 per cent of the occupied population in 1901 and 1911 respectively.

44. Barry: Percentage Distribution of Small and Large Houses, 1913

District	Small terrace	All large houses
Barry Island	77·6	22·4
Barry	67·3	32·7
Barry Dock	80·2	19·8
Cadoxton	92·9	7·1
Total	79·7	20·3

GIGGS, unpublished Ph.D. Thesis, p. 37.

45. Between 1899 and 1902 5,700 labourers left Barry Dock and Cadoxton after the completion of No. 2 Dock in 1899. *Ibid.*, p. 32.

46. 'So much has been said and written respecting immorality in the more notorious streets of Barry Docks and Cadoxton that my suggesting a remedy is my excuse in thus writing. I am the owner of nearly two-thirds of the houses in Gueret Street which has an unenviable reputation. I am prepared, if the agents or owners of the other houses will help me, to get rid of all the objectionable tenants, repair the houses, and then let them to respectable people. Of course this would mean a pecuniary loss, but in a little while we shall be repaid by seeing our property increase in value by being cared for by good tenants. Necessarily, we should require the cooperation of the police authorities to carry out our intention, but, knowing the trouble they have had in this and similar streets, I feel sure they will do so.' *Barry Dock News*, 4 January, 1895.

47. SULLENGER, T. E., 'The social significance of mobility', *Am. J. Sociol.* 1950, pp. 559–64.

CHAPTER 7

SUBURBANISATION IN RURAL WALES:

A CASE STUDY

Gareth J. Lewis

Intimate relationships have always existed between urban areas and the surrounding countryside.[1] Those relationships, both economic and political, were tenuous in a temporal sense and were characterised by specialisation by both elements of society. Hence the urban and rural communities were physically and economically separate and distinct entities. Industrialisation led to the breakdown of this polarisation and to the expansion of urban areas into the countryside on a mammoth scale. Today the development of all forms of communication binds the rural areas more closely to the urban orbit. As a consequence the once clearcut division between rural and urban is now a blurred and indistinct zone of transition.[2]

The process of urban expansion and suburbanisation has been most intensively studied in North America,[3] where it has led to the recognition of a distinct area round the city, which has both urban and rural characteristics. Fewer studies of such phenomena have been made in Britain[4] though two recent surveys in Hertfordshire clearly typify the processes involved. Coppock[5] has succinctly outlined the advent of suburbanisation in the parish of Radlett, and Pahl[6] has analysed the consequent social and economic changes in three parishes in the centre of the county. The emphasis in all these studies has been upon the increasingly closer tie between the rural community and the urban community. People move out to reside in the countryside, and the character of the local society changes with the introduction of these people with new ideas and codes of behaviour. Therefore in many instances a new type of community has evolved, neither rural in function nor urban in location.

British studies have been concerned with suburbanisation in areas adjacent to large cities; the situation in sparsely populated areas surrounding small towns is less well documented.[7] Such areas are still regarded as agricultural in function and way of life, and a series of postwar socio-anthropological studies[8] has tended to emphasise this view. This picture is rather distorted, since in sparsely populated areas the urban centre, even if small, acts as a significant agent of social change. Already studies in Wales,[9] Ireland,[10] and parts of southern England,[11] for example, have emphasised the role of the small town as a provider of social amenities but knowledge of its social and economic effect on the surrounding rural communities is still scanty

It is with such a problem in Mid-Wales that this essay is concerned. A 'middle-order' town,[12] Aberystwyth, and its surrounding hinterland of villages and hamlets is selected for study, and the field investigation upon which the study is based was carried out during 1963 and 1964. The principal aim is to assess the degree of incorporation of these rural communities into the urban community, and to analyse the consequent changes within their social structure and way of life. An attempt to place the study in a wider context by comparing it with certain suburbanisation concepts follows, and finally, an indication of the feasibility of the outlined pattern as a basis for the planning of future settlement forms in rural areas will be made.

THE SOCIAL AND ECONOMIC BACKGROUND

Mid-Wales is one of the largest areas in the British Isles which has consistently lost population since the latter part of the nineteenth century.[13] Despite a fall in population from 185,729 in 1951 to 178,546 in 1961 and an increasing rate of decline after that date, some areas within the region have increased their population since the Second World War.[14] One of these is the town and rural district of Aberystwyth, the area which forms the core of this study.

The population growth in this area can largely be accounted for by the increasing employment opportunities available in the town. Originally Aberystwyth was a castle town. During the eighteenth century it became a port of significance, and with the coming of the railway during the nineteenth century, added an important resort function.[15] As a result of improved transport facilities it began to assume the role of a commercial and service centre for the surrounding rural communities. This process was accelerated by the failure of the village crafts to compete with factory-made products and the location of government-sponsored social services in the town. Since the Second World War these processes have proceeded apace, and as a consequence the service functions of the surrounding villages have declined even more. In addition, there has been a marked extension in the administrative function of the town, exemplified by numerous commercial, insurance, and government offices, whilst the continuing expansion of the University College of Wales provides additional economic support

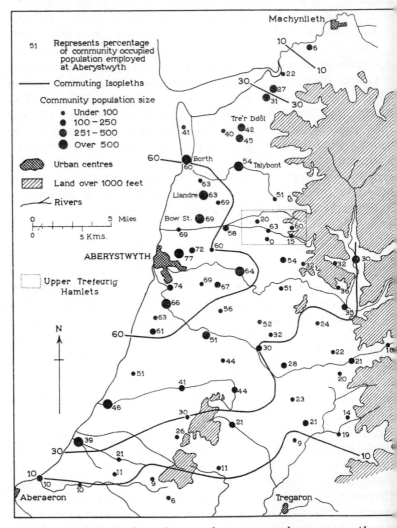

Fig. 7.1. North Cardiganshire settlements: employment at Aberystwyth.

Indeed the University is now the largest single employer within Aberystwyth.

The nature of the employment opportunities available in the town can best be understood from its present occupational structure (Table 7.1). Those connected with transport and public utilities, distribution, professional and public services are particularly significant but there is a noticeable absence of workers involved in any form of manufacturing industry. Aberystwyth suffers from a paucity of local resources, and its isolation from major industrial areas makes any significant manufacturing development unlikely.

These changes within the functional structure of Aberystwyth are reflected in its present extensive urban field. On the one hand, it provides social provisions and services for a large part of Cardiganshire, as two recent surveys clearly show,[16] and on the other hand, it is a source of employment for a similar, though slightly smaller area.[17] The villages and hamlets are heavily dependent upon the town for employment (Fig. 7.1).[18] It is only within a few miles of the small

TABLE 7.1. *The employment structure of Aberystwyth Municipal Borough and Rural District in 1961*

Socio-economic group	Administrative areas	
	Aberystwyth Municipal Borough	*Aberystwyth Rural District*
	Proportion per 1,000 inhabitants in each case	
1. Employers and Managers (large establishments)	46	16
2. Employers and Managers (small establishments)	77	49
3. Professional—self-employed	27	25
4. Professional—employees	77	47
5. Intermediate non-manual	100	36
6. Junior non-manual	185	58
7. Personal service	23	8
8. Foremen and supervisors	15	25
9. Skilled	239	181
10. Semi-skilled	58	60
11. Unskilled	66	104
12. Workers on own account (other than professional)	46	49
13. Farmers	—	127
14. Agricultural workers	15	68
15. Armed Forces	—	3
16. Others	23	16

Based on *Census 1961 England and Wales, Occupation, Industry and Socio-Economic Groups: Cardiganshire*, Table 5, p. 11.

centres of Machynlleth and Aberaeron that Aberystwyth ceases to be a major centre of employment, whilst to the east it is limited by the uplands of Pumlumon. This employment field may be described in terms of three zones. In the inner zone of villages, over 60 per cent of their occupied population travel daily to Aberystwyth. Around this is an intermediate zone of villages with over 40 per cent commuting to the town, and to the south-east, a minor zone with only 20–30 per cent. Beyond there is a surrounding fringe zone.

The structure of Aberystwyth's urban field, as estimated by the service and employment needs of the surrounding communities bears immediate comparison with Martin's model-like pattern.[19] It consists of a central area of communities immediately adjacent to the town, which are socially and economically dependent on it. Surrounding this is a larger area of communities which are less dependent on the town, and an even larger peripheral area with communities dependent on a number of urban centres.

This model is useful because it focuses attention upon the two factors of 'focality'[20] and 'urban orientation',[21] which are significant in any social and economic differentiation of communities within this urban field. The relationship of these two factors give the communities their present character, and are represented within each community by their distance from the town, their population size, the number of social facilities[22] they possess, and the proportion of their occupied population employed at Aberystwyth. In order to gain some insight as to the pattern of relationships, product moment correlation coefficients (Table 7.2) and regression relationships (Fig. 7.2), were calculated for the four indices.

TABLE 7.2. *Relationships between the four indices: product moment correlation coefficients*

	(a) Distance	(b) Population	(c) Social facilities	(d) Employment
Distance	—	−0·52	−0·06	−0·70
Population	−0·52	—	+0·56	+0·23
Social facilities	−0·06	+0·56	—	+0·05
Employment	−0·70	+0·23	+0·05	—

The analysis indicated varying patterns of relationships. As would be expected, the most significant correlation, even at the 0·1 per cent level, is that between distance from the town, and the proportion of occupied population employed at the town. The absence of any marked deviation from the regression line clearly confirms this relationship. Similarly, the larger villages tend to be nearer the town, indicated by a negative correlation, significant at the 0·1 per cent level. However, there are certain deviants from the general pattern, the most notable being Ponrhydfendigaid in the south-eastern part of the urban field, and the main-road communities of Llanrhystud and Llanon to the south of Aberystwyth (Fig. 7.1). The former, due to its relative inaccessibility from the town, has been able to maintain many of its original functions. The latter, due to their main road location, have increased their connection with Aberystwyth despite a distance much greater than many other communities. In turn, there is a positive correlation between population size and number of social facilities possessed by the communities, significant at the 0·05 per cent level, but as indicated by the regression line, a certain number of the larger villages, in particular those near Aberystwyth, deviate from this pattern. In many cases, the town has taken over many of their social and economic functions, and the indirect effect of this has been to produce an insignificant correlation between distance from the town and the number of social facilities possessed. In addition, there is little correlation between the proportion employed in the town, and either population size or number of social facilities possessed by the communities.

From this analysis four significant points emerge. First, the villages and hamlets within about ten miles of Aberystwyth have a high proportion of their employed persons commuting daily to the town. Secondly, the number of social facilities possessed by a settlement has been shown to be controlled by size and to a lesser extent, distance from the town. Thirdly, the range of social facilities possessed by these settlements is comparatively limited, and fourthly, distance from the town, in the form of accessibility, provides a vital factor influencing all other variables.

These four indices indicate in varying degree the influence of 'focality' and 'urban orientation' in the social and economic differentiation of the communities, and it is considered that these relationships, in turn, can be an important indicator of the status a community may possess within the Aberystwyth hinterland. In the present circumstances these indices are more meaningful in a classification than service function[23] or population size, since the town has not only eroded many community functions but has become the social and economic

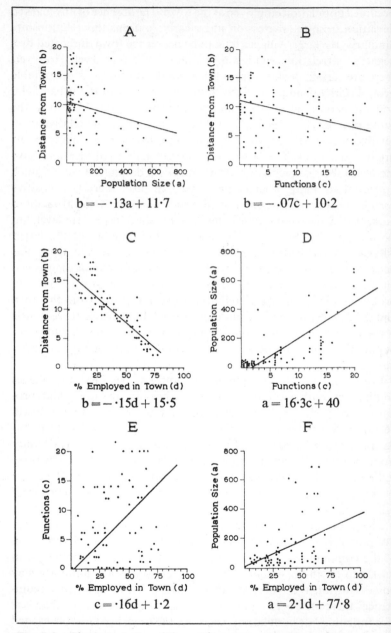

Fig. 7.2. Characteristics of the settlements: regression relationships.

focus for the surrounding communities, either enhancing or lowering a settlement's status within the area. Therefore this classification will not only indicate the relative status of the communities in relation to

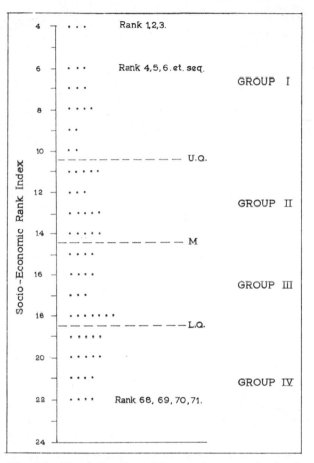

Fig. 7.3. North Cardiganshire: socio-economic classification of settlements. Rank 1 to 71 relate to settlements in the study area and run consecutively.

the town but also provide a better insight into the type and nature of the communities.

The procedure for this socio-economic status classification was as follows: all the seventy settlements within the Aberystwyth hinterland

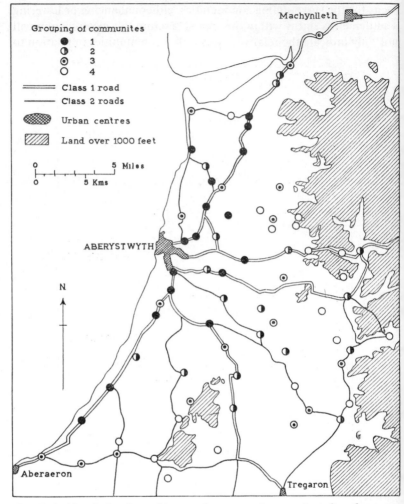

Fig. 7.4. North Cardiganshire: socio-economic grouping of settlements.

were ranked under the four indices of population size, proportion
employed at the town, distance from the town, and number of social
facilities. The four resultant columns were then divided into sectiles,
and points on a scale of 1 to 6 were applied to each settlement according to its position in each ranking column. These were totalled for each
settlement and ranked. Finally, a quartile division of the grouped
ranking was made (Fig. 7.3).

The resultant grouping of communities has a number of distinguishing features (Fig. 7.4). Group I, for example, contains all the communities with both a high 'urban orientation' and 'focality' e.g. Bow Street, Talybont, Llanfarian, and also contains settlements with a very high 'urban orientation' but with a corresponding lower 'focality index', e.g. Rhydyfelin, and Y Waun Fawr. The latter have but recently developed on the fringe of Aberystwyth, and their location in relation to the town has not warranted any marked central place functions. Spatially this group of communities is located in a ring around the town with extensions to the north and south along the main roads. In many ways they form the core of the central area described earlier in the service and employment field model. In many ways, Group II is similar, but at a lower level of significance. It contains communities with a corresponding lower degree of 'urban orientation' and 'focality index', and also those with a high 'focality' tendency but a corresponding low 'urban orientation', for example Ponterwyd and Pontrhydfendigaid. In general, the former constitute part of the middle area of the urban field, and the latter, part of the periphery. Groups III and IV are much smaller in population size, all are below 200, and they possess very few 'focality' tendencies. Their degree of orientation towards Aberystwyth varies markedly, since they are dependent upon a number of central communities. For example, Ffair Rhôs looks towards the nearby larger village of Pontrhydfendigaid, the smaller centre of Tregaron, and then, Aberystwyth. In general, they form the outer fringe of the urban field.

Analysis of the contemporary social and economic structure of the area fails to give an adequate explanation of these patterns; reference must be made to the historical development of the settlements. Originally the area was typically one of scattered farmsteads and isolated hamlets,[24] and the principal nucleating factor, particularly in the northern and eastern part of the hinterland, lay in the lead mining industry of the eighteenth and nineteenth centuries. In some cases nearby landed estates were important influences.[25] From the nineteenth century onwards these factors became particularly operative, and as a consequence the population of the area grew rapidly.[26] The villages expanded, and basic functions of services and crafts increased. These tendencies towards centralisation led to a growth in the importance of the nucleated settlement in the life of the rural area. However, during the latter part of the nineteenth century, the mining activity declined coincidently with an agricultural depression.[27] This led to an exodus from the area to the industrial areas of South Wales and the Midlands as well as abroad.[28] Naturally this decline affected some villages more than others. For example, the settlements in the upper part of the Trefeurig parish suffered markedly compared with many in lowland areas, such as Talybont and Bow Street. The decline of villages was hastened during the early part of this century by the concentration of more and more services at the urban centre. These processes were facilitated by the increasing mobility of the individual with the coming of the railway, bus service, and latterly, the motor car. During the post-war period, increasing centralisation of functions within towns has led not only to a continuing diminution in village functions but also to an economic and social orientation of the rural communities towards the town.

Up to this point it has been stressed that the villages and hamlets within the hinterland of Aberystwyth are heavily dependent on the town for their economic survival. The majority have now markedly lost their functions, and increasingly look towards the town. In such circumstances, the action of the town as an agent of social change must be potent, and the next section of this essay will concern itself with the resultant process of suburbanisation.

It is thought that this process is best explained by reference to a limited number of villages and hamlets so that the specific nature of the suburbanisation may be readily understood. The two adjoining villages of Llandre and Bow Street were selected as being typical of Group I type of communities and as a contrast the five hamlets of the upper Trefeurig parish of Group III and IV.

THE PROCESS OF SUBURBANISATION: TWO CASE STUDIES

In the following two case studies emphasis will be placed on the increasing economic and social links between the town and the rural community and the effect this has had upon the local community structure. This theme led to a questionnaire study of the local population. Questions were asked about the social and geographical background of the population, the nature of their journey outside the village for employment and pleasure, and their social activities within the village.[29] There has been little attempt to analyse the data at a sophisticated statistical level since such a procedure proved inadvisable with such small figures.[30]

Today the hamlets of the upper Trefeurig parish show completely different patterns from the villages of Bow Street and Llandre, though it must be stressed that these differences were not so marked in the past. During the mid-nineteenth century, the Trefeurig hamlets had a combined population of 556 compared with 432 at Bow Street and 296 at Llandre; in each case the majority of their occupied population was involved, directly or indirectly, in the lead mining industry of their hinterlands.[31] It is to more detailed characterisation of these differences that we must now turn.

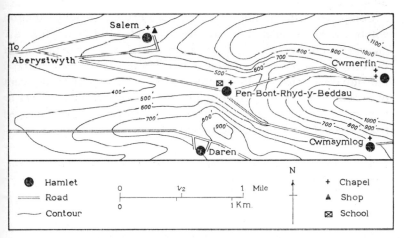

Fig. 7.5. Location of the upper Trefeurig hamlets.

Upper Trefeurig hamlets

The five hamlets of Cwmerfin, Cwmsymlog, Banc-y-Daren, Salem, and Penbontrhydybeddau, are located on the eastern side of the Trefeurig parish (Fig. 7.5). They are sited in the upper reaches of two narrow valleys along the western slopes of Pumlumon, and the constricted nature of these valleys has resulted in a series of small ribbons of development, consisting of haphazardly located houses.

The hamlets exhibit certain similarities both in their present structure and historical development. In 1964 the total population of the five amounted to only 173, and the economic and social facilities they possessed were limited to a general store, a school, four chapels, and two social organisations.

It has already been observed that the hamlets had a much larger population during the nineteenth century, a period when they all had

a close affinity with the surrounding area. The lead mines of the neighbourhood were reaching their zenith,[32] and people had migrated into
the hamlets from considerable distances.[33] It would seem that the
growth of this industry was instrumental in the formation of these
communities in something like their present form and location. With
the decline in mining activity after the 1880s the hamlets lost population rapidly, and people left for the industrial areas of South Wales
and the Midlands. This process of out-migration has continued to
afflict the hamlets.[34]

Compared with the mid-nineteenth century the present situation
within the five hamlets is markedly different. Collectively they are
dependent not only on the surrounding 'locality'[35] for employment
but also on Aberystwyth (Table 7.3).[36] However, there are marked
individual variations in this pattern. For example, over 60 per cent
of the employed from Cwmerfin and Penbontrhydybeddau travel to
the town for employment, but less than 20 per cent of the employed
from Salem, Cwmsymlog, and Banc-y-Daren.

TABLE 7.3. *The employment structure of the Trefeurig hamlets (percentages)*

Form of employment		Place of employment	
Professional	—	Village	7
Intermediate	8	Locality	59
Skilled	26	Aberystwyth	34
Partly Skilled	19	Elsewhere	—
Unskilled	47		
	—	Total	100
Total	100		

It is difficult to account for this contrast, since the differences in
distance from the town are minimal and all have a similar public
transport service. Probably the older age structure of the second group
is largely responsible. However, despite the overall dependence upon
the locality for employment the opportunities there are limited. The
only significant opportunities are in forestry, agriculture (which has
declined markedly due to recent farm amalgamation and purchases by
the Forestry Commission) and an agricultural research station at the
lower end of the parish.[37] Inevitably in such a situation commuting
has become of significance.

Despite this increasing dependence on two sources of employment
the occupations of the Trefeurig hamlets are predominantly limited to

the manual variety (Table 7.3). Those trained for white-collar posts have continued to leave, and very few from outside have been attracted to reside within the hamlets. In such circumstances little wealth is introduced into the area.

Since the turn of the century the population of the five hamlets has continued to fall, creating an age structure akin to rural communities which have suffered from depopulation over a long period of time.[38] Those in the lower age brackets, particularly between twenty and

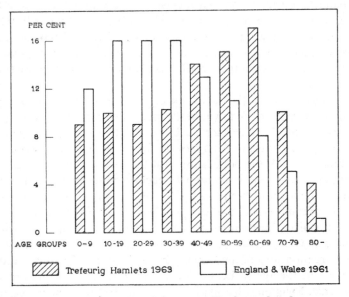

Fig. 7.6. Age structure of the upper Trefeurig hamlets.

forty, are notably absent, and there is a corresponding heavy preponderance of persons in the upper age groups (Fig. 7.6). This depopulation might have been more severe but for the general shortage of houses within the Aberystwyth area from 1945 onwards and certain socio-economic difficulties within the communities themselves. Only a few of the houses have been modernised, despite the availability of a grant, indicating a probable insufficiency of capital. Thus the difficulties of selling become almost insurmountable, and since there is a high proportion of owner-occupied property alongside a lower level of income, the possibilities of migration to better located villages are limited. However, by 1964 there were several unoccupied houses in the area and only a few had been developed as summer residences.

In such a situation population movement is slow and local in character. People from afar have not been attracted to the hamlets in any large numbers, and any change is outwards, particularly to the town or 'better' located villages. The origin of the present population is local, 72 per cent of the in-migrants come from the Trefeurig parish or the adjoining ones, and this has the effect of retaining people of similar backgrounds within the local community. Therefore, none of the hamlets appear to possess a class structure in a socio-economic sense, and even the traditional Welsh *buchedd*[39] is relatively weak. They possess neither professional persons, as Table 7.3 indicates, nor an estate landlord. The nearest to such a status group would be the local farmers, but even these could hardly qualify as a separate social class.

In many respects the local society is inward looking. Despite economic links with the town, in the form of employment, few significant social links have developed. For example, less than a quarter of the housewives travel to Aberystwyth for shopping once a week, and less than a fifth of the population visit the town in any one week for entertainment. This could largely be accounted for by the difficulty of travel to the town without a car, since the bus service is limited. Moreover the preponderance of older people in the communities makes the desire for visits to the town much less than in a community with a significant young element. The hamlets have a limited number of social organisations of their own, such as Women's Institutes and an 'Aelwyd' of the Welsh League of Youth, and the majority are well supported. Religion still plays a vital role in the life of the people, and the services are well attended. Many of the characteristics of the traditional Welsh way of life are preserved here and this is emphasised by the fact that 91 per cent of the population are Welsh-speaking and that the majority prefer to converse in their mother tongue.

Nevertheless, it must be stressed that the Welsh way of life in these small communities is in decline, not from social change emanating from the town, but rather through economic stagnation. Its disintegration results from a social malaise. The hamlets have not been able to exploit their proximity to Aberystwyth by creating a new type of society. Despite the fact that a significant number of their inhabitants commute to the town, the hamlets have not developed as 'dormitory' centres in the sense of a community in which the social and economic

life is markedly oriented towards a neighbouring town. The relative
short distance to Aberystwyth has certainly allowed some of the
employed to commute daily, but poor sites, difficulties of transport
and general inaccessibility have encouraged a large number to migrate
to better located centres, and at the same time discouraged others from
moving to reside in the hamlets. Despite this economic link with the
town these communities have not developed parallel social links, and
so the stimulant of an urban centre to growth has been absent. It
would seem that stagnation had entrenched itself prior to the increasing
influence of the town, and proximity to an urban centre in itself does
not necessarily stimulate social change.

In conclusion, it may be said that these Trefeurig hamlets, despite
economic dependence on the town, exhibit at the same time a social
stability and a demographic instability. In many ways they are typical
of communities in decline.[40] They are still peculiarly isolated and decaying, despite close proximity to Aberystwyth with its employment
and social opportunities, and can be regarded as examples of 'insular'
poverty.[41] The pattern outlined above is in contrast to the situation to
be described below.

Bow Street and Llandre

The two adjoining villages of Bow Street and Llandre are located
between four and five miles north of Aberystwyth, the former in a
relatively wide valley along the main north–south trunk routeway,
and the latter in a much narrower valley on a secondary road which is a
link to the small seaside resort of Borth. Morphologically both are
of a one-street character, though they do have a number of side roads.[42]
By now Bow Street and Llandre have nearly coalesced, though the gap
between them in the neighbourhood of Rhydypennau is sufficiently
wide to regard the two as distinct communities (Fig. 7.7).

In 1963 Bow Street and Llandre had a population of 686 and 502
respectively, and as such were two of the largest settlements within the
survey areas. As indicated earlier, these two villages are oriented, both
socially and economically, towards the town, and it is this theme that
the following paragraphs will outline under six principal headings:
(1) the economic links with the town; (2) the social links with the
town; (3) the demographic structure; (4) the social and geographical
origins of the population; (5) the evolution of a class structure; (6) the
development of a social and geographical segregation.

12

1. *Economic links with the town.* The increasing influence of a town
can best be understood in terms of the employment structure of the
rural community, since it can be a vital determinant of the effectiveness
of suburbanisation, particularly when the community is physically
distinct from the urban centre.

From Table 7.4 it can be seen that both Llandre and Bow Street are
heavily dependent upon Aberystwyth for employment. The villages
themselves, their surrounding localities, and 'other' areas are relatively

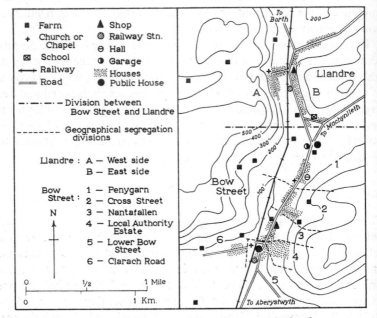

Fig. 7.7. Locational features of Bow Street and Llandre.

insignificant employment centres. However, the degree of dependence
upon the town varies significantly between the various occupational
types.

In both villages dependence on Aberystwyth varies directly with
increase in social class, as does the use of the car as a mode of travel to
work. If anything, Llandre reveals a slightly greater dependence on
professional and managerial occupations, and Bow Street on skilled
and unskilled occupations. The contrast is largely accounted for by
the fact that the latter has a large council housing estate, which has

TABLE 7.4. *Bow Street and Llandre: The employment structure and place of work*

A. The Employment Structure (percentages)

	Professional	*Intermediate*	*Skilled*	*Partly skilled*	*Unskilled*	*Total*
BOW STREET	9	25	41	14	11	100
LLANDRE	12	36	28	11	12	100

B. The Place of Work (percentages)

	Professional	*Intermediate*	*Skilled*	*Partly skilled*	*Unskilled*	*Total*
BOW STREET						
Aberystwyth	89	74	74	65	63	69
Village	2	8	12	12	9	11
Locality	9	18	14	21	22	16
Elsewhere	—	—	—	2	6	4
Total	100	100	100	100	100	100
LLANDRE						
Aberystwyth	84	77	55	53	51	63
Village	—	6	14	10	12	9
Locality	11	17	22	29	29	22
Elsewhere	5	—	9	8	8	6
Total	100	100	100	100	100	100

attracted a high proportion of 'non-white collar' workers, while in the former, even during the interwar period a greater proportion of middle-class type houses were erected. However, compared with the Trefeurig hamlets, both Bow Street and Llandre have proportionally more white-collar occupations, and in this respect they exhibit affinity to suburban communities on the fringe of large cities.[43] Apart from a nearby agricultural research station, the town is the only employment centre for this type of occupation, and so those employed in or around the villages are skilled and unskilled workers and tradesmen. The relative absence of this latter group indicates the insignificant service functions possessed by both villages.

Despite a certain significant difference in the employment structure of Bow Street and Llandre, there is little or no difference in the employment mobility of the 'newer' and the 'older' members of the two communities. People of varying occupational status have been attracted to reside in these villages, and all the categories, except for agriculture, look towards the town. In other words, the whole economic well-being of these two villages is tied to the town, and they have only been able to survive and grow as a consequence of this increasing link.

2. *Social links with the town.* Up to this point it has been shown that the majority of the employed population travel daily to Aberystwyth, so the next question is to what extent does the local population travel to the town for pleasure or social contact. In other words, has the economic link with the town become a social link? To this end three specific questions were chosen.

Respondents were first of all asked about the frequency of their visits to Aberystwyth for shopping. Both villages have one general store of their own, but local shopping is not particularly significant, though all respondents maintained that these facilities are used for occasional needs. Weekly grocery shopping is equally divided between the local stores and those of the town. Any other form of shopping is heavily dependent on Aberystwyth (Table 7.5). The frequency of shopping

TABLE 7.5. *Frequency of shopping visits to Aberystwyth by housewives (percentages)*

Frequency	Bow Street	Llandre
Once per week or less frequent	20	30
Twice or three times per week	66	51
More frequent	14	19

visits to the town by housewives shows that over three-quarters from Bow Street, and slightly less from Llandre, travel at least twice a week. This slight difference between the two villages in the frequency pattern of shopping visits could largely be accounted for by the better public transport available from Bow Street. The 'shop at the door' facility is proportionally less significant for these two communities than for the Trefeurig hamlets.

Secondly, questions were asked as to the frequency of visits to the town for pleasure. There is a wide range of social activities at Aberystwyth and members of both communities make good use of these facilities (Table 7.6); certain sections of the population, particularly the young, make greater use of these facilities than others. Thus, people between fifteen and twenty are attracted by the cinema, dances, and coffee bars whilst certain middle-class families are attracted by concerts, drama, and music societies. The increasing popularity of these facilities means that local-based social activities

TABLE 7.6. *Frequency of visits to Aberystwyth for entertainment (percentages)*

Frequency	Bow Street	Llandre
Once a week	21	27
Once a month	33	39
Less frequently	46	34

have declined rapidly, as will be seen later, though the coming of television has also been an important factor in this decline.

The third question, when and from where did the last visitor come to the household for a meal, can be regarded as an index of social contact. Unfortunately, it was much more complex to assess. It was realised immediately that the majority had come from the town but the frequency of this occurrence was impossible to deduce. There seems to be little contact of this nature between households within the villages but it must be emphasised that such a phenomenon does not necessarily reflect a lack of sociability. In this social environment entertainment to meals is unusual and seems to extend only to those from outside the village. Neither length of residence nor occupation appears to affect the incidence of this form of social activity which is not practised in Bow Street or Llandre to the same extent as in communities on the fringe of the metropolitan area.[44]

From the limited discussion so far it is obvious that much of the social life of Bow Street and Llandre is oriented towards Aberystwyth, and it means that the life of these small communities is outward rather than inward looking.

3. *The demographic structure.* In such a situation the demographic structure of both communities differs markedly from the traditional rural pattern. They have an equal proportion of males and females, and their age structure is not overweighted by persons in the older age brackets (Fig. 7.8). Both have a significant proportion of their population aged between thirty and sixty, along with a significant element below fifteen, though Llandre proportionally has more over fifty than Bow Street. This contrast can be explained by the slightly differing migrational patterns they have experienced within the last fifteen years or so. Both have become centres of in-migration, usually of persons in their middle age. In addition, Llandre in particular has had a significant in-migration of retired persons, and Bow Street, of young married couples. At the same time, those aged between eighteen and thirty

continue to leave the two communities in search of types of employment not found within the area, further education, or marriage, though it should be noted that this out-migration is not as marked as in many other Welsh rural communities,[45] due to the employment opportunities available at Aberystwyth.

This in-movement has had the effect of introducing persons of differing social and geographical backgrounds into the two communities

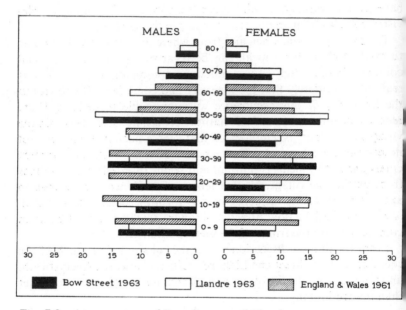

Fig. 7.8. Age structure of Bow Street and Llandre.

with new codes of behaviour and attitudes. Therefore, the next section will outline these backgrounds and the motivation for deciding to reside within Bow Street and Llandre.

4. *Social and geographical origins of population.* Up to the Second World War the in-migrants of Bow Street and Llandre were local in origin but during the last twenty or so years the source of the migrants has become more distant. At the time of the field investigation several streams of invasion could be discerned (Table 7.7). First, there are those originating from the parishes that surround the two villages, secondly, the town, thirdly, the rest of Mid-Wales, and finally, the rest

TABLE 7.7. *Previous place of residence of the adult population (percentages)*

Area	Bow Street	Llandre
Locality	27	19
Aberystwyth	18	15
Rest of Cardiganshire	17	11
Rest of Mid Wales Counties	11	19
Rest of Wales	11	11
England	13	16
Other areas	3	9
Total	100	100

of the British Isles, Compared with the last century, the source of the present migrants was more distant,[46] though Bow Street still has a significant group originating from the locality. These are represented by young married families, attracted by the availability of a house at the council estate. The various in-movements can be categorised as follows:

(*a*) Movement into the village from the town;

(*b*) Movement into the village by those seeking employment in the town but preferring rural residence;

(*c*) Movement into the village from adjoining areas;

(*d*) Movement for retirement.

The motives of these migrants in deciding to reside in Bow Street and Llandre proved difficult to summarise since varied replies were received, but an attempt has been made in Table 7.8.

TABLE 7.8. *Motivation among in-migrants*

Category of in-migrant	Principal reasons in order of importance[47]
(*a*)	Attracted by village life Desire for rural residence Suitable house
(*b*)	Proximity to town Village life Rural residence
(*c*)	Availability of house Proximity to work and social facilities of town
(*d*)	Proximity to friends and relatives Home area Village life

The majority of the migrants desired residence outside the town but none were prepared to reside at too great a distance away. Those in categories (a) and (b) were not influenced by a desire for residence in a specific village; so long as it had a suitable house and was close to the town they were satisfied. Those in category (d) were much more specific in their selection of location, and those in category (c) were influenced by the availability of a house, particularly a council estate one. Many were attracted to life in the countryside and the small-scale nature of village community life, and in this respect were typical of suburban people. However, this pattern was complicated at Llandre and Bow Street by the in-migrants from more isolated neighbourhoods, who in many ways were taking the first step towards urban residence.[48] Thus there was a contrasting attitude among these in-migrants towards residence at these two villages. On the one hand, those that had moved from more isolated parts considered the commuters 'urban', due to their proximity to the employment and social facilities of the town; on the other hand, those that had moved out from the town or from some other urban centre, considered the communities 'rural' since they were small villages located in the countryside. In other words, the latter were attracted by 'village' life and the former by 'urban' living.

5. *The evolution of a class structure.* These in-migrants, with their different backgrounds, have introduced new attitudes and codes of behaviour into the two communities. Added to these, new values emanate from the towns, and so stresses and strains have appeared in the communal life of Bow Street and Llandre. Both are characterised by an 'established' and a 'newcomer' element.[49] The latter are only accepted as village people after a lengthy period of residence, though this may be shortened if they are Welsh-speaking and are prepared to partake in village social activities. In addition, a more complicated class system has been built upon this structure. Welsh rural society in

TABLE 7.9. *Length of residence and social class*

Class[50]		BOW STREET			LLANDRE	
		Newcomers	*Established*		*Newcomers*	*Established*
Middle	34	62	38	48	79	21
Lower	66	31	69	52	14	86
Total	100	47	53	100	47	53

the past has been pictured as being relatively classless, in the sense that status was based upon non-material factors such as *buchedd,* and it would seem that this was the situation Bow Street and Llandre until the interwar period. However, with the advent of professional and managerial people and the increasing link with Aberystwyth, greater value is being placed upon material things, and as a consequence awareness of economic status has been introduced (Table 7.9).

Both communities are characterised by a relatively high proportion of middle-class people, in particular, among the newcomer element. If anything, Llandre has proportionally a greater number of middle-class than Bow Street, and this can largely be explained by a slightly differing pattern of in-migration.

As recent studies have outlined, such a situation is typical of suburban communities, and it has been created here by the in-movement of new people, often with middle-class values, consequent on the increasing economic and social links with the town, and thus allowing the town's role as an agent of social change to become effective.

6. *Geographical and social segregation.* The effect of the imposition of this class structure on life at Bow Street and Llandre has been to create a certain degree of social and geographical segregation, and this section will attempt to outline these contrasts.

The geographical segregation of the middle and lower classes, a feature so typical of suburban living, is clearly apparent in the spatial structure of these two communities. However, it should be emphasised that the evolution of such a pattern was determined not only by the changing attitudes and motives of the population but also the availability of suitable land. The pattern of this geographical segregation has been summarised in Table 7.10, and it shows that the segregation

TABLE 7.10. *Geographical distribution of population according to class*

BOW STREET			LLANDRE		
Subdivisions	Middle class	Lower class	Subdivisions	Middle class	Lower class
Penygarn	31	69	West side	21	79
Nantafallen	12	88	East side	81	19
Lower Village	32	68	Talybont road	79	21
Housing estate	18	82			
Cross Street area	72	28			
Clarach road	51	49			

layout of Llandre and Bow Street differs to a certain extent. At Llandre there is a clear dichotomy between the middle class of the eastern side of the main road, and the predominantly lower class of the western side. The former is characterised by large detached and semi-detached houses, and the latter by an admixture of cottages, bungalows, terrace houses, small detached and semi-detached houses, as well as a small council housing estate. At Bow Street the pattern is much more complex. The three original nuclei, and the new council housing estate are mostly lower class, and the middle class are predominantly located along the two side roads and an area between the two original nuclei (Fig. 7.7). The pattern, therefore, is much clearer at Llandre

TABLE 7.11. *Percentage of families participating in local social activities*

	BOW STREET			LLANDRE		
Activity	*All groups*	*Middle class*	*Lower class*	*All groups*	*Middle class*	*Lower class*
Eisteddfod	30	45	14	28	26	32
Women's Institute	20	35	3	19	27	14
Y.M.C.A.	13	22	10	6	2	10
Local government	5	7	2	4	11	2
Choir	13	12	6	10	9	11
Literary meetings	24	35	14	21	15	27
Carnival	36	35	39	31	33	30
Chapel teas	40	54	25	21	13	29
Extramural class	1	5	—	3	7	2
Young Peoples' Association	10	5	8	8	9	6
None	34	16	57	42	45	40

but the existence of such a phenomenon is a good expression of changing desires and attitudes brought about by the town, and typifies the influence of suburbanisation.

Having determined the extent to which the middle and lower classes have created a geographical segregation within Bow Street and Llandre it is now necessary to assess the degree to which they also determine a social segregation. It was thought necessary to discuss this by reference to the degree of participation in local social organisations and events, and attendance at religious services (Table 7.11).

At the time of the field investigation Bow Street had twelve social organisations and events of its own. These varied from weekly meetings, such as the Young Farmers' Club, to annual events, such as the Carnival, but Llandre had only one such organisation, the Women's

Institute, and an occasional event connected with the church. Therefore, the people of Llandre had to share the social activities of Bow
Street, but they do not participate in these social activities to the same
extent as those of Bow Street, and this may be due to the greater
distances involved. In general, support for these social activities came
from a greater range of the society of Bow Street than at Llandre.
However, the principal participants from the former tend to be middle-
class and Welsh-speaking, and from the latter lower-class and Welsh-
speaking. This contrast is due to two principal reasons. First, the
Llandre middle class are predominantly English-speaking compared
with those of Bow Street, so they are hindered from partaking in these
events because they are held in the Welsh tongue, and secondly,
Bow Street has a relatively high proportion of lower-class newcomers,
a group that is not prepared to partake readily. Therefore, it would
seem that within the sphere of social participation the middle class of
Llandre are socially more isolated than those of Bow Street.

Religious adherence was at one time an essential part of community
life in rural Wales,[51] but if frequency of attendance is any indication
then this aspect has declined markedly within these communities.
Bow Street has two chapels, Presbyterian and Congregationalist in
denomination, while Llandre has a Church and a small branch

TABLE 7.12. *Frequency of attendance at Sunday services*

Frequency of attendance (percentage)	BOW STREET			LLANDRE		
	All groups	Middle class	Lower class	All groups	Middle class	Lower class
Once a week	25	29	21	21	24	18
Once a month	21	22	19	16	18	14
Once in 3 months	14	19	10	15	14	17
Less frequent	11	10	12	19	18	20
Not at all	29	20	38	29	26	31
Total	100	100	100	100	100	100

Presbyterian chapel. Members of any other denomination have to
travel outside the communities. In both Bow Street and Llandre the
most frequent attenders are those in the middle class,[52] and in older
categories of the population (Table 7.12). Members of the middle
class are also developing as the leaders within the church and the
chapels. However, in general, these services are not as significant in
community life as they were in the past.

Therefore, in both communities, class determines to a certain extent the degree of interest in religion and social activities, though its full effect is distorted by the influence of language. The decline in interest in these two activities and the beginning of the development of a social segregation along class lines typifies a community under the influence of suburbanisation.[53] Thus, social and geographical segregation seems increasingly to be an essential feature of life at Bow Street and Llandre, clearly exhibiting the influence of the town as an agent of social change, though the process has not advanced as far as in many suburban communities on the edge of large cities.

Conclusion

In Bow Street and Llandre it has been demonstrated that the socially and economically self-contained communities of the past have collapsed. Commuting to Aberystwyth for employment and pleasure pursuits is vital to their well-being. As this process proceeds in-migration is becoming more selective, and more middle-class people are moving in. The effect is to create a class distinction within the local society which is segregated along social and geographical lines. Hence both communities are linked very closely to the outside world through their local town, and apart from their geographical location they are to all intents and purposes incorporated into the urban community.

SUBURBANISATION AND PLANNING IMPLICATIONS

Throughout this study an attempt has been made to isolate the forces at work in bringing about the suburbanisation of a rural area, and a selected number of the consequent changes were considered in the two case studies. It was seen that not all the communities had developed in the same way, since the reaction of people in different places varied significantly. Among the forces that determined these forms were: accessibility to the town, economic pressure, social desires, planning legislation, and local factors such as land ownership, attractiveness of the area, housing, and the local community structure. Within these forces individual and group decisions were also important determinants.

The analysis has provided another example of the increasing network of connections[54] between rural communities and the surrounding towns. Within this present study these links were limited to the social and economic sphere. In Bow Street and Llandre economic and social activities were locally based in the part and so the network of relations tended to coincide. But with the increasing connection with the town, these networks of social relations, for example, interest, friendship and kinship, have become larger and more diffused, and do not overlap. On the other hand, in the Trefeurig hamlets these social networks still tended to coincide, probably because of their relatively unchanged social structure and geographical isolation.[55] So within the latter social relations tended still to be primary and face-to-face, but at the former this kind of contact had declined, tending rather to be secondary and segmented.[56] In these terms, therefore, these two groups of communities could be regarded as being at different levels on an urban-rural continuum.[57]

Throughout the study the town has been seen as an agent of social change, influencing the surrounding communities, changing their internal structure, their relationship to each other, and re-sorting their viability. The consequent changing of community structures is creating a new pattern in the social geography of rural communities in Mid-Wales. This pattern is proceeding along two complementary lines. The local communities are evolving from a traditional Welsh rural society, the pattern of which has been so expertly summarised by Rees in his study of Llanfihangel yng Nghwynfa,[58] into either a type of 'urban residential community'[59] such as Bow Street and Llandre, or into a decaying structure, such as the Trefeurig hamlets. Thus the impact on communities in a sparsely populated area is twofold. On the one hand it leads to growth and a new type of community, and on the other to decline and a social disintegration of the traditional society.

With such a pattern developing as a consequence of the continued growth in the town's influence it is considered that such changes have potential for planning future settlement forces, on a local and a regional scale, within rural areas.

On a local scale, it is argued that the process of re-sorting the viability of the villages and hamlets by the town should be encouraged by allowing development only in the better located ones. The development of 'key' villages is not a new idea but it does seem critical to base their selection upon their relationship with the town. Such a policy would not only have the advantage of encouraging residence in the countryside but would also provide an outward looking society which did not suffer from isolation and poverty of social intercourse.

On a regional scale the planner in Mid-Wales[60] is faced with the problems of a continually falling population. Recently the Government has intimated that it proposes to arrest this drift by introducing greater employment opportunities, but there is little agreement as to how such development can be made to benefit the whole region. It is suggested, on the basis of this study, that such developments should be concentrated in a number of existing towns rather than at one major centre[61] because such a policy has the advantage of extending the existing pattern. It has been shown that Aberystwyth acts as the central commuting focus with a distinct hinterland, made up of a series of commuting satellites, so if development were concentrated at the commuting focus the increase in population would occur not only at the centre but also in the hinterland villages. This could be adopted for the existing towns in Mid-Wales, since they have administrative and commercial functions and commuter hinterlands similar, though on a smaller scale, to those of Aberystwyth. The advantage of such a policy is that it attempts to maintain a spatial balance of population throughout the region, and is an expansion in form of existing conditions. Many would object to such a policy on the grounds that an increase in village dormitory function would mean a decline in community life, as outlined at Bow Street and Llandre, and therefore the whole scheme would be considered undesirable. Against this, it must be emphasised that dormitory communities exist there already and if nothing is attempted, the distinctive local communal life would itself disappear, as at the Trefeurig hamlets.

If such policies, in conjunction with the recommendations of the Mid-Wales Investigation Report,[62] were rigorously applied, only then would the full potential of the area be realised and the region rationally reorganised along successful lines. The future pattern of the social geography of rural communities in Mid-Wales[63] will depend largely on local planning policy and the extent of the regional developments proposed.

REFERENCES

1. DICKINSON, R. E., *West European City*, Routledge, 1961.

2. HAUSER, P. M., 'Folk urban ideals', in Hauser, P. M. and Schnore L. F., eds., *The Study of Urbanization*, Wiley, 1965, pp. 503–17.

3. Among the numerous studies include those of Dobriner, W. M. *The Suburban Community*, Putnam, 1958, and *Class in Suburbia* Prentice-Hall, 1963.

4. CRICHTON, R., *Commuters Village*, Macdonald, 1964; COPPOCK J. T., 'Dormitory settlements around London', in Coppock, J, T. and

Prince, H. C., eds., *Greater London*, Faber, 1964, pp. 265–91; MASSER, F. I. and STROUD, D. C., 'The metropolitan village', *Tn Plann. Rev.*, **36**, 1965, pp. 111–24; PAHL, R. E., *Urbs in Rure: the metropolitan fringe in Hertfordshire*, London School of Economics, 1965; ELIAS, N. and SCOTSON, J. L., *The Established and the Outsiders: a sociological enquiry into community problems*, Cass, 1965.

5. COPPOCK, 'Dormitory settlements around London'.

6. PAHL, *Urbs in Rure*.

7. FRANKENBERG, R., *British Communities*, Penguin, 1966.

8. REES, A. D., *Life in a Welsh Countryside*, University of Wales Press, 1950; WILLIAMS, W. M., *The Sociology of an English Village: Gosforth*, Routledge 1956; DAVIES, E. and REES, A. D., eds., *Welsh Rural Communities*, University of Wales Press, 1960; WILLIAMS, W. M., *A West Country Village: Ashworthy*, Routledge, 1963; LITTLEJOHN, J. *Westrigg: The Sociology of a Cheviot Parish*, Routledge, 1963.

9. CARTER, H., *The Towns of Wales*, University of Wales Press, 1965, pp. 105–40.

10. NEWMAN, J., ed., *The Limerick Rural Survey*, Tipperary, Muintir Na Tire Rural Publications, 1964, pp. 248–306.

11. BRACEY, H. E., *Social Provisions in Rural Wiltshire*, Methuen, 1952.

12. ROWLEY, G., *Middle Order Towns in Wales*, unpublished Ph.D. thesis, University of Wales (Aberystwyth), 1967.

13. *Report of the Committee on Depopulation in Mid-Wales*, HMSO, London, 1964, p. 1.

14. *Ibid.*, pp. 3–4.

15. LEWIS, W. J., 'Some aspects of the history of Aberystwyth', *Ceredigion*, **3**, 1959, pp. 283–318; **4**, 1960, pp. 19–33.

16. CARTER, H., and DAVIES, M. L., 'The hierarchy of urban fields in Cardiganshire', *Tijdschr. voor econ. soc. Geogr.*, **54**, 1963, pp. 181–6; ROWLEY, unpublished Ph.D. Thesis, 1967.

17. LEWIS, G. J., 'Commuting and the village in Mid-Wales', *Geography*, **52**, 1967, pp. 294–304.

18. A detailed fieldwork survey of the population size and occupational structure of the villages and hamlets within the Aberystwyth hinterland was carried out in 1963. Each house was visited in order to determine the number of inhabitants, the number of gainfully employed, the form and place of employment, and the mode of transport to work.

19. MARTIN, W. T., 'Ecological change in satellite rural areas', *Am. sociol. Rev.*, **22**, 1957, pp. 173–83.

20. The term 'focality' refers to the number of facilities such as social provisions, services, and organisations that a community possesses. Note the more general term, 'centrality', as used by Davies and Lewis in Chapters 2 and 9.

21. 'Urban orientation' refers to the degree that a community's social and economic life depends upon an urban centre. Within this essay the urban centre is Aberystwyth.

22. This refers to the range of social provision facilities and social organisations and events a community possesses.

23. For an example of this approach see Bracey, *Social Provisions in Rural Wiltshire*, 1952; and the same author's 'Towns as rural service centres—an index of centrality with special reference to Somerset', *Trans. Inst. Br. Geogr.*, **19**, 1953, pp. 95–105.

24. JONES-PIERCE, T., 'Medieval Cardiganshire—a study in social origins', *Ceredigion*, **3**, 1957, pp. 265–79.

25. HOWELLS, J. M., 'Crosswood Estate 1683–1899', unpublished M.A. Thesis, University of Wales (Aberystwyth), 1956.

26. *Census Reports 1801–1871: Cardiganshire.*

27. THOMAS, T. M., *The Mineral Wealth of Wales and its Exploitation*, Oliver and Boyd, 1961, pp. 195–7.

28. BOWEN, E. G., 'Welsh emigration overseas', *Adv. of Sci.*, **46**, 1960, p. 261.

29. The field investigation within these communities was carried out during 1963, 1964, and 1965. Each house was visited at least once, and the head of the household was interviewed from a detailed questionnaire schedule.

30. For an example of a detailed statistical analysis of a small rural community see Gadourek, E., *A Dutch Community*, Leiden, H. E Stenfert Krooss, 1956.

31. Public Record Office, *Census Enumeration Schedules 1861*, H.O 107/1372–2486.

32. LEWIS, W. J., *Lead Mining in Wales*, University of Wales Press 1967, pp. 170–204.

33. Public Record Office, *Census Enumeration Schedules, 1861.*

34. *Census Reports 1871–1961: Cardiganshire.*

35. The term 'locality' refers not only to the parish that a community is located within but also the parishes that surround it.

36. Based upon Registrar General's Classification of Occupations 1960.

37. This is the Welsh Plant Breeding Station, a part of the University College of Wales, Aberystwyth.

38. SAVILLE, J., *Rural Depopulation in England and Wales 1851–1951*, Routledge, 1957.

39. 'The Welsh term *buchedd* denotes behaviour, either actual or ideal, and this corresponds broadly to the English term, way of life. The same overall pattern of social life is found within each *buchedd* group.' High status is bestowed upon those associated with the chapel or church and low status upon those frequenting public houses. See JENKINS, D., 'Aberporth', in Davies and Rees, eds., *Welsh Rural Communities*, 1960, p. 13.

40. Compare with MITCHELL, G. D., 'Social disintegration in a rural community', *Human Relations*, 3, 1950, pp. 279–306.

41. GALBRAITH, J. K., *Affluent Society*, Penguin, 1958, pp. 262–4.

42. For example, Bow Street originally was made up of three small nucleii, Nantafallen, Penygarn and 'Old' Bow Street, and with expansion have coalesced into a linear form.

43. BOTT, E., *Family and Social Network*, Tavistock Publications, 1957.

44. Contrast with PAHL, *Urbs in Rure*, pp. 60–1.

45. Contrast with the Trefeurig hamlets and the communities studied in Davies and Rees, eds., *Welsh Rural Communities*.

46. LEWIS, G. J., 'The demographic structure of a Welsh rural village during the mid-nineteenth century', *Ceredigion*, 5, 1967, pp. 290–304.

47. There was a good deal of overlap and so no attempt was made to scale order the replies.

48. BEIJER, G., *Rural Migrants in Urban Setting*, The Hague, Martinus Nijhoff, 1963.

49. The 'established' group were considered to be *the* village people, and the 'newcomers' were not regarded as such until about ten years of residence within a community.

50. This was based upon the Registrar General's Classification of Occupations 1960. The 'middle class' consisted of Groups I and II, and the 'lower class' of Groups III, IV, and V.

13

51. REES, *Life in a Welsh Countryside*, pp. 109–12; Davies and Rees eds., *Welsh Rural Communities*.

52. The frequency of church-going becoming markedly less common with a decline in the social order has also been noted by CAUTER, T and DOWNHAM, J. S., *The Communication of Ideas*, Chatto & Windus 1954, p. 261.

53. Compare with PAHL, *Urbs in Rure*, pp. 46–52.

54. BARNES, J. A., 'Class and committees in a Norwegian parish' *Human Relations*, 7, 1954, pp. 39–59.

55. WILLIAMS, W. M., 'Changing functions of the community', *Sociologia Ruralis*, 4, 1964, pp. 299–310.

56. COOLEY, C. H., *Social Organization*, New York, Schocken Books 1925.

57. PAHL, R. E., 'The urban-rural continuum', *Sociologia Ruralis*, 6 1966, pp. 299–327.

58. REES, *Life in a Welsh Countryside*.

59. HOEKVELD, G. A., 'A theoretical contribution to the Construction of Models for use in the Geography of Settlements', *Tijdschr. voor econ. soc. Geogr.*, 56, 1965, pp. 201–8.

60. LEWIS, C. R., Chapter 10 of this book.

61. One proposal suggests the siting of a major new urban centre in Mid-Wales, see *Consultant's Report on a New Town in Mid-Wales* HMSO, London, 1966; and another, the expansion of a single existing centre; for a contrary opinion as to which existing town see EVERSLEY D. E. C., 'A new town for Mid-Wales', *Town and Country Planning*, 3, 1965, pp. 45–6; and MOUNFIELD, P. R., 'Aberystwyth: growth point *Town and Country Planning*, 34, 1966, pp. 261–5.

62. Ministry of Agriculture, Fisheries and Food, *Mid-Wales Investigation Report*, HMSO, London, 1956.

63. LEWIS, G. J., *Socio-Geographical Changes in the Welsh Borderland Since the Mid Nineteenth Century*. Unpublished Ph.D. thesis, Univ of Leicester, 1969.

CHAPTER 8

A SMALL TOWN COMMUNITY IN MID WALES:

AN INTRODUCTORY STUDY

Morgan L. Davies

In an environment increasingly dominated by metropolitan centres it is not surprising that the spotlight of attention should be focused on the large cities. However, one should not overlook the fact that the small towns, the lowest order of the urban hierarchy, also have many problems to overcome at the present time. In the past, when communications were more difficult and people were less mobile, each small town played an important role, serving a rural hinterland with essential goods and services as well as forming a focal point for social and cultural activities. In many ways small towns tended to provide the best of two worlds, for their size meant that an urban way of life could be followed without the loss of close 'face to face' relationships that could not be maintained in the large city complex. Hence it satisfied an ideal along the rural-urban continuum[1] by providing the countryman with a taste of urban civilisation without becoming too far removed from the peasant culture which had nurtured him. It also crystallised the dream of many town dwellers of enjoying an urban way of life in an essentially rural setting.

Modern scientific advance, combined with individual affluence have, however, undermined many of the advantages of small towns. Today a more mobile and sophisticated population find few of their social and economic needs satisfied within such centres. Hence a vicious circle is created; people move away from the countryside and small towns because the opportunities available are so limited. This in turn erodes the position of the small centres even further. Thus the spiral of relative decay is accelerated.

Many studies have been carried out in Britain in an attempt to understand the detailed nature of these problems and to suggest ways of revitalising the countryside. The Scott Report published in the early 1940s maintained that growth areas should be established in rural

districts and that these should be located around existing small towns
'Where industries are brought into the country areas they should be
located in existing or small towns and not in villages or the open
country.'[2] Such an attitude was re-emphasised at a conference held in
1943 to consider the part country towns should play in a national
planning policy. The final report of the conference pointed out that
'the existing country towns of Britain present opportunities of develop
ment capable of catering for a considerable measure of decentralisa
tion of industry, business and population from large towns and
congested areas'.[3] The Town and Country Planning Act of 1947 con
tinued this line of thought and stressed the need for dispersal from
large cities, with the countryside becoming a reception area. In 195
White expressed the view that the problems of rural areas and country
towns were being overlooked: 'a superficial age which tended to judge
success by mere size has condemned many of them as failures, the
main stream of life has passed them by'.[4]

A number of pilot surveys and reports[5] dealing specifically with
small towns stemmed from a reassessment of the role of smaller com
munities. Some dealt with the reasons for the decline of small centres
others discussed the problems brought about by the expansion of
country towns.[6] Moreover the need for integrated planning led to
several workers stressing the need to integrate the demands of rural
areas with plans for dispersal from overcrowded cities.[7] In all these
reports a common feature was the prominence given to the fact that
any individual plan should be closely geared to the social and economic
characteristics of the region if it was to have any chance of success
Thomas and McLoughlin, for example, stated that 'a town is a special
event in the region and can no more be fully understood in isolation
than a word in a sentence'.[8] Hence no universal panacea was con
ceived; the problems of small towns will 'vary from one part of the
country to another, with the greatest difficulties lying in the more
isolated parts of the South-West and Wales'.[9] It is one of these areas
Mid-Wales, that provides the location for this particular study.

In Mid-Wales all the difficulties that have been looked at on
national scale are clearly in evidence. Numerous small centres class
fied as 'subtowns' or 'urban villages', the intermediaries between rural
and urban settlement,[10] are facing a crisis that has caused considerable
concern for some time. In the early 1950s the Beacham Report[11]
attempted to show why there were so many cases of 'arrested develop
ment' among Welsh country towns. In 1957 a specific attempt was

made to deal with the problem, a Mid-Wales Industrial Development Association was set up,[12] its main objective being to attract industry to small towns in the area. The Association suggested that a comparative analysis of various towns in Mid-Wales should be made in order to help define the ones that had possibilities for development. Twelve towns were selected as being suitable, but the scheme was never put into action, mainly because of the limited financial support available.

Meanwhile rural depopulation was accelerating[13] and in order to combat it a new and more ambitious plan was submitted. Instead of developing a series of small towns, it was visualised that a new town should be established in the area. This was described by the consultants who proposed the idea, as 'a novel type of new town, combining traditional manufacturing functions with recreational and resort functions.'[14] It would take the form of a linear town fourteen miles long. Such a grandiose scheme did not materialise. Once again the existing urban framework became the key element in the development plan for the area, though it was stressed that 'it would be both unwise and unrealistic to contemplate the significant expansion of each of the twenty-one towns in Mid-Wales'.[15]

In a new attempt to deal with rural decay a Mid-Wales Development Corporation was formed in 1966. One of its first announcements was a plan for doubling the size of Newtown, with other towns scheduled for expansion later. However, the report warned that the problem of developing small country towns 'is a matter on which there is all too little practical experience and know-how available'.[16] Since it has often been pointed out that 'it is not possible to lay down a detailed standard method for planning individual small towns'[17] it would seem essential to understand the existing structural characteristics of Mid-Wales towns, if any acceptable plans are to be formulated. Once these characteristics are understood the nature of the problems will become clearer and plans may be dovetailed into the present pattern instead of being proposed with little understanding of existing conditions.

This chapter does not attempt to make a sophisticated analysis of the problems of all Mid-Wales towns. Instead a case study of the initial results of a complete survey of one town, Aberaeron, is presented. Some of the basic data used in this study could have been obtained from the 1966 Census record[18] but the aggregation of available data on a county basis, as well as the sample framework used in this Census has meant that a great deal of potentially valuable information

is either not available or of dubious validity for such a small area
Hence recourse was made to a 100 per cent coverage of the town in
order to derive the basic data. This will be used to build up a detailed
picture of the social and economic elements operating within a small
community representative of other urban centres in Mid-Wales. Few
attempts have been made to develop extensive generalisations from
this one example; such generalisations would only be useful if they
were derived from a comparative study of towns.

ABERAERON

Aberaeron in the early years of the nineteenth century was still a small
hamlet with few central functions. The physical attributes of its site
and location were partly responsible for its development, an expansion
based first of all on its harbour and later on the railway.[19] This prosperity was shortlived and today the town exists primarily as a small
holiday resort with certain administrative and low order retail functions. Like that of many other Mid-Wales centres its future is vague
and uncertain and the area would seem to be a suitable one for a case
study.

In line with the comments made above the intention is to examine
certain contemporary social and economic characteristics of the town
in order to develop a more complete understanding of the characteristics of a town of this size as an aid to planning forecasts. Before the
various features are examined it is important to note that planning is
not a development new to Aberaeron.[20] The town was planned from
the beginning of its growth, though the planning was a matter of
physical rather than economic or social control.

Population structure

No analysis of a small town can be complete without a study of its
population structure. Not only does the study provide a basic back

TABLE 8.1. *Age structure*

					Age group					
0–9	10–19	20–29	30–39	40–49	50–59	60–69	70–79	80–89	90+	*Total*
					Males					
58	65	35	49	60	50	43	35	13	—	408
					Females					
58	60	40	53	55	85	74	64	16	2	507

round to all facets of a small town society, but it demonstrates the
mpact of past trends and provides a useful indication of future
evelopments. Table 8.1 provides a breakdown of the age structure of
Aberaeron, a structure that is remarkably unbalanced. This lack of
alance is due to a number of reasons, reflecting both local and
ational characteristics (cf. Fig. 7.6).

One of the most striking features of the age distribution is the
omparatively small number of people in the 20–39 age category. This
eflects the paucity of employment opportunities in a small town. Once
ducation has been completed and the children enter the labour market
here is no alternative for many of them other than migration to places
ffering a wider range of employment opportunity. Inevitably this
tructural characteristic has a feedback effect that has powerful reper-
ussions on the community. It is this age group that forms the main
hild-bearing group. Loss of these people means that the natural
eplacement element in a population is lost and a downward trend in
ommunity size is inevitable, unless in-migration fills the gap. More-
ver the loss of the most physically and mentally active element of the
opulation leads to a further erosion of community well-being.

Allied with the deficiency of numbers in the 20–39 age group is the
oncentration of people in the older age categories. No less than 28
er cent of the population of Aberaeron are over the age of sixty.
aturally this reflects one of the characteristic economic features of
he town, its function as a retirement centre. The dominance of females
n these age categories is primarily due to the favourable mortality
ates for females as opposed to males, but also reflects the attraction
f Aberaeron for elderly female in-migrants.

TABLE 8.2. *Marital status of the population*

	Single	Married	Widowed	Divorced	Separated
Male	161	228	16	—	3
Female	185	228	89	2	3

TABLE 8.3. *Age groups of single persons*

Age group	0–9	10–19	20–29	30–39	40–49	50–59	60–69	70–79	80–89	90+
Male	58	65	16	5	4	3	2	6	2	—
Female	58	60	14	3	4	5	22	15	3	1

Table 8.2 provides more detailed evidence of this characteristic. Although many of the females in the 'single' category are under twenty and have not yet reached the age of marriage, it is apparent that over one-third of the single females are over the age of twenty and 10 per cent are over sixty (Table 8.3). Added to this is the high proportion of females in the 'widow' category (almost 90 per cent of all widowed) again demonstrating a top-heavy demographic structure.

TABLE 8.4. *Number of persons per household*

Total number persons	1	2–4	Over 5
Dwellings	90	222	42

TABLE 8.5. *Marital status of persons living on their own*

	Single	Widowed	Separated
Male	5	7	—
Female	25	52	1

TABLE 8.6. *Age structure of persons living on their own*

Age group	0–9	10–19	20–29	30–39	40–49	50–59	60–69	70–79	80–89	90+
Numbers	—	—	1	1	6	16	21	34	9	2

Knowledge of the features described above makes Table 8.4 more intelligible. Over one-quarter of the households in Aberaeron contain only one person and, in view of the discussion so far, it will be expected that the majority are elderly females (Tables 8.5 and 8.6). Hence these demographic characteristics mean that the housing stock of the town is being considerably underused because of yet another top-heavy element in the community structure.

Migration characteristics

To the demographic patterns revealed above must be added the characteristics shown in Table 8.7.

Again a pattern of concentration is revealed, for over a third of the inhabitants were born in the town and another third were born within the county of Cardiganshire (cf. Chapter 7). Clearly there are intimate connections between the town and its surrounding area.

TABLE 8.7. *Place of birth of Aberaeron residents*

Place	Aberaeron	Rest of Cardiganshire	Rest of Wales	Outside Wales
Number	331	284	199	101
Percentage	36	31	22	11

In order to examine the spatial variations in the location of these birthplaces Fig. 8.1 was constructed. This shows the number of people born at various distances from Aberaeron. In general terms the familiar pattern of 'distance-decay' is revealed,[21] though the actual curve deviates from the ideal exponential condition. The first interruption

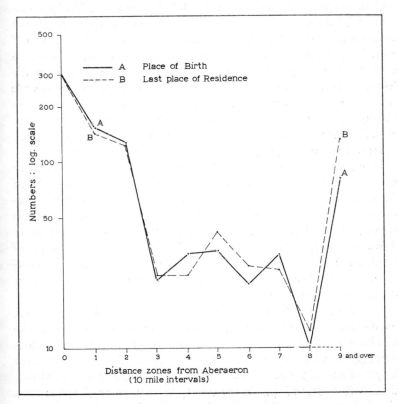

Fig. 8.1. *Birthplaces and last place of residence of Aberaeron population.*

from the straight line condition shown in Fig. 8.1 occurs in the zones twenty to forty miles from Aberaeron. Much of this zone is unoccupied or sparsely populated because it is composed of the mountain core of Wales (cf. Table 7.7). The second distortion, the plateau of values between forty and seventy miles from Aberaeron, seems to be due to the influence of the South Wales industrial area. This area represents a large population concentration and seems to act as one zone in the provision of people to Aberaeron. Certainly no distance-decay factor can be recognised here. Finally, some comment is needed about the upturn in values at the end of the graph. This is due to the summation of all birthplaces at distances greater than ninety miles from Aberaeron in this zone.

The analysis of birthplaces is, however, only a crude way of dealing with the migratory flows to the town. Ideally one would like information on all the individual movements made from place to place, but such detail is virtually impossible to obtain. In an attempt to add another dimension to the problem of in-migration, the Aberaeron survey noted the last place of residence of each inhabitant. From the 'place of birth' analysis it has been shown that almost two-thirds (64 per cent) of the inhabitants have moved into the town. Again Cardiganshire provided the largest single total with 47 per cent, though a quarter of the total came from the nearest urban places, namely Aberystwyth, Lampeter, Newquay and Llandyssul.

In distance-decay terms, Fig. 8.1 reveals that last place of residence shows an almost identical pattern to the one provided by birthplaces, for a *chi*-squared test failed to record any significant difference between the two distributions. It would seem, therefore, at least in this particular case, that our attempt to extend the analysis of migratory flows by incorporating the additional parameter of 'last place of residence' has failed to add any extra spatial variation to our knowledge of these flows. There seems to be a spatial uniformity in these distributions, irrespective of our parameter.

Figure 8.2 shows how long the present residents of Aberaeron have lived in the town. It proved useful to differentiate between those who had been born in the town and those who were born outside. Not surprisingly, in view of the comments made above about Table 8.1, the length of stay of the people born in the town parallels the age distribution, with a marked gap in the twenty to sixty years of age groups. Fig. 8.2 reveals a different distribution for those people who have migrated to the town. A regular exponential decay characterised the

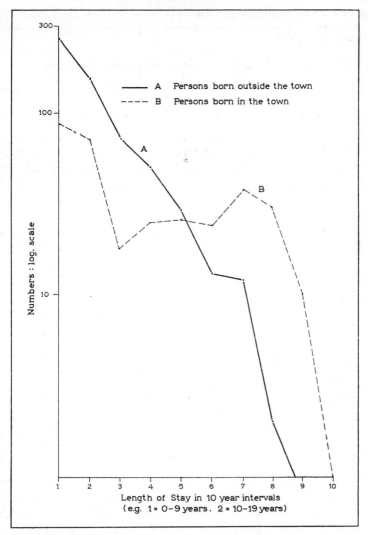

Fig. 8.2. Aberaeron residents: length of stay in town.

length of stay of these migrants. Comparatively few of them had been in the town any length of time (68 per cent have been there under twenty years). In view of the high proportion of elderly people who have retired to the town this, of course, may be expected though the uniformity of the distribution does seem noteworthy.

TABLE 8.8. *Employment status of residents*

Aberaeron residents

In full-time education	230	Not gainfully employed	180
Retired	205	Employed	300

Employment structure

Given the characteristics revealed in the first section, one would expect Aberaeron to possess a high dependency ratio in terms of its economic structure. This is confirmed in Table 8.8 for it shows that only one-third of the total population of the town are gainfully employed.

TABLE 8.9. *Occupational characteristics of Aberaeron workers*

Occupational groups	Aberaeron residents	Living and working in Aberaeron	Commuting out of Aberaeron	Commuting into Aberaeron	Numbers employed in Aberaeron
Professional	76	64	12	37	101
General office work	26	21	5	61	82
Retail and commercial	81	79	2	10	89
Technicians and craftsmen	34	29	5	25	54
Transport workers	13	10	3	13	23
Labourers	23	20	3	25	45
Personal service and others	28	27	1	—	27
Agriculture	16	11	5	—	11
Fishing	3	3	—	—	3
Total	300	264	36	171	435

Even the employed population is largely concentrated in one or two sectors (Table 8.9). Thus the professional and office sector accounts for over a third of the total work force, whilst the retail and commercial sector takes another quarter. At first this situation is rather surprising in view of the size of the town. Certainly the retail and commercial employment reflects Aberaeron's importance as a small market centre for the surrounding countryside (the reader is referred elsewhere for an analysis of this function[22]), but another factor accounts for the high professional and office sector, namely the decentralised nature of Cardiganshire's county council functions. As Aberaeron possesses the county planning offices as well as many other county administrative services this inevitably gives a considerable boost to the local economy.

Table 8.9 shows that the town is not the only place to benefit from this artificially high office sector. A considerable number of people (one-third of the total number of people employed in the town) commute daily to the town, though the length of these flows is not particularly great. Thus almost three-quarters of the total live within five miles of the town (cf. Chapter 7). Occupationally, it must be stressed that the large 'office' element has its effects on the surrounding area for a very high proportion of commuters are in this category. On the other hand, numbers of retail workers and professional people are significantly lower in this daily migration.

This daily flow of workers into the town is not balanced by any large compensating outflow. A very limited out-migration from Aberaeron occurs, though it might be noted that over a third of the group are in the professional occupational category and work in the nearest higher order towns, Aberystwyth and Lampeter.

In view of these top-heavy occupational characteristics, it is obvious that Aberaeron and district is not at present in a particularly healthy economic state. The recent White Paper on administrative boundary readjustment in Wales[23] proposed a merger between Cardiganshire, Pembrokeshire and Carmarthenshire, and there is a possibility that Aberaeron will lose some of its council offices. Hence an administrative reorganisation designed to improve the efficiency of services in rural Wales would have a drastic impact on the employment structure of one small town, an impact that would have considerable multiplier effects leading to the withdrawal of professional workers and probably to the closure or rundown of many of the existing commercial services that are dependent on the sector. The small villages round Aberaeron would also be hard hit in any administrative centralisation, for it is precisely in the 'general office' category that the majority of commuters into the town are found. It would seem, therefore, that the employment situation is delicately balanced, with the prospect of even greater rural depopulation in the area around the town if Aberaeron loses its county council offices. Certainly there is little evidence of any potential economic growth.

Social organisations

The concentration of social and cultural organisations in a town is one of the hallmarks of urbanism,[24] a feature that contrasts with the relative paucity of such organisations in the countryside. Aberaeron has thirty social organisations attended by adults and fourteen organised for children. All these societies operate on a 'face to face' basis and provide an important cohesive force in bringing about community integration. Given the size of Aberaeron, it is not surprising that few opportunities exist for duplication of organisations. Only one organisation can exist at once, for there is little scope for competition between identical social units.

Although the religious organisations gained the greatest support in the town, the quantitative pattern of this support presents a rather different picture from the usual impression of the nature of Welsh communities.[25] Thus, only 25 per cent of the population (189 adults and 38 children) considered themselves regular participants in the two chapels, and only 20 per cent (148 adults and 32 children) attended church regularly. Even allowing for exaggeration in frequency of attendance, the most probable source of survey error, these figures seem remarkably small, though they do reflect the pattern revealed in the villages analysed in Chapter 7 (Table 7.12). Given the fact that in a third (117) of all the households in Aberaeron religious participation proved to be the only form of organised social contact within the town, it is apparent that the closely integrated community ties based on religion have been broken down in this urban environment (cf. Chapter 7).

In view of the preliminary nature of this essay, no further attempt will be made to estimate the support for all the other social organisations in the town or to examine the overlapping roles of the participants, the traditional approach to the social analysis of small towns.[26] However, it was thought useful to examine briefly several

TABLE 8.10. *Characteristics of the community leaders*

Age categories (years)	Number	Length of stay (years)	Numbers
10–19	1	0–9	14
20–29	3	10–19	16
30–39	10	20–29	4
40–49	10	30–39	6
50–59	15	40–49	6
60–69	8	50–59	3
70–79	5	60–69	2
80–89	1	70–79	2
Total	53	Total	53

characteristics of the two ends of the membership spectrum, namely the leadership and non-participant elements.

Table 8.10 reveals that the age distribution of the leaders of the social organisations in Aberaeron is almost normally distributed, with the largest number of leaders in the 50–59 year-old age group. Given the large proportion of people in the higher age categories (Table 8.1), it might be expected that significantly more community leaders would come from these older categories. This suggestion was not borne out. A *chi*-squared test between the number of leaders in each age category and the number of the town population in these categories revealed that there was no significant difference between the two distributions. If anything, therefore, the older residents (in terms of age) were under-represented in the leadership distribution.

Table 8.10 also shows the length of residence within Aberaeron of each leader of a social organisation. Clearly the distribution is remarkably skew, for almost 60 per cent of the leaders have been living in the town under twenty years. In other words, the migrants to Aberaeron seem to take a more active part in community organisations. As a large white-collar element exists in this migrant group this finding is not, perhaps, particularly surprising. After all, it is precisely this group that has experience of organisations. Moreover as many of this group are retired they have the time to deal with such activities and might be expected to take an active part in organised activities.

At the other end of the social spectrum are the people who fail to belong to any social or cultural organisation. Members of seventy-nine households (22 per cent of the total) fall into this category. As over one-third of the group live on their own, and the majority are over seventy years of age, it is apparent that a quite considerable number of socially isolated people exists in the town. They are part of the urban community but fail to contribute to any social expression of its functioning. Clearly it is not only in the large cities that the problem of socially isolated and elderly people raises its head. Hence Aberaeron has a particular problem in this sphere as well, though the existence of more extensive non-formalised relations within a small town might mitigate the problem.

CONCLUSION

This introductory analysis of a small town community in Mid-Wales has probably raised more problems and questions than it has proved possible to solve at this stage. But it is to be hoped that the characteristics revealed for this one town contribute towards an awareness of its problems and will lead to the support of some future comparative survey of the structural characteristics of existing urban areas in Mid-Wales. (It might be noted at this stage that only in terms of central place structure does a considerable body of comparative information exist on the towns of Mid-Wales.)[27] Out of such a comparative study generalisations may be developed, so that future planning proposals can be formulated against a background of knowledge.

In many ways, of course, towns like Aberaeron are products of another society, a society that is fast disappearing. This does not imply that small towns do not play a useful role in the structure of modern society. They are still functionally active, albeit it at a lower level than in the past. Thus Aberaeron has been shown to be a focal point for its surrounding hinterland, a focality that exists not only in a commercial sense, whilst its role in the provision of accommodation for an increasing number of summer visitors provides an additional economic prop. Hence its removal or further rundown would hasten the decay of the surrounding countryside, for without Aberaeron's employment and retirement opportunities, rural depopulation in the area would be accelerated.

Given all these considerations, it might be concluded that any positive planning policy should try to get beyond mere 'head counting' as a measure of the problems of an area, and even perhaps to circumvent the current obsession with greater growth as a panacea for all small towns. Self-sustaining growth would probably not be achieved even if all the towns of rural Wales doubled or trebled in size overnight. Instead, a careful selection of potential growth points should be made while the limited role played by other units should be accepted. These centres could then concentrate on improving the functions that are already carried out with some success. In Aberaeron's case this might imply the catering for in-migration of retired people by the provision of modern and more easily managed houses which would, in time, release on to the market many of the present underoccupied premises.

REFERENCES

1. SCHNORE, L. F., 'The rural-urban variable—an urbanite's perspective', *Rural Sociology*, **31**, 1966, pp. 131–43; DUNCAN, O. D., 'Community size and the rural-urban continuum', in Hatt, P. K. and Reiss

A. J., eds., *Cities and Society*, Free Press of Glencoe, 1957, pp. 35–45.; HAUSER, P. M., 'Observations on the urban-folk and urban-rural dichotomies as forms of western ethno-centrism', in Hauser, P. M. and Schnore, L. F., eds., *The Study of Urbanisation*, Wiley, 1965, pp. 503–15.

2. *Report of the Committee on Land Utilization in Rural Areas*, Cmd 6378, HMSO, London, 1942, p. 70.

3. DARON, S., ed., *Country Towns in the Future England*, Faber, London, 1943, p. 134.

4. WHITE, L. E., *Small Towns and their Social and Community Problems*, London, National Council of Social Service, 1951, p. 5.

5. CROSS, D. A., 'Small town survey', *Town and Country Planning*, **34**, 1966, pp. 223–8; SEALE, A., 'The plan for the small town', *J. Tn Plann. Inst.*, **47**, 1961, p. 19; THORBURN, A. and SWINDALL, A. T., 'The plan for a small town—a practical approach', *J. Tn Plann. Inst.*, **47**, 1961, p. 101.

6. RILEY, D. W., 'Expansion of small towns, planned and unplanned', *J. Tn Plann. Inst.*, **44**, 1958, pp. 106–9.

7. HIRSCH, G. P., 'Country towns and their function in the rural pattern', *Town and Country Planning*, **19**, 1951, pp. 210–14.

8. THOMAS, M. P. and MCLOUGHLIN, J. B., 'The planning of small towns —a plea for method', *J. Tn Plann. Inst.*, **47**, 1961, pp. 294–6.

9. WIBBERLEY, G. P., 'The economic and social role of the country town', *Town and Country Planning*, **32**, 1964, p. 414.

10. CARTER, H., *The Towns of Wales*, University of Wales Press, 1965, p. 146.

11. BEACHAM, A., *Industries in Welsh Country Towns*, Oxford University Press, 1951, p. 1.

12. Mid-Wales Industrial Development Association First Annual Report, Aberystwyth, 1958.

13. OGDEN, W. M. and BEACHAM, A., *Depopulation in Mid-Wales*, HMSO for Welsh Office, 1964, p. 19.

14. Economic Associates, *A New Town for Mid-Wales*, HMSO, London, 1966, p. 1.

15. Mid-Wales Industrial Development Association, Ninth Annual Report, Aberystwyth, 1966, p. 22.

16. *Ibid*.

17. THOMAS and MCLOUGHLIN, *J. Tn Plann. Inst.*, 1961, p. 296.

14

18. 1966 Sample Census, *County Report; Cardiganshire*, HMSO, 1967.

19. HOWELL, J. M., 'The birth and growth of Aberaeron', *Trans. Cardiganshire Antiq. Soc.*, 4, 1926.

20. CARTER, *The Towns of Wales*, p. 295.

21. MORRILL, R. L. and PITTS, F. R., 'Marriage, migration and mean information field', *Ann. Ass. Am. Geogr.*, 57, 1967, pp. 401–22.

22. CARTER, H. and DAVIES, M. L., 'The hierarchy of urban fields in Cardiganshire', *Tijdschr. econ. soc. Geogr.*, 54, 1963, pp. 181–6.

23. *Local Government in Wales*, Cmnd. 3340, HMSO, Cardiff, 1967.

24. BURGESS, E. W. and BOGUE, D. J., *Contributions to Urban Sociology*, University of Chicago Press, 1964, pp. 201–324.

25. DAVIES, E. and REES, A. D., *Welsh Rural Communities*, University of Wales Press, 1960.

26. KUENSTLER, P., *Community Organisation in Great Britain*, Faber, 1961.

27. See Chapter 10, footnote 61, and ROWLEY, G., *Middle order towns in Wales*, unpublished Ph.D. dissertation. University of Wales, Aberystwyth, 1967.

CHAPTER 9

TOWARDS AN INTEGRATED STUDY OF CENTRAL PLACES:

A SOUTII WALES CASE STUDY

Wayne K. D. Davies

ystems analysis has proved to be a liberalising force in geographical tudies. Not only has it stressed the need to specify the state of any patial system by identifying (and measuring) the various elements of hat system, but, by emphasising the study of functional organisation nd dynamic processes, it has opened up comparatively new dimenions of geographical analyses.[1] Moreover, the attention paid to the ntegration of the various dimensions of study has refocused attention pon the geographic whole rather than presenting a series of often iscordant studies of individual parts.

Within the field of urban geography, workers who have investigated ne pattern of central places have come closest to the ideals of systems nalysts. But despite the success and the popularity of the central place eld[2] comparatively few investigators have dealt with more than one imension of analysis. Most workers have been content to establish a .nctional classification of places and/or their spheres of influence. 'ertainly, the diurnal functioning of the system, or the growth and evelopment of the system have received short shrift, though recent /orkers such as Morrill[3] have made some breakthrough in the latter eld. Moreover, many central place studies are locally orientated and nly achieve local relevance. They tend to concentrate on the characeristics of individual centres rather than treating the whole network.

In view of these problems this chapter has a twofold objective. In ne first place it focuses attention on the form of the whole system and utlines the general system properties, before dealing with the haracteristics of individual places. Hence all places are viewed as a et of interdependent parts rather than as isolated individuals. By earching for the empirical regularities of the whole network in this way ne study seeks to attain more than just local relevance. Secondly, the

network of central places is considered from several different perspec
tives. Only by specifying, and indeed measuring, all the relevant vari
ables can a coherent picture of the central places be attained. It is t
the specification of these variables that we must now turn.

PERSPECTIVES FOR THE STUDY OF CENTRAL PLACES

Each individual commercial function, by virtue of being a focal poin
for people who require this function, is in practice a 'central place'

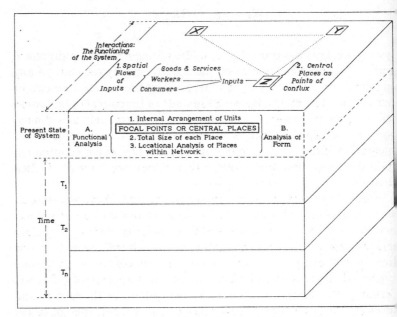

Fig. 9.1. An elementary paradigm of central place studies.

though the term is more usually applied to those clusters of com
mercial functions known as Central Business Districts (C.B.D.s
commercial cores, or shopping centres. Such clusters can be studie
either in terms of the functions carried on at that place or in terms c
the morphology of the buildings in which these functions are pe:
formed. Once this distinction, unfortunately a very real one in urba
geographical analysis, is established, it is possible to view these foc:
points in terms of the internal arrangement of individual units (wheth
form or function) or in totality, each centre being ranked according t

its functional or formal size, whilst a third approach would be to study the location of these centres or units within the general network of places. It is the study of the relative functional status of one central place in a network of places that has formed the core of the empirical study of central place. A paradigm of the major possible approaches to central place analysis is provided by Fig. 9.1, though it must be stressed that possible variations in the definition of 'function' and hence the associated functional parameters recently defined by the author[4] and extended by C. R. Lewis (Chapter 10), are not shown in detail on this diagram.

Such approaches, however refined in input and technique, only concentrate on the static structure of central places. Yet these relationships can be established for any period in the past. By evaluating the status of each central place at past periods the various states of the central place system can be determined, the whole analysis forming another dimension to the study of central places.

Incorporation of the temporal element certainly provides a dynamic perspective for central place analysis, but this dynamism is limited to the changing form and function of a centre. Indeed, all that has been outlined so far are the properties of the central places that result from the temporal process. Another focus of study is provided by the diurnal functioning of the system. Since every central place can only function if it is provided with an inflow of goods for sale, workers to operate the establishment and customers to buy the goods, analysis of any of these parameters provides another perspective on the nature of central places. Selected aspects of these parameters form a traditional part of central place study. Thus, investigation of the home location of customers provides one basis for the study of the spheres of influence of central places,[5] while the aggregative analysis of consumer behaviour within centres, as revealed by pedestrian flows, has also been the subject of many enquiries,[6] even though the results have not usually been interpreted with reference to central place theory.[7] Ultimately it is the decision about where the consumer spends his money (as well as the amount of money that is available) that forms the ultimate determinant of any central place system. Consequently it is appropriate that the spatial analysis of consumer spending patterns, not in one centre, but with reference to a set or system of places, forms the current frontier of central place studies.[8]

In this essay an attempt is made to analyse the structure of a central place system from several rather different perspectives. Completeness,

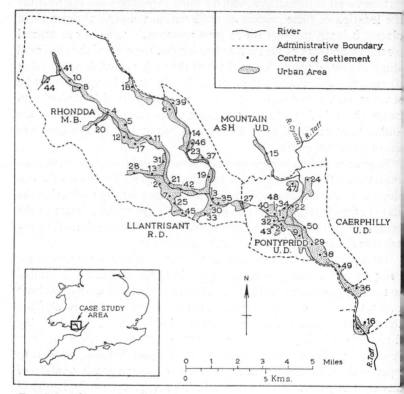

Fig. 9.2. The case study area.

Numbers in Figure relate to the following settlements.

1. Pontypridd	17. Gelli	34. Lanover and Berw
2. Tonypandy	18. Maerdy	Roads
3. Porth	19. Ynyshir	35. Brittania
4. Treorchy	20. Cwmparc	36. Nantgarw
5. Pentre	21. Trealaw	37. Wattstown
6. Ferndale	22. Trallwn	38. Hawthorn
7. Penygraig	23. Pontygwaith	39. Blaenllechau
8. Treherbert	24. Cilfynydd	40. Hopkinstown
9. Treforest	25. Williamstown	41. Blaenrhondda
10. Tynewydd	26. Graig	42. Dinas
11. Ystrad	27. Trehafod	43. Maesycoed
12. Ton	28. Clydach Vale	44. Blaencwm
Pentre	29. Rhydyfelin	45. Edmonstown
13. Blaenclydach	30. Cymmer	46. Stanleystown
14. Tylorstown	31. Llwynypia	47. Glyncoch
15. Ynysybwl	32. Pwllgwaun	48. Pantygraigwen
16. Taffs Well	33. Trebanog	49. Upper Boat
		50. Glyntaff

especially in the sense of a causal explanation of the network changes, cannot be the end product of study because of the insufficiency of historical data dealing with consumer behaviour. Instead, it is hoped that introduction of these several perspectives will lay bare the structural skeleton of central places and will thereby extend understanding of the central place system.[9]

THE CASE STUDY AREA

Central places, like any set of towns, cannot exist independently, but are bound together in an intimate network of relationships. Hence any study of one area must represent some abstraction from reality simply because of this process of abstraction. But if there is some rationale behind the choice of area, and the case study is referred back to the wider regional setting, the dangers of spatial abstraction, and with it, the closed system approach, may be mitigated.

In this essay a case study is made of the Rhondda–Pontypridd area of the South Wales Coalfield (Fig. 9.2). Industrialisation came late to the area. The small scale and scattered developments in the early nineteenth century—ironworks at Pontypridd, tinworks at Treforest (1837) and small colleries at Dinas (1809) and Gelliwion, near Trehafod—represented overspill from the growth points around Merthyr and were stimulated by the presence of the Glamorganshire Canal (1794).

By 1830 most of the area was still in rural isolation, though the junction of the Rhondda and Taff Valleys was occupied by a small collection of houses near which a small market was held. The size of this development may be gauged from Fig. 9.3 and was certainly insignificant when compared with the booming iron town of Merthyr and the developing port and commercial centre of Cardiff. Despite this regional insignificance it is important to note that Pontypridd (or rather the settlement to be named Pontypridd in 1858) had achieved a local importance and had outgrown its other competitor in the area, the small but historic market centre of Llantrisant.

During the 1830s, and for the next thirty years, the Aberdare Valley joined Merthyr as the boom area of South Wales, a development at first based on iron, but soon superseded by the extensive development of the coal measures.[10] This new economic upsurge was accompanied by the development of a new form of transport, the railway. The Taff Vale Railway was built to Merthyr and branch lines were extended to

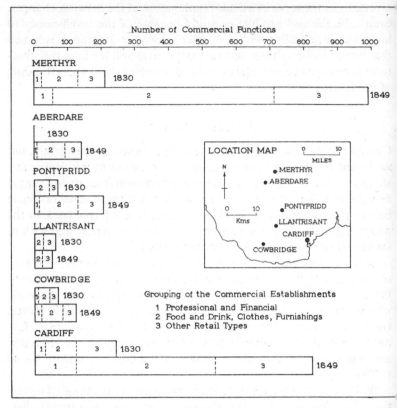

Fig. 9.3. Numbers of commercial functions at principal places in east Glamorgan, 1830 and 1849.

Aberdare and Trehafod (1841). Eight years later, the line was extended to Dinas Rhondda.

Figure 9.3 shows that the continued development of the area led to an increasing concentration of commercial functions in Cardiff and especially Merthyr, though it is significant that more professional and financial concerns were located in Cardiff by mid-century. Pontypridd clearly outpaced the older market centres, and Llantrisant actually declined in the period, reflecting the loss of part of its hinterland to Pontypridd. Moreover, despite the development of the Cynon Valley, Pontypridd remained considerably larger than the new focal point of Aberdare.

This general outline takes us to the verge of one of the world's most spectacular mining booms, a history that has been ably documented by E. D. Lewis.[11] It was initiated by the proving of steam coal measures at Treherbert in 1855 and the subsequent extension of the Taff Vale Railway to this place. In 1862 Ferndale, and hence the Rhondda Fach Valley, was similarly linked to the main line.

At first development was hesitant. The parish of Ystradyfodwg, which covered most of the Rhondda Valleys, attained a population of only 3,025 in 1861, though even this was a significant advance on the rather stagnant pattern revealed by totals of 542 in 1801 and 951 in 1851. By 1871 the population of the parish reached 16,914 and from this date onwards expansion was phenomenal, the Rhondda Urban District attaining a population of 169,000 in 1924.

This development (the inset to Fig. 9.4 shows the population change in the whole area) was focused exclusively upon the exploitation of the coal measures (67 per cent of the males over twelve years of age in 1924 were engaged in mining). Pontypridd shared in this expansion, though south of Treforest only scattered developments can be traced, leaving considerable areas in farm land, a factor of some importance for industrial and residential development in subsequent years.

After the peak population year of 1924 an almost continuous depression set in. In 1939 coal production was only one-third of the 1913 total and in 1932 unemployment of the male population reached 52·9 per cent. Building came to a standstill, and the inevitable result of the unemployment was a considerable population loss. Between 1921 and 1951, 36·1 per cent of the population (over 60,000 people) left the Rhondda Urban District. Pontypridd suffered similarly, though not quite so badly, because it was less dependent upon the mining industry.

Immediately before the war steps were taken to alleviate this unemployment. In 1936 an industrial estate was built south of Treforest, whilst other new factories were scattered throughout the area. After the war this trend continued, though nationalisation of the mines gave a new boost to the coal industry. Rationalisation of the mining industry consequent upon changing energy requirements has led to the closure of many pits. Now only four mines are still working in the study area, only two in the two Rhonddas above Porth, a far cry from the sixty working in 1913.[12] Unemployment is still above the national average and causes increasing concern given the deficiency in the employment spectrum and the limited space available for rebuilding in a narrow valley environment. Hence recent developments have taken place in the lower Taff Valley, and future developments are likely to be sited in the Llantrisant area. Recent proposals for the re-organisation of local government boundaries make a great issue of this fact.[13] Our concern, however, is not so much with the planning impli-cations of change, rather with the state of the central place system in the 1960s, and the general process of this development in an area that has developed under the influence of one major economic stimulus.

Precise and detailed indices upon which to base the study of the changing central place system are difficult to establish until the last quarter of the nineteenth century. Census figures are based on parishes that bear little relevance to the newly emerging settlement pattern and meaningful totals for individual settlements are difficult to establish. Moreover, the early commercial directories tend to be rather vague in their locational descriptions. However, the publication of a fairly comprehensive commercial directory[14] in 1868 and the first Ordnance Survey Maps at a scale of 1:2500 in 1875 make it possible to obtain a reliable picture of the situation from these dates.

THE GROWTH OF THE CENTRAL PLACE SYSTEM

Population change

The particularistic account of the economic development of the study region developed in the previous section stresses, albeit briefly, the spatial variation in the distribution of economic activities and popula-tion but does not permit any coherent and aggregative description of the internal pattern of growth and decline. Fig. 9.4 attempts to deal with this problem by presenting the population change of the area in terms of distance from the major focal point, Pontypridd. Moreover, instead of dealing with absolute figures, the population totals of each settlement are expressed in terms of their percentage contribution to the whole area. In this way the readjustments *within* the area will not be swamped by the great outflow in the 1930s and will be placed in the perspective of a local study.

As the major stimulus to the development of the area proved to be the number of jobs provided in each mine, it is the locational decisions made in siting the mines that provides the basic control over settlement. The effect of chance discoveries (certainly many mines were specula-tive ventures[15]), local geological conditions and land ownership com-plications will all have some locational influence, whilst the scarcity of building land in a difficult incised valley environment provides another control to the expansion of any one area.

The detailed analysis of these locational decisions is outside the scope of this inquiry, but the effect of these decisions, the changing population distribution, forms a crucial backcloth to any central place

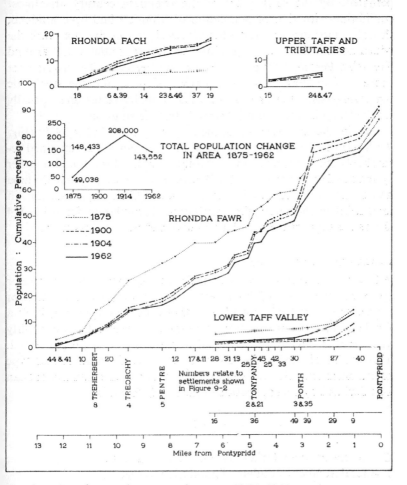

Fig. 9.4. Population changes in the area, 1875–1962.

investigation. At first (1875) the population curve demonstrates the influence of the initial discovery of steam coal in the Upper Rhondda Fawr. This initial pattern was gradually erased once the almost insatiable demand for coal led to an increasing number of mines, jobs and associated houses. Given the urbanisation of the area, the process of development in this period of growth corrected these initial deviations so that the effect of the initial mining discoveries was not perpetuated. By the early years of the twentieth century an almost equilibrium situation of population distribution had been attained, though minor distortions on the curves shown in Fig. 9.4 mark the widening of the valley (leading to larger settlements) around Treorchy, Pentre, Tonypandy, Porth and Ferndale. Thus, given the process of infilling, a limited number of sites, and the stochastic temporal basis to this process, the most probable state was eventually reached, in this case an almost straight line distribution.

Despite the great reversal of the migratory flows in the 1930s (Fig. 9.4 inset) the general form of the population curve has remained remarkably constant, reflecting a stability that has been found in other systems and at other times.[16] By 1962 the economic changes in the area and the new job opportunities in the Vale of Glamorgan and Cardiff area had their effect upon the distribution of population, for as Fig. 9.4 shows the slope of the population curve had become less steep.

General functional change

A functional measurement of central places applicable to any time or space has been derived by reverting to the original conception of centrality.[17] The basic postulate is that each establishment, itself a focal point for the distribution of goods and services, has a centrality value that is directly proportional to the number of people served. This will be reflected in the relative abundance of outlets of each type of establishment. Hence a centrality value for each establishment can be calculated by the application of the simple formula:

$$C = \frac{t}{T} \cdot 100$$

C = centrality value for any type of establishment t.
T = total number of outlets of good t in the region.
t = one establishment of type t.

Once the numbers and type of establishments present in each settlement are known, application of this formula gives the centrality rating of each establishment. By summing all these values an index (called a functional index) of the importance of a settlement is obtained. This index represents a crude measure of the importance of places, because it does not incorporate into the analysis any data on the size of individual establishments. Such drawbacks seem unavoidable in view of the limited nature of the historical record. Moreover, it must be stressed that the temporal analysis is concerned with the functional size of settlements not commercial centres, a limitation made necessary by the imprecision of the locational descriptions given by some directories.

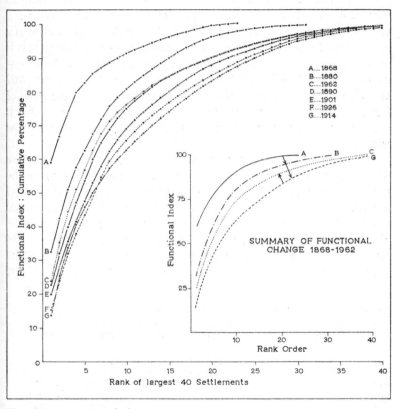

Fig. 9.5. Functional change in the area, 1868–1962.

Functional indices for each settlement were calculated at approximately ten year intervals until the Depression: 1868, 1881, 1890, 1900, 1914 and 1926. In the absence of the more recent directories the only point of comparison in the modern period is 1962, a year in which a detailed field survey of the area provided the basic information. Once the functional index for each settlement was obtained, these were converted to percentages, ranked and plotted as lorenz curves (Fig. 9.5).

Scrutiny of Fig. 9.5 and the data on which it is based reveals the complete dominance of Pontypridd in the area in 1868. The only other settlements of any functional size were Treherbert, Ystrad and Treforest, reflecting the only other population concentrations at this date. With the urbanisation of the whole area this primate pattern became less marked, the influx of new central place functions tended to follow the spread of settlement with the inevitable consequence of a progressive deconcentration in the functional patterns, though this is only a relative change. This is shown by the flattening of the lorenz curves in Fig. 9.5. After 1926 a reversal of this trend occurs, the 1962 curve becomes steeper. In other words, an increasing centralisation of function occurs in the larger centres. Graphically it is apparent that it is the middle-ranking settlements that showed the greatest losses at this time.

A matrix of correlation coefficients showing the change in the rank of the settlements for each pair of years was prepared to measure the degree of change (Table 9.1). McQuitty's[18] linkage analysis was applied to this matrix. This showed that from 1880–1914 the functional distribution in every decade was closer to the previous decade. The reciprocal relationship existing between the years 1926 and 1914 meant that these periods were closer to each other than to any other period in terms of their settlement rank, whilst the reversal of the

TABLE 9.1. *Matrix of correlation coefficients between the years*

	1962	1926	1914	1901	1891	1881
1962	1·000	+0·9164	+0·9362	+0·8724	+0·7992	+0·4843
1926		1·000	+0·9616	+0·9099	+0·7533	+0·5424
1914			1·000	+0·9213	+0·8587	+0·4966
1901				1·000	+0·9107	+0·5914
1891					1·000	+0·4445
1881						1·000

Linkage relations: First orders connections.

$$1926 \rightleftarrows 1914 \leftarrow 1901 \leftarrow 1891 \overset{*}{\leftarrow} 1881$$
$$\uparrow$$
$$1962$$

* Not significant at 0·1 per cent level.
(The coefficients are Spearman's rank order correlation coefficients based upon the changes in the rank of individual settlements between the years indicated.)

deconcentration trend since the last war (as shown by the 1962 curve) is represented by the closer fit of the 1962 distribution to the 1914 curve.

As all the correlation coefficients proved to be significant at the 0·1 per cent level, except those between 1880 and all other years, it is apparent that the period to 1890 was the one in which the maximum change in central place character occurred. From 1890 the changes in the distribution, though not unimportant, are comparatively minor and by 1914–26 a condition of stability was established.

Although the numbers of commercial establishments increased throughout the period and most settlements showed absolute increases in numbers of functions, the relative effect of their growth was to diminish the influence of the largest centre, Pontypridd. Given the relative functional distribution in 1868, the general trend to 1926 was one of increasing entropy throughout this period of growth, the initial deviations represented by excessively high order places were reduced. After 1926 the centralisation processes operating within the system increased the relative information content (functional size) of the high order places, so that deviation amplification (morphogenesis) becomes the new characteristic.[19]

Detailed changes in settlement status from 1914

Now that the general form of the functional pattern has been established, it is important to look at the changes that have occurred in the individual status of settlements, though for reasons of space only the largest places are looked at in detail.

The fact that the period to 1890 provided the time of greatest change is demonstrated again in Fig. 9.6. This shows the changes in status of the largest focal points in the area and it is apparent that the basis of the present day organisational structure had developed by 1890. Six of the centres shown in Fig. 9.6, Tonypandy, Porth, Pentre, Ferndale, Treherbert and Treorchy, had crystallized out of the general functional array, all of them it must be noted, centres of the increased population concentrations found where the valley widens. By 1914 the first three of this group possessed a considerably higher functional status than the others, though by 1926 Pentre was lost from this group. In 1926, therefore, Porth and Tonypandy formed a set of major focal places, with four other settlements and Penygraig forming a lower order cluster. It is significant that in the Upper Rhondda three of these settlements, Treherbert, Treorchy and Pentre, had achieved some sort of equivalence in status, though each had had its period of dominance.

The situation here is explained by the fact that the growth of these largest places after 1890 was controlled not by their immediate access to their own population concentration but by their ability to dominate other settlements and hence other central places. In other words they were able to gain access to the higher order purchases of consumers. In the Upper Rhondda Fawr the spatial contiguity of these three

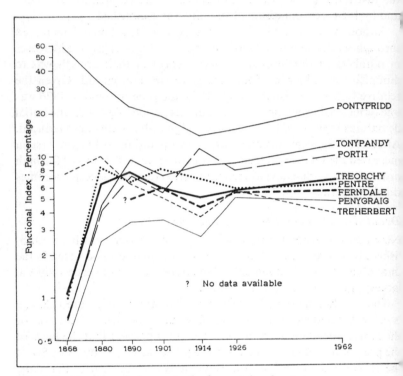

Fig. 9.6. Functional change in the largest focal points.

settlements heralded a period of competition between them. All possessed some important stimulus to growth unique to itself. Treherbert was the first centre to be developed, Treorchy was midway between the other two and able to capture trade from the others—or to lose it— whilst Pentre achieved greater importance by being the administrative centre of Rhondda Urban District because the old hamlet centre of Ystradyfodwg was located near here. It has been shown that from 1926 a major centralisation process occurred in the study area, and i has been Treorchy that has crystallised out as the most important centre of the area, primarily due to its centrality in relation to Cwmparc and Treherbert. It is to the detailed description of this centralisation trend and to the effects it has had on all the settlements that we must now turn.

Figure 9.7 shows the general change in the status of the settlements over the last fifty years. Part of the data on which this figure is based is

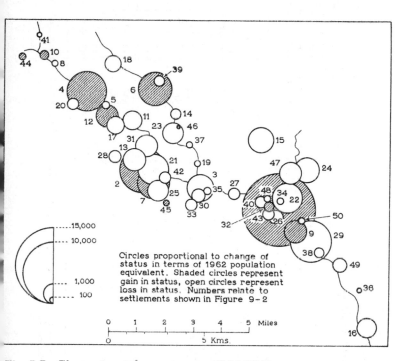

Circles proportional to change of status in terms of 1962 population equivalent. Shaded circles represent gain in status, open circles represent loss in status. Numbers relate to settlements shown in Figure 9-2

Fig. 9.7. Change in settlement status, 1914–1962.

shown in Table 9.2. By converting the 1914 and 1962 data for functions and population into coefficients, a direct comparison between these two elements at each date, and between the two years, is possible. This change can also be partitioned into that due to functional change and that due to population change. One example may serve to clarify this technique. Over the period 1914–62 Pontypridd increased its functional status by a population equivalent of 13,991. Relatively, therefore, the centre has gained quite considerably, though such a change could be

15

TABLE 9.2. Change in status of settlements 1914-62

| Largest 15 places in 1962 | 1962 Functional index (1) | 1962 Functional coefficient (2) | Difference between population and functional coefficients | | Difference between columns 3 and 4 (5) | Population equivalent (1962 figures) (6) | Composition of the population equivalent of the 1914-62 change. Column 7—relative population change. Column 8—functional change (population in brackets) | |
			1962 (3)	1914 (4)			(7)	(8)
1. Pontypridd	1152·78	23·53	+23·30	+13·56	+9·75	+13,991	−0·12 (172)	+9·62 (13,810)
2. Tonypandy	565·82	11·55	+9·76	+5·92	+3·84	+5,503	−0·76 (1091)	+3·08 (4,421)
3. Porth	445·32	9·09	+4·20	+5·52	−1·32	−1,891	−0·88 (1256)	−2·19 (3,144)
4. Treorchy	326·20	6·66	+1·90	−0·93	+2·83	+4,060	−1·16 (1667)	+1·67 (2,397)
5. Pentre	295·76	6·04	+3·63	+3·74	−0·10	−144	−0·79 (1133)	−0·89 (1,278)
6. Ferndale	272·47	5·56	+1·85	−0·18	+2·03	+2,916	−0·77 (1107)	+1·26 (1,809)
7. Penygraig	230·34	4·70	+0·75	−1·09	+1·84	+2,647	+0·20 (283)	+2·04 (2,928)
8. Treherbert	190·76	3·89	+0·64	+0·72	−0·08	−118	+0·27 (382)	+0·19 (273)
9. Treforest	142·25	2·90	−0·81	−1·85	+1·04	+1,496	−0·75 (1075)	+0·29 (416)
10. Tynewydd	100·36	2·05	−0·08	−0·22	−0·14	+207	−0·02 (23)	+0·13 (187)
11. Ystrad	95·51	1·95	−1·39	−0·81	−0·58	−838	+0·19 (277)	−0·39 (560)
12. Ton Pentre	93·60	1·91	−0·43	−1·30	+0·87	+1,242	−0·47 (668)	+0·40 (574)
13. Blaenclydach	92·43	1·89	−1·82	−1·02	−0·80	−1,141	+0·20 (290)	−0·59 (847)
14. Tylorstown	67·29	1·37	−1·25	−1·03	−0·22	−316	−0·33 (469)	−0·55 (790)
15. Ynysybwl	67·02	1·37	−1·19	−0·03	−1·16	−1,671	+0·48 (692)	−0·68 (976)

(N.B. Columns 7 and 8 show the composition of the change between 1914 and 1962 in terms of the population change (col. 7) and the functional change (col. 8) during the period.)

the result of either a decrease in the population of the centre with the same functional composition, or an increase in the function of the centre with the same population, or indeed any combination of these factors. In fact, columns 7 and 8 of Table 9.2 reveal that the majority of the change is due to a relative increase in the functional status of the town, though a slight decrease in population in the central area heightens this change in functional status.

In view of the comments made above, it is not surprising that it is the largest centres that have gained in importance. In this case 'large' relates to those settlements possessing a functional excess in both years; incidentally, this in itself is an indication of the focal importance of these settlements. Pontypridd in particular has gained considerably in importance, an increase that outweighs all the others combined. This type of change, which is due to a relative increase in functional equipment, also occurred in Treorchy, Tonypandy, Penygraig and Ferndale. Porth, Pentre and Treherbert on the other hand although still 'central' by the definition of column 3 in Table 9.2 show various rates of decline, and it seems possible to interpret these differences in the light of their relative location. Thus whilst Treorchy has grown in status in the Upper Rhondda, Pentre and Treherbert, both immediately adjacent settlements have declined. The decline is mitigated to some extent by the fact that the relative loss of population is above average. Consequently, even if the same functional equipment were present, an apparent gain in the discrepancy between population and function would be registered. It seems, however, that Pentre and Treherbert have declined at the expense of Treorchy, probably because the forces of centralisation combined with the population decline has meant that too many large centres existed in the area. Porth also has shown a relative decline, but the effect is certainly intensified by the exceptional gain in status this settlement made in the decade before 1914. Despite such a mitigating circumstance, the proximity of Porth to Pontypridd must be noted. It certainly looks as if it is declining in the face of the dominance of Pontypridd, a decline largely due to the failure of the settlement to accrete the functional equipment that would attract the population of the lower Rhondda Fach settlements.

Most of the other settlements have decreased in importance, though there are exceptions. It is convenient to look at these results by reference to the basic principles that seem to account for them. Where any one of the central settlements (those with a functional excess in 1962) has declined over the period, the settlements around seem either to increase slightly in status, or to decline less than average. There is, in effect, a counterbalancing effect to the decline of a large centre. The smaller foci within the hinterland of high order places increase in compensation, because the declining centres become less attractive Tynewydd, Ynyshir and Ton Pentre provide examples of this trend in relation to Treherbert, Porth and Pentre respectively. Other settlements that are almost purely residential, in the sense that they lacked any service centre of their own, and have been completely dependent upon another large centre, have also declined considerably—Llwynypia Blaenclydach and Trealaw to Tonypandy, and Trallwn to Pontypridd So the rise in status of the larger centres has had a detrimental effect upon the dependent places that are immediately adjacent. But one strange effect remains to be accounted for, the relative growth of Penygraig and Treforest in the shadow of Tonypandy and Pontypridd respectively. In the case of Treforest the explanation lies in the con siderable relative population decline in the settlement, but probably it proximity to the highly functionally deficient area of Rhydyfelin (with its numerous postwar houses) constitutes a significant explanation In the case of Penygraig, the fact that this settlement has attracted th lower order function formerly exercised by Williamstown is important though in return it has not acquired the higher order functions charac teristic of Tonypandy. Reference to the composition of the functiona index solves the problem. Thus Penygraig dominates Williamstow but it is in turn dominated by Tonypandy.

The other settlements that have declined in status can be classed int two groups. On the one hand there are the places that did not decline great deal before 1914 because of their initial resistance to incorpora tion within the orbit of the larger centres. The resistance was the resu either of their remote location (Taffs Well) or their size (Cilfynydd Ynysybwl has been affected by both factors. As all these settlemen are relatively large, demand could be concentrated more easily. Henc retailers were attracted to these places; the influence of the large focal places was not so great. Between 1914 and 1962 this resistanc gradually broke down, leading inevitably to the declining function status of these places.

The second group of settlements showing large discrepancies i their population/function ratios over the period are the areas that hav acquired new housing estates. Though population totals showe spectacular increases their acquisition of functions has been extreme slow. Rhydyfelin, Glyncoch, and Hawthorn are the most important settlements in this group.

Finally some comment needs to be made about the rest of the settlements. Although the majority have experienced a decline, a few have slightly increased their relative importance, though the change in all cases has been very small. Yet two settlements in the Rhondda Fach valley do not fall very neatly into the classes outlined. The middle portion of the valley (Pontygwaith and Wattstown) has always been characterised by a functional discrepancy. Whilst the area has never been fully incorporated into the absolute hinterland of Porth, it has also failed to develop an important service centre of its own. A functional discrepancy is, therefore, perpetuated, simply because of this maladjustment.

Throughout this discussion mention has been made of the relative nature of the changes investigated. From 1914 to 1962 the actual number of commercial establishments declined by 40·4 per cent. The absolute decline was greatest in the middle ranks of the settlements. The eight major focal centres, although gaining relatively in function, certainly lost considerable numbers, though the percentage decline in these places was only 34 per cent, compared to 47 per cent in all the other settlements. Basically these changes may be attributed to the loss of the small back-street type of shop and the effect of the Depression.[20] These shops (mainly general dealers) were originally scattered throughout the area, but with the interwar loss of population and changes in retail organisation fewer were needed. Furthermore, they were of relatively greater importance to the settlements with lower functional status. So the focal points in the eight highest order settlements, by keeping their main cores almost intact, only lost the side street shops. It is this that accounted for their lower absolute decline in numbers.

So far the analysis has concentrated on the functional status of settlements, though reference has occasionally been made to the service centres within the settlements. A detailed study of these centres was not possible until 1962, when input data could be obtained from a field survey rather than from a limited historical record. Since the various sizes of premises and the market in Pontypridd (an extremely important addition to its status) were incorporated into the analysis, a measurement that is fairly close to reality was achieved.

Objective grouping tests applied to the 1962 data revealed a distinct hierarchy of central places. The distribution of these various grades (which provided a more rational situation than those proposed by previously existing studies) is shown in Fig. 9.8. These results have been the subject of detailed discussion elsewhere and it is superfluous to repeat them here.[21] However, the fact that these findings, a series of hierarchical steps, seem to conflict with the continuum of values presented in this analysis does need explanation. This may be compared with the parallel confusion created by the analogous situation of the elemental versus the aggregative level of enquiry.[22]

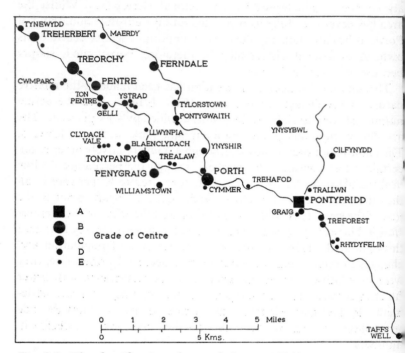

Fig. 9.8. The classification of central places in 1962.

Any analysis of the status of settlements rather than individual central places is bound to blur the stepped nature of the distribution. Moreover, the discovery of a hierarchy does not, in practice, imply that each level of centre is exactly equivalent in size, only that the members of this group are closer to each other than to other centres. The minor fluctuations within each step level, itself a feature of the inevitable differences in the nature of individual hinterlands, together with the temporary imbalances provided by the processes of growth

and decline working within the functional system, are enough to distort
the nature of the functional hierarchy. Hence a continuum of values
rather than an obvious hierarchy should be expected once the places
are looked at in rank size terms rather than by reference to their
locations.

THE MORPHOLOGY OF THE CENTRAL PLACES

The conceptual distinction between the form and function of central
places that was indicated in Fig. 9.1 is one that has a long history in
urban geography. Judging from the relative volume of literature on
both these aspects[23] it would seem that central places only possess a
functional existence, though it is quite apparent that they possess a
distinctive, if complicated, formal expression as well. Some writers
have taken a pessimistic view of the possibility of analysis of the zone,
believing that one must accept this area as a morphological zone with
a functional basis, 'leaving to verbal description and pictorial illustration the rest of the characterisation of a highly individual and complex
association of forms'.[24] However, just as the heterogeneity of functions present within central areas can be reduced to one expression by
measuring its centrality, it proved possible to derive a measurement of
the form of buildings within the zone.

It has already been shown that the case study area is basically the
product of a forty-year mining boom. One result of this rapidity of
growth and similarity of economy was the relative uniformity that
emerged in the morphological pattern of the area. Ninety per cent of
the residential area is composed of the basic two-storey terrace house
built of Pennant Grit, though minor variations in style can be traced.[25]
Out of these serried rows of residential areas the central places gradually crystallised. By occupying existing premises, conversion, or
by rebuilding, commercial establishments gradually made themselves
dominant in the central places. Given the individual choices involved
in this adaptation over a ninety-year period it is not surprising that a
confusion of building styles characterise each central place.

The basic terrace house was accepted as a morphological norm in
the area and partitioned into its four basic components: size, building
style, building material, and function. To each of these components a
scaling measurement was applied. This is shown in Table 9.3. Hence
an ordinary two-storey Pennant Grit terrace house will score 0000.
Once the various scores of these four components are added together a

measure of the degree of deviation from the morphological norm is provided. By mapping these building scores the degree of morphological intensity and variation within central areas can be clearly seen.

TABLE 9.3. *Composition of the morphological points index*

Major components	Detailed elaboration	No. of points allocated
Number of storeys	1–2 Storeys	0
	3 Storeys	1
	4 Storeys	2
Building materials	Pennant Grit	0
	Brick or other material	1
Building style	Terrace style	0
	Other styles	1
Sign of commercial activity	No morphological alteration	0
	Ordinary shop front (large wooden frame)	1
	Modern shop front (modern conversion in wood or stone)	2

Fig. 9.9 shows an example of this technique. As the total characteristics of the centres, rather than their internal variations, represent the primary concern of this essay, the reader is referred elsewhere to a more detailed analysis of these variations and their theoretical background.[20]

The addition of the morphological scores attained by each building in the central places gives a measure of the morphological intensity of each place. Their correlation with the functional index attained by the same set of centres is shown by Fig. 9.10. A significant correlation coefficient was established between the two parameters, though one centre, Pentre, showed a considerable deviation from the general trend. Recourse to the previous sections of this essay explains why the morphological rating is so much higher than expected. Pentre achieved a high functional status in the early years of this century and possesses a number of buildings of three or more storeys in its central area. These are built out of materials other than Pennant Grit and in styles rather different from the traditional terrace type. Since the Depression the settlement has declined in the face of competition from Treorchy and new buildings are rare. The old buildings remain in Pentre, a constant reminder of its past status; functionally the settlement exists at a considerably lower level.

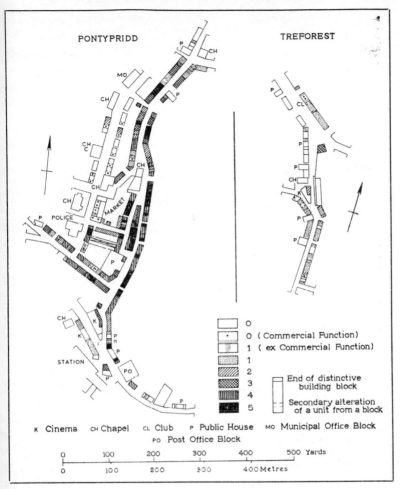

Fig. 9.9. The morphology of two central places: Pontypridd and Treforest. The numbers 0–5 relate to the number of morphological points scored by each building.

This section has demonstrated that the form of the central places reflect their function, though the timelag in the interrelations between the two must be stressed.[27] Form changes less rapidly than function so that adequate appreciation of the pattern is only obtained by a correlation of the two, stressing both the actual and changing functional form.

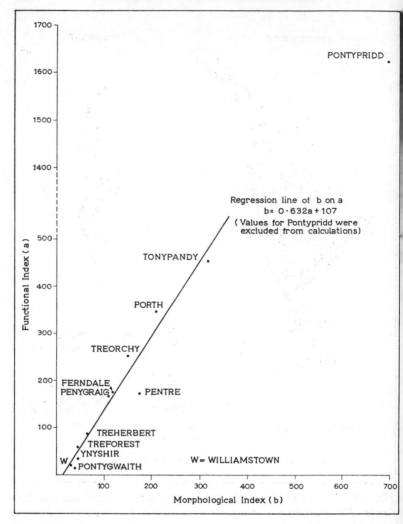

Fig. 9.10. The correlation between the morphological and functional indices.

THE CENTRAL PLACES AS ZONES OF CONFLUX

So far this essay has concentrated on the functional and morphological measurement of the central places. This should not obscure the fact that it is the day to day functioning of the centres that gives them vitality. It is this functional organisation and interaction of a set of central places that forms the third perspective of this study.

Most studies of the interaction and interchange between a set of central places concentrate on the definition of generalised trade areas or on the delimitation of trade area boundaries for various types of goods and services. Such concern with the whole area is outside the scope of this study, concerned as we are with the central places themselves. Given this restriction, analysis of any of the inputs shown in

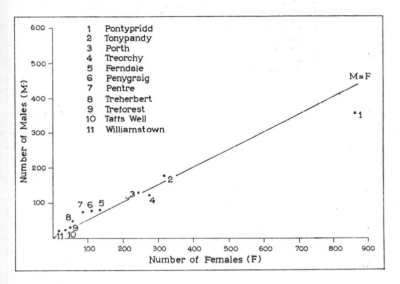

Fig. 9.11. Central place workers: sex ratio.

Fig. 9.1 (namely goods and services, shoppers or workers) would fall within our frame of reference as all of them contribute to the central place as a zone or area of conflux. As very few studies of journey to work patterns in commercial places at more than the descriptive level of daily ebbs and flows have been made, this aspect of the conflux was chosen for analysis. Again this theme has been the subject of a longer report.[28]

A complete survey of the largest places in the study area revealed that 1902 workers were employed in the retail establishments of the A, B and C grades of centre. The sex ratio of the workers in each place proved to be remarkably uniform as Fig. 9.11 demonstrates. Only Pontypridd has a higher female ratio, a consequence of the large size of premises (and hence work-force). However it is notable that Pentre, and to a lesser extent Treherbert, have lower female ratios, a reflection of the decline in status of these settlements over the last thirty years.[29]

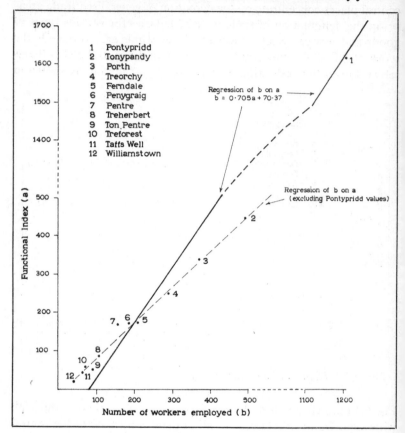

Fig. 9.12. The correlation between functional index and numbers of workers employed.

Figure 9.12 shows the correlation between the functional size of places and the total number of workers in each place. A significant correlation existed, though Pentre again proved to be rather different from the other places by possessing fewer workers than one might expect. This also can be attributed to its decline in status.

Analysis of the home addresses of the workers revealed a fairly uniform decline with distance from the workplace (Fig. 9.13). Given

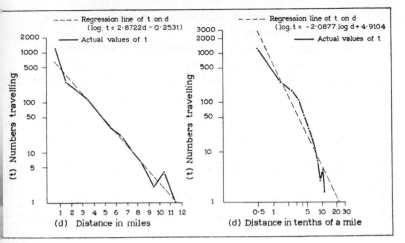

Fig. 9.13. The journey to work: distance decay.

the relatively low wages of workers in the retail trade it is not surprising that the majority of workers live in close proximity to the places in which they worked, a finding that corroborates the conclusions of other people who have studied low wage industries,[30] though a considerable degree of interchange still occurred at greater distances. Also, relatively longer journeys to work were undertaken by the male sector of the labour force, a feature that parallels the findings of investigators who have studied the patterns associated with secondary industry.[31] In this case the flows reflect the fact that most of the males occupy the higher paid and more senior positions in the retail trade.

From the empirical evidence obtained from this survey a descriptive model of the journey to work patterns was constructed. Although this model uses a gravity model framework,[32] it is comparatively sophisticated in that it incorporates the attraction provided by all the central places in the area. The mathematical formulation of the model is given by the formula:

$$T_{ij} = N_i - \frac{\dfrac{E_j}{d_{ij}^{x}}}{\displaystyle\sum_{j=1}^{9} \dfrac{E_j}{d_{ij}^{x}}}$$

where T_{ij} = number of workers travelling from settlement i to central place j.

N_i = total number of retail workers living in settlement i.
E_j = size of central place j.
d_{ij} = distance between settlement i and central place j.
x = an exponent applied to the distance variable.
(It must be noted that this can only be a partial model as only the nine highest order central places are used in this study.)

The model shown above states that the number of workers living in settlement i and working in centre j is:

(*a*) in direct proportion to the number of workers living in settlement i (N_i).
(*b*) in direct proportion to the size of the central place j (E_j).
(*c*) in inverse proportion to the distance between the settlement i and central place j (d_{ij}).
(*d*) in inverse population to the competing centres, i.e.

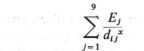

$$\sum_{j=1}^{9} \frac{E_j}{d_{ij}{}^{x}}$$

Once this model is applied to each settlement in turn, an estimate of the number of workers travelling to each central place is obtained. Summation of these results on the basis of the central places gives an estimate of the size and distance of the journeys to work to these places.

This model was run several times using different input data and the results of the best fit attained to date are shown in Fig. 9.14. Operationally these results were obtained from the following input data:

(*a*) N_i = number of retail workers in each settlement.
(*b*) E_j = size of the central places in terms of the numbers of retail workers.
(*c*) D_{ij} = distance in miles between each settlement and each central place.
(*d*) x = exponent applied to the distance variable.

All the data were derived empirically and the value of the distance exponent x was calculated from the aggregative relationships between numbers travelling and distance travelled (Fig. 9.13).[33] Certainly a fair degree of correspondence between the actual numbers working in any place and the values expected from the model was obtained as Fig. 9.14 shows. However, the results of the journey-to-work patterns from individual settlements proved less convincing, for the model underestimated the numbers travelling short distances, a feature that was expected in view of the distribution shown in Fig. 9.13. Thus it would seem that a linear regression formula used as the distance exponent is insufficient to account for the variation in flows from individual settlements.

Descriptively, therefore, this journey-to-work model would seem to be rather useful, though if it is to possess more than short term

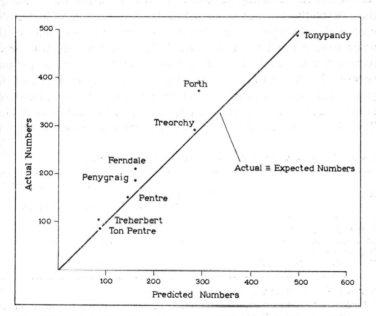

Fig. 9.14. Actual and predicted numbers of workers.

predictive value the input data should be capable of being derived from information obtained from outside the system of actual journey to work flows. However, such considerations lead us beyond the scope of this study. It is enough to have demonstrated another line of enquiry into the nature of central places [incidentally an aggregative one]. Again the close correlation between the functional size of places and another parameter, in this case the degree of conflux, has been shown and this has meant that the deviant places are seen in their true perspective.

THE SURROUNDINGS OF THE CENTRAL PLACE SYSTEM

The dangers of spatial abstraction were explicitly noted at the beginning of this essay. Now that the main results of the analysis have been presented, it is necessary to return to consider the case study as part of the wider system of which it forms a part. Unless the study is replaced within the wider network a purely closed system interpretation may be placed on the results that have been obtained. Already the growth of settlements south of Pontypridd and in the Rural District of Llantrisant reflect the changing balance of population distribution, though these developments are not attracting any great growth of high order central place functions, a situation that will change if, or rather when, a new town is developed in the area.[34] Then, perhaps, the wheel may have turned full circle and a return to the central place competition between Pontypridd and the Llantrisant area may be heralded. Of greater immediate relevance to the functioning of the case study area is the proximity of Cardiff, the largest commercial centre in Wales. Table 9.4 shows the result of a survey carried out in April 1966, in

TABLE 9.4. *The journey to shop: visits to Cardiff and Pontypridd*

Area	Total*	No. visits to either centre	At least 1 visit to centre	
			Cardiff	Pontypridd
Upper Rhondda Fawr	169	77	62	55
Mid. Rhondda Fawr	137	61	44	54
Rhondda Fach	114	46	36	48
Porth and Lower Rhondda	70	26	20	40

Source: *Field Work*, April 1966.
* Figures in rows do not add up to the total number of people interviewed because some people visited both centres.

which a total of 490 households (approximately a 2 per cent sample) randomly distributed in each settlement in the Rhondda Valleys were asked whether they had visited Cardiff or Pontypridd for shopping trips in the previous month. Two-fifths of the households had visited one or other of the places, but it is significant that the total number of visits made to Cardiff was not very much below the figure for Pontypridd. Pontypridd dominates the nearest settlements in terms of number of visits, but at greater distances, visits to Cardiff become more and more frequent. In the Upper Rhondda Fawr the number of visits to Cardiff seem on this evidence to be the same as those to Pontypridd.

Even allowing for the limited sample size, it is apparent that the case study area is not a closed system for high order goods, but is becoming more closely linked to Cardiff. Any model attempting to predict retail trade patterns would need to incorporate the influence of Cardiff as a major variable.

The dominance of Cardiff was also revealed by analysing the residences of people working in the commercial core of Pontypridd. On balance there is a great daily outflow of commercial workers from Pontypridd to Cardiff, but a reverse flow (or countercurrent, to use Ravenstein's terminology[35]) does occur. In total this flow from Cardiff is insignificant, contributing only 3 per cent to the total number of workers in Pontypridd. In influence or control, it is of great importance, for two-thirds of the number are owners or managers of commercial premises. This means that 15 per cent of the establishments in Pontypridd are controlled by residents of Cardiff, a figure that is over twice that for any other single settlement.

Although this essay has not attempted to delve very deeply into the metropolitan influence of Cardiff, these two examples serve to demonstrate the increasingly intimate network of communication between the study area and its nearest regional centre. By discussing the surroundings of a system in this way the dangers inherent in abstracting one area from the larger reality may be mitigated (a problem that exists at all scales of analysis) and another perspective on the nature of a central place system will be revealed.

CONCLUSION

By concentrating on examples drawn from three different levels of perception this essay has isolated and measured several major structural characteristics of a system of central places. However, the principal object of this exercise has been to demonstrate the need to study places not as a set of independent places and independent variables, but as an integrated system. By utilising this approach, a coherent picture of the structure and functioning of the system has been developed and individual deviations are placed within the perspective of the whole.

Though the description of change has formed an integral part of this enquiry, no causal explanation of this change has been attempted. Adequate data on the key behavioural variables of consumer mobility and consumer expenditure, as well as the nature of the options and

16

decisions open to the commercial entrepreneurs, would be needed for such a task, and such information proved impossible to obtain for any period in the past. Hence it proved impossible to conclude this essay with a predictive and behavioural model of future changes for the area that is soundly based on its past development. However, one attempt was made to develop a structural model of the functional size of places in 1914 by means of a multiple regression framework incorporating five independent variables.[36] As insignificant correlation coefficients even at the 10 per cent level of significance were obtained, it is apparent that the analysis proved abortive. It would seem that the case study area did not provide enough examples of the necessary range and type of settlements from which to draw meaningful generalisations of individual change[37]; it is only large enough to specify the various forms of the whole system.

Although a comparatively successful model of journey-to-work movements was developed in the final section of this essay, the drawbacks to this sort of descriptive model must be emphasised. It is dependent on empirically derived data (especially the exponent applied to the distance variable) and there is no reason to suppose that such key variables will remain constant in the distant future, a criticism which applies to most gravity model frameworks.[38] Yet despite this problem the very success of the description demonstrated here may mean that the model is applicable to other areas in South Wales at this time, and it may be useful as a short term predictive tool. By varying the input data the effects on the whole system may be gauged.

Despite these rather unfashionable conclusions, unfashionable at least in the light of many current research efforts devoted towards aiding prediction of future states of the system, it must be stressed that some of the results of this study do have considerable planning potential. The establishment of an objective method of ranking service centres is important in itself, as is knowledge of its past states, while this data goes a long way towards fulfilling the often neglected requirements of any behavioural model of change. People do not satisfy their demands for goods and services or consider their employment opportunities within a vacuum, but within a life space that encompasses a set of central places. Measurement of this network, and knowledge of its past states, are a necessary part of the coherent appreciation of a system of central places and form an essential part of the input data for any model, simply because all behaviour, past, present and future must be constrained by the existing structure.

REFERENCES

. BERRY, B. J. L., 'Approaches to regional analysis: a synthesis', *Ann. Ass. Am. Geogr.*, **54**, 1964, pp. 2–11.

. As evidenced by the considerable literature in the field. BERRY, B. J. L. and PRED, A., *Central Place Studies: A Bibliography of Theory and Applications*, Regional Science Research Institute, Philadelphia, 1961; BARNUM, H. G., KASPERSON, R. and KIUCHI, S., *Central Place Studies: A Supplement Through to 1964*. Regional Science Research Institute, Philadelphia, 1965.

. MORRILL, R., 'Simulation of central place patterns over time', in Norberg, K., *Proceedings of I.G.U. Symposium in Urban Geography 1960*, Gleerups, Lund, 1963, pp. 109–20.

. DAVIES, W. K. D., 'Some considerations of scale in Central Place Analysis', *Tijdschr. econ. soc. Geogr.*, **56**, 1965, pp. 221–7.

. BERRY and PRED, *Central Place Studies*, pp. 41–51.

. JOHNSON, R. J. and RIMMER, P. J., 'The competitive position of a planned shopping centre', *Australian Geogr.*, **11**, 1967, pp. 160–8.

. DAVIES, W. K. D., 'Central Swansea: a pilot survey of pedestrian flows', unpublished discussion paper. University of Swansea, 1967.

. RUSHTON, G., *Spatial Pattern of Grocery Purchases by the Iowa Rural Population*, University of Iowa Studies in Business and Economics, New Series No. 9, 1966.

. A more comprehensive outline of approaches to central place analysis is provided by DAVIES, W. K. D., 'The study of central places: an overview', *Institute of British Geographers Study Group in Urban Geography*, Durham Meeting, 1967.

0. CARTER, H., 'The growth of industry 1750–1850', in Bowen, E. G., ed., *Wales: A Physical Human and Regional Geography*. Methuen, 1956, pp. 204–19.

1. LEWIS, E. D., *The Rhondda Valleys*, Phoenix House, 1959.

2. *Ibid.*, p. 102.

3. *Proposals for Administrative Re-organization in Wales*. HMSO, Cardiff, 1967.

4. *Slater's Commercial Directory for South Wales*, 1868.

5. In the final period of sinking the Parc Colliery in Cwmparc, the workmen volunteered to work for a week without pay as the owner, David Davies of Llandinam, was in financial difficulties. It was in this

period in March, 1866, that coal was struck; see THOMAS, I., *To, Sawyer: biography of David Davies of Llandinam*, Longmans, 1938 p. 146.

16. MADDEN, C., 'On some indications of stability in the growth o cities in the U.S.A.', *Economic Development and Cultural Change*, 4 1956.

17. DAVIES, *Tijdschr. econ. soc. Geogr.*, 1965, pp. 221–7.

18. MCQUITTY, L. L., 'Elementary linkage analysis for isolating ortho gonal and oblique types and typal relevancies', *Educ. psycho. Measur.* (Baltimore), **17**, 1957, pp. 207–29.

19. BERRY, B. J. L., 'Cities as systems within systems of cities', i Friedman, J. and Alonso, W., *Regional Development and Planning A Reader*, Massachusetts Institute of Technology Press, 1964.

20. DAVIES, W. K. D., 'Discrepancies in source material: a case study i South Wales in 1914', unpublished discussion paper, Universit College of Swansea, October 1966.

21. DAVIES, W. K. D., 'Centrality and the central place hierarchy', *Urba Studies*, **4**, 1967, pp. 61–79.

22. BERRY, B. J. L. and BARNUM, H. G., 'Aggregate patterns and ele mental components of central place systems', *Journal of Regiona Science*, **4**, 1963, pp. 65–106.

23. See the literature cited in footnote 2.

24. SMAILES, A. E., 'Some reflections on the geographical descriptio and analysis of townscapes', *Trans. Inst. Br. Geogr.*, **21**, 1955, p. 10

25. DAVIES, W. K. D., 'The hierarchy of commercial centres', unpub lished Ph.D. dissertation, University of Wales (Aberystwyth), 1964.

26. DAVIES, W. K. D., 'The morphology of central places', *Ann. Ass Am. Geogr.*, **58**, 1968, pp. 91–110.

27. DZIEWONSKI, K., 'Typological problems in urban geography *Volume of Abstracts, 20th International Geographical Congres* London, 1964, p. 321.

28. DAVIES, W. K. D., 'Journey to work movements and central plac patterns', unpublished discussion paper, University College c Swansea, 1967.

29. DAVIES, *Tijdschr. econ. soc. Geogr.*, 1965, pp. 221–7.

30. LONSDALE, R. E., 'Two North Carolina commuting patterns *Econ. Geogr.*, **42**, 1966, pp. 114–38.

31. CARROLL, J. D., 'Some aspects of home: work relationships of industrial workers', *Land Econ.*, **25**, 1949, p. 414.

32. LAKSHMANAN, T. R. and HANSEN, W. G., 'A retail market potential model', *J. Am. Inst. Planners*, **31**, 1965, pp. 133–43.

33. It may be noted that better results were derived from the exponential curve (log: actual values) than from log normal curve (log: log values).

34. Many government planning reports have suggested that a new town should be sited at Llantrisant. The most recent report to suggest this idea is *Wales: The Way Ahead*, HMSO., Cardiff, 1967.

35. RAVENSTEIN, E. G., 'The Laws of Migration', *Jl Roy. statist. Soc.*, **52**, 1889.

36. The dependent variable was that part of the functional index composed of retail functions. The independent variables were: (*a*) the population in 1914, (*b*) the distance from Pontypridd, (*c*) the distance from the nearest B or C centre, i.e. the secondary focal points in the area, (*d*) the size of this nearest B or C centre, (*e*) the functional index (retail part) in 1891.

37. One of the most recent and successful studies of central place change is HODGE, G., 'The prediction of trade centre viability in the Great Plains', *Pap. reg. Sci. Ass.* **15**, 1965, pp. 87–115.

38. DAVIES, *Tijdschr. econ. soc. Geogr.*, 1965, pp. 221–7.

CHAPTER 10

THE CENTRAL PLACE PATTERN OF MID-WALES AND THE MIDDLE WELSH BORDERLAND

C. Roy Lewis

The division of space into functional regions is accepted as one of the tasks of the urban geographer, and has given rise to a variety of terms to describe the dependent areas of central places as well as an even greater variety of indices to draw boundaries. Although arguments may arise over the suitability of analytical tools, the findings of most studies reveal disparity between existing planning units and areas of human interaction (Chapter 2). In the light of these obvious anomalies it is not surprising that when the notion of regional planning comes to the fore on a wave of political fashion, the geographer feels that he has something to contribute in the reconstruction of planning units.

The successful operation of regional planning bodies depends on the selection of meaningful regions, and, perhaps more important, on the selection of investment nodes within those regions. In Britain debate continues as to what kind of region should be adopted as the new administrative tier between national government and local government. (A summary of the wide range of regional institutions and organisations in England is given in a publication by the Acton Society Trust.[1]) In the first article of the first issue of *Regional Studies*, Self attempts to rationalise this debate by suggesting three criteria which must be taken into account in any system of planning regions— economic planning, city or urban regions, and administrative and cultural factors.[2] The second of his criteria embodies the contributions of numerous geographers and economists, both at the theoretical level, as in the locational models of Christaller[3] and Lösch,[4] and in empirical studies, as in the works of Fawcett, Gilbert, Taylor, and Dickinson.[5] Whilst many of these studies first saw the light of day as academic exercises, illustrating hierarchies of central places, it would appear that city regions are now proving of interest to planners on both sides of the Atlantic.[6] In line with this current interest, the aim of this chapter is to examine the central places of Mid-Wales and the middle Welsh Borderland as the constituent elements of an urban system.

THE STUDY AREA

The area of this study, straddling the administrative division between England and Wales through the lowland corridors of the Severn and Wye valleys, encompasses several different planning regions.

The counties of Shropshire and Herefordshire lie within the West Midland Region, a region which has shown considerable planning enterprise since the formation of the West Midland Group in 1941 under the auspices of the Bournville Village Trust. Reports on the region suggest that the western boundary is an arbitrary divide. The rural west, which looks to Shrewsbury and Hereford for urban services (see Figs. 2.2, 2.3), 'has something in common with the hillier and even less populous adjoining counties of Mid-Wales itself' for 'both look to the Birmingham conurbation rather more than to any other major city; both receive from the conurbation a substantial proportion of visitors, weekenders and retired people; and these features are reflected in their major lines of communication'.[7]

Mid-Wales, other than being a general geographical description of part of the Welsh Planning Region, formally exists as a planning unit in its own right. In 1957 the County Councils of Cardiganshire, Merioneth, Montgomeryshire, and Radnorshire set up the Mid-Wales Industrial Development Association, and were joined in 1958 by Breconshire County Council. This area shows general agreement with the Mid-Wales County, proposed by the Local Government Commission for Wales in 1963.[8] One of the aims of the Association is to attract industry to the area, and the West Midlands must be viewed as an obvious recruitment region, bearing in mind the overspill needs of the Birmingham conurbation. In terms of service provision, reports for the Mid-Wales area suggest that consumer orientation from its eastern counties is towards the West Midlands. In the Beacham Report of 1964 it was noted that 'as Third Order, Major Regional Centres, Shrewsbury and Hereford extend their influence across the Welsh boundary into east Montgomeryshire, south-east Radnorshire and south-east Breconshire', and 'as exterior Second Order, Provincial Centres, Birmingham and Cardiff draw into their wider, or more superficial spheres of influence, Montgomeryshire on the one hand and Breconshire on the other'.[9] Thus, even a superficial study of the

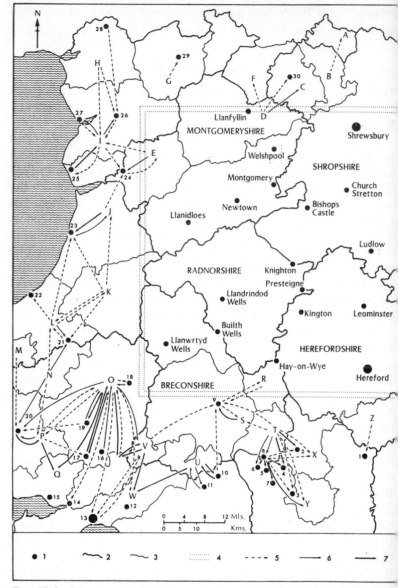

Fig. 10.1. Movement of workers across administrative boundaries outside the study area, 1951.

1. Urban Areas. 2. County Boundaries. 3. Rural Districts. 4. Study Area.
Numbers of Workers: 5. = 1 to 99. 6. = 100 to 199. 7. = 200 and over.

Index to administrative areas:

URBAN AREAS

Monmouthshire:
1. Monmouth M.B.
2. Abergavenny M.B.
3. Pontypool U.D.
4. Blaenavon U.D.
5. Nantyglo and Blaina U.D.
6. Ebbw Vale U.D.
7. Abertillery U.D.

Breconshire:
8. Brynmawr U.D.
9. Brecknock M.B.

Glamorgan:
10. Merthyr Tydfil C.B.
11. Aberdare U.D.
12. Neath M.B.
13. Swansea C.B.
14. Llwchwr U.D.

Carmarthenshire
15. Llanelly M.B.
16. Cwmamman U.D.
17. Ammanford U.D.
18. Llandovery M.B.
19. Llandeilo U.D.
20. Carmarthen M.B.

Cardiganshire:
21. Lampeter M.B.
22. Aberaeron U.D.
23. Aberystwyth M.B.

Montgomeryshire:
24. Machynlleth U.D.

Merioneth:
25. Towyn U.D.
26. Dolgellau U.D.
27. Barmouth U.D.
28. Blaenau Ffestiniog U.D.
29. Bala U.D.

Shropshire:
30. Oswestry M.B.

RURAL DISTRICTS

Flintshire (Det.):
A. Overton

Shropshire:
B. Ellesmere
C. Oswestry

Montgomeryshire:
D. Llanfyllin
E. Machynlleth

Denbighshire:
F. Ceiriog

Merioneth:
G. Penllyn
H. Deudraeth
I. Dolgellau

Cardiganshire:
J. Aberystwyth
K. Tregaron
L. Aberaeron
M. Teifiside

Carmarthenshire:
N. Newcastle Emlyn
O. Llandeilo
P. Carmarthen
Q. Llanelly

Breconshire:
R. Hay
S. Brecknock
T. Crickhowell
U. Vaynor and Penderyn
V. Ystradgynlais

Glamorgan:
W. Neath

Monmouthshire:
X. Abergavenny
Y. Pontypool

Herefordshire:
Z. Ross and Whitchurch

literature of these adjacent planning units demonstrates that their common boundary can be discounted as a satisfactory divide for the analysis of central places in the eastern Welsh Marches.

But the problem of defining a meaningful study area, embracing part of the Welsh highlands and the neighbouring lowlands of Shropshire and Herefordshire, still remains. The type of area sought is a polarised region which, as described by Boudeville, 'enables one to define, formally, interdependent and polarised groups, each with an internal hierarchy'.[10] For almost a century the upland rural areas of Wales have experienced depopulation, and central places, in the absence of industrial development, have been faced with lower demands from their agricultural hinterlands. Naturally enough, from within the area the civic pride at each centre will seek to perpetuate the existing central place pattern. By studying a settlement in isolation it is possible to make out a *prima facie* case for development investment. What is required is an analysis which will reveal the potential role of each settlement in the regional structure, as called for in the concluding sentence of the Beacham Report. The validity of the conclusions drawn from such an analysis will depend on the definition of the study region, for, as Davies points out, 'the hierarchy should not be abstracted from the spatial framework in which it is found, otherwise one is introducing a difference in scale which apparently distorts the basic functional organisation'.[11]

This multi-dimensional problem of defining composite systems of central places, incorporating hierarchies of settlements from provincial capitals down to rural villages, has been tackled by many workers. The most familiar techniques involve plotting the trade areas of a range of central place functions, such as local newspapers, and bus passenger services. Because of the essentially subjective delimitation of urban networks on the basis of these indices, it is desirable for the urban geographer to have an objective measure at his disposal. In this context Nystuen and Dacey[12] and Boudeville[13] claim that telephone communications may be considered an acceptable single index.

Trunk telephone data for Wales and adjacent areas have been analysed in Chapter 2. In the middle Welsh borderland, Shrewsbury and Hereford stand out as nodal points, and their influence extends westwards into Mid-Wales along the Severn and Wye valleys respectively. Because of inadequacies in the raw data, the total pattern is not revealed, but bearing in mind the quotations taken from planning reports, justification is given to the selection of the Severn and Wye valleys and the adjoining parts of Shropshire and Herefordshire as a distinct functional region.

In order to test the validity of the telephone index as a measure of city regions, an analysis of journey-to-work patterns has been carried out, using data contained in the Usual Residence and Workplace Tables of the 1951 Census. Figures for 1951 seem more acceptable than the 1961 data despite their age, since the latter derive from a sample survey that was not stratified for occupational types. The main flows of workers across administrative boundaries are to Shrewsbury, Ludlow and Hereford in the borderland, Welshpool and Newtown in the Severn valley, and Llandrindod Wells in the Wye valley. In Fig. 10.1 work flows have been plotted for areas adjacent to the study area. It can be seen that movements across the boundaries of the study area are small, and this emphasises its unity.

In the study area (Fig. 10.2), twenty-one centres have been selected for analysis:

1. Llanidloes	8. Hay-on-Wye	15. Hereford
2. Newtown	9. Presteigne	16. Leominster
3. Welshpool	10. Shrewsbury	17. Kington
4. Montgomery	11. Ludlow	18. Knighton
5. Rhayader	12. Bishop's Castle	19. Llanwrtyd Wells
6. Llandrindod Wells	13. Craven Arms	20. Caersws
7. Builth Wells	14. Church Stretton	21. Llanfyllin

(These reference numbers are standardised throughout this chapter.)

The distribution of centres clearly reflects the physical build of the area, with a band of settlements fringing the eastern foothills of the Welsh highlands and two lines of settlements extending westwards along the corridors of the Severn and Wye valleys. To the north the area is bounded by the Berwyn mountains, to the west the Pumlumon range rises to over 1,800 feet, and to the south lie Mynydd Eppynt and the Black Mountains. The valley corridors are separated by the uplands of Clun Forest and Radnor Forest. The historical development of the entire Welsh borderland has reflected its physical characteristics, namely, the meeting of highland and lowland in a series of valley embayments. To the north and south of the Welsh highlands coastal lowlands take the place of valley routeways.

Geographers have long been concerned with classifications of borderlands, frontiers, and boundaries,[14] and in central place analysis transitional zones must be regarded as significant variables in conditioning spatial patterns. Christaller stresses the importance of 'physiographically conditioned deviations' from his central place pattern around Stuttgart and Munich in southern Germany,[15] and Lösch considers the impact of political boundaries on regular networks of market areas.[16] Numerous other empirical studies may be cited which describe urban patterns in frontier areas. The effect of the boundary between the Republic of Ireland and Northern Ireland, dating from the Anglo-Irish Treaty of the 1920s, on urban hinterlands has been examined by Thomas,[17] and in Platt's study of the Dutch-German Border it is noted that 'Dutch economy and German economy are two separate systems meeting at the boundary, in contact but not

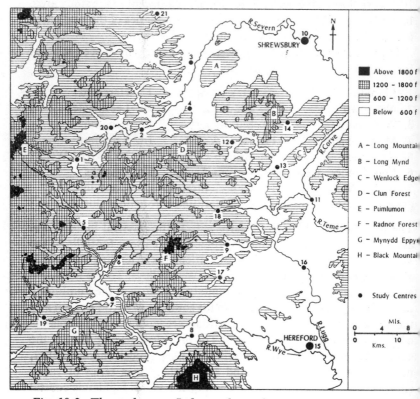

Fig. 10.2. *The study area. Index to the study centres is given in the text.*

coalescing', with the result that shoppers do not usually cross the boundary, even though the journey would be more convenient in terms of distance.[18]

HISTORICAL DEVELOPMENT OF CENTRAL PLACES IN STUDY AREA

The central place pattern of the study area must be viewed against the background of a physical borderland. Since the Norman Conquest no firm political line has separated the upland and lowland regions.

The Roman invasions against the Welsh highland core were halted at the eastern borderland. A line of forts from Chester through Wroxeter to Caerleon effectively defined the civil zone of Roman Britain, from which military incursions were made into the highland area to the west. The fort at Caersws in the upper Severn valley was established during the Roman infiltration along lowland routeways. But until the Norman invasions, Welsh princes were able to maintain a form of political separatism from the neighbouring lowlands, a separatism heightened by the looting raids romanticised in borderland tradition. Following a series of devastating raids between A.D. 705 and 709, the rulers of the neighbouring kingdom of Mercia raised earthworks along the borderland, culminating with the construction of Offa's Dyke towards the end of the eighth century.[19]

How effective this earthwork was as a political frontier during the Dark Ages is difficult to ascertain, but soon its north to south alignment was to be transgressed by Norman armies, and in the middle borderland a period of colonisation was initiated which was directly related to the east–west orientation of the valley routeways. The Norman conquest was accomplished by the systematic subjugation of territories from castle strongholds. Rebellions by the Welsh hampered occupation, but before the end of the thirteenth century the north-west and west of the Principality had been divided into shires, and by the Acts of Union of 1536 and 1542 Wales was formally united with England. Although a political line divided Montgomeryshire and Radnorshire from Shropshire and Herefordshire in the middle borderland, functional patterns have evolved with east to west associations, disregarding the north to south alignment of that divide.

In their evolution, the central places of Shropshire and Herefordshire may claim longer and more continuous histories than many of those in the Severn and Wye valleys. For instance, Hereford's foundation can be traced to a Roman fortress located on Watling Street, leading from Wroxeter to Caerwent.[20] At the time of the Domesday survey a settlement existed at Hereford, of a size estimated at six hundred inhabitants,[21] clustered around a religious house founded c. A.D. 680. This wattled edifice can be regarded as the forerunner of the present cathedral. However, accepting the observations made by Pirenne, which dispel the idea of urban agglomerations prior to the Carolingian era in Europe,[22] it may be unwise to associate marketing activities with this settlement during the Dark Ages. Carter emphasises this general statement, pointing out that to regard the three foci of settlement nucleation in Wales—the Roman *castrum*, religious houses, and fortified royal residences—'as anything more than preurban nuclei is to exaggerate their importance.'[23]

If towns are equated with marketing points, rather than with simple agglomerations of dwellings, then it must be stressed that the Norman Conquest was instrumental in laying the framework for the distribution of central places in the eastern Welsh Marches. The political subjection of the Severn and Wye valleys, directed from the strategic centres of Shrewsbury and Hereford, was brought about by castle towns, which were assimilated by the conquered territories as market towns.

Whilst military considerations were of paramount importance in the precise siting of castle towns, geographical accessibility determined their prosperity as central places. By the end of the thirteenth century the Principality had been reduced to a state of uneasy peace, and castle towns sought chartered recognition as market and fair centres. Records for the borough of Llanidloes, located in the upper Severn valley, list tolls collected on market and fair days as early as 1293.[24] But peaceful conditions were interrupted by local skirmishes or widespread revolution. The Glyndŵr Rebellion of the early fifteenth century impoverished the Principality, and market trading was disrupted. Fair tolls at Llanidloes decreased from 133 shillings and 5 pence in 1374 to 40 shillings in 1401, and to 13 shillings and 4 pence in 1421, whilst market tolls fell from 200 shillings in 1374 to 40 shillings in 1401, and to 10 shillings in 1421. In the suppression of the Glyndŵr Rebellion, Shrewsbury and Hereford were again the bases of the English campaigns.

Although the Severn and Wye valleys functioned as distinct military arenas during the Norman Conquest, the castle towns themselves, as central places, exerted only local spatial influence. In the eastern lowlands, where peaceful conditions were obtained soon after the Norman Conquest, the commercial influence of market towns was limited. A scatter of locally orientated trading nuclei existed, and out of this has crystallised the present central place pattern, in which Shrewsbury and Hereford, as shown by the analysis of functional connections in Chapter 2, have assumed regional importance.

The sixteenth and seventeenth centuries witnessed the gradual decline of military functions at the castle towns and the increasing importance of commercial functions. It is difficult to measure the relative importance of centres, for, other than noting the presence of marketing and legal activities, one must turn to the impressionistic topographical descriptions of noted travellers for supplementary information.[25] Rather than follow this line of research, it is sufficient to note that whilst markets established themselves and urban trade was organised around guild institutions, the total domination of the valley routeways by fewer central places was hampered by the poor state of transport.

The spacing of markets in the Middle Ages must be seen as a function of walking distance, and in this context, Bracton, a thirteenth-century lawyer, gave six and two-thirds miles as the legal spacing for market centres.[26] This distance is incorporated in some market charters, as in that granted to the corporation of London in 1327: 'No market from henceforth shall be granted by us or our heirs, to any within seven miles in circuit of the said city'.[27] The distance clause must be also interpreted in the light of the periodic operation of markets, as a possible safeguard against the clashing of market days in two neighbouring centres. Undoubtedly, market towns assumed control over local hinterlands, and Pease and Chitty refer to two court cases, one of which was the Leominster Fair Case of 1285, where objections were raised to the establishment of neighbouring markets.[28] The payment of tolls, or stallage, for the privilege of trading on market day, was often avoided by sellers, who offered their wares outside the market place. This action, known as forestalling, was seen to undermine the prosperity of the centres, and measures were taken to preserve local trade for the benefit of the central markets. In the Hereford Presentments for the early seventeenth century, a case for 1632 reads: 'Ite(m) we doe present for foorestallinge of the Markett in buyinge butter and cheese . . . wthoute Ine gate, Reece Jones alias Thomas.'[29] It is clear from cases such as this that market centres sought to establish their territorial supremacy.

The evidence suggests that within the study area commerce was carried out around a close mesh of market towns up to the end of the seventeenth century. This distribution can be related to restricted communications and the simple exchange of commodities between producer and consumer. But from this period onwards the market towns were to draw apart in terms of relative status, so that by the start of the twentieth century trade was concentrated at fewer points. Beginning with the eighteenth century, roads were improved, as witnessed by the numerous Acts passed for establishing Turnpike Trusts. In the eastern borderland road improvement appears to have been geared to the needs of through traffic, producing an east to west network of routes, running up the valley corridors from the 'gateway' towns, and over the highland core to the west coast of the Principality. Among these was the turnpiked road from the border town of Leominster, through Rhayader and the Elan valley, to Aberystwyth. Where a castle town had been built in the uplands proper its importance was now undermined by a neighbouring lowland centre. In Radnorshire the town of New Radnor, situated in the uplands of Radnor Forest, lost its county importance to the town of Presteigne, located in the lowlands of the Lugg Valley.[30] Comparatively few similar examples exist. Only one or two market towns were located away from the turnpiked roads, for in their siting the control of the Severn and Wye lowlands had been a strong military consideration.

In the early days of road mending the market towns were only provided with link roads, and communication in their local hinterlands still remained difficult. The Turnpike Trust formed in 1767 in Radnorshire was responsible for through routes in the county, but away from these the condition of tracks leading to the markets prompted Howse to observe that local farmers used runners rather than wheels on their carts in order to negotiate mud and rough surfaces.[31] Bowen, after describing the transportation situation in the first part of the eighteenth century, concludes that 'it was easier to move out of Wales than within Wales'.[32]

However, by the early 1800s wheeled traffic, both between market centres and to market centres from their hinterland areas, was extensive. Town gazetteers show that regular passenger services were in operation on market days and national commercial directories contain the timetables of carriers' carts between centres. In the study area, Shrewsbury and Hereford gained importance as entrepôts for goods conveyed by road from London and the Midlands. From these two centres a net of carrier services distributed commodities to surrounding markets, including those of the Severn and Wye valleys. Changes were taking place, too, in the commercial structures of the market towns. By the middle of the nineteenth century auction sales became a feature of the livestock trade,[33] and retail outlets began to carry stocks of goods brought in by carriers and to rely less on simple bespoke provision.

Railway construction in the second half of the century emphasised the transportation pattern established by the carrier services. By 1853 the railway had reached Shrewsbury, Ludlow, and Hereford, and from the border towns tracks were built to the market towns in the valley hinterlands to the west. The railway mesh simply reflected the distribution of market towns. Only Montgomery was bypassed, for the station was built a mile away from the town. Also, in one instance, the railway was responsible for the creation of a market centre, Craven Arms in Shropshire, at the junction of the Shrewsbury to Hereford line and the Central Wales line.

While transport innovation in the nineteenth century established the border towns of Shrewsbury and Hereford as major foci for the Mid-Wales hinterland, the market towns of the valley lowlands were able to maintain their status almost to the end of the century. But their local importance was related as much to industrial 'base' functions as to central place functions. In particular, the woollen industry ensured their prosperity. By the early nineteenth century the woollen trade had freed itself from the control of the Shrewsbury Drapers,[34] and flannel manufacturing became concentrated at market towns in the Severn valley, with the markets of neighbouring counties supplying raw materials. This industry flourished during the first part of the century, until competition from the textile industries of Lancashire and Yorkshire caused a gradual decline.

In many ways the growth and subsequent collapse of woollen manufacturing bears resemblance to other industries which acted as stimuli to settlement growth in rural Wales. Lead mining in Cardiganshire in the nineteenth century gave temporary prosperity to the rural scene (see Chapter 7). Within the study area, the centres of Church Stretton, Llandrindod Wells, Builth Wells, and Llanwrtyd Wells gained importance as spa resorts at the end of the nineteenth century. The most spectacular development was at Llandrindod Wells in Radnorshire. At the beginning of the century Llandrindod was a village in a parish of that name, the population of which was 192 in 1801. By 1841 the population was 270, and the Parish returns record thirty-four visitors at boarding houses near the mineral water springs. Its development as a spa resort began after 1865, when the railway reached Llandrindod. In the early 1890s parts of the civil parishes of Cefnllys and Llandrindod were amalgamated into the urban district of Trefonen, which was afterwards renamed Llandrindod Wells.[35] A peak population of 4,596 was reached in 1921, but then, as spa resorts fell from favour, the centre experienced decline.

This brief account demonstrates that the central places of Mid-Wales and the middle Welsh Borderland cannot be compared one with another as distribution points for central place functions alone in the nineteenth century. Local industrial activities played an important part in their prosperity.

FUNCTIONAL ANALYSIS

The twenty-one centres selected for analysis range in size from small service villages, illustrated by Caersws and Montgomery, to the regional centres of Shrewsbury and Hereford, with populations of 49,566 and 40,434 respectively, in 1961. In seeking to analyse the dynamic nature of central place systems the researcher is faced with the problem of data collection. In order to establish the status of centres in the nineteenth century reference has been made to Trade Directories, and data for the contemporary functional pattern were obtained by personal field survey at the twenty-one centres in 1964.

The reliability of directory entries, particularly at the beginning of the last century, can be questioned on a number of counts.[36] The classifications of functions may vary from year to year, and even from place to place in the same year; traders are sometimes listed under several trade headings; and groups of centres may be omitted in the final compilation. But by careful checking of the trade lists it is possible to derive tabulations of commercial outlets[37] for the central places. The problem of classification of outlets in field survey was overcome by enumerating establishments according to the main commodities offered for sale.

For the purposes of this study it was decided to make a comparison between the grading of centres in the early and mid-nineteenth century, and the hierarchy of settlements derived from 1964 data. In order to establish an acceptable grading for the former period, directories were consulted for 1791, 1811, 1822–23, 1828 and 1830–31, and 1850. It was found necessary to analyse a wide spread of source material since all centres were not given at any one date. In Table 10.1 the twenty-one study towns are listed and the availability of directory information is indicated. Llandrindod Wells and Llanwrtyd Wells do not appear at any date on this list as they only became important as spa towns at the end of the century. Craven Arms is also absent, as its growth was due to the railway, whilst no information exists for Caersws, which was only a small village settlement in the upper Severn valley.

For each of these dates and for 1964 the numbers of commercial establishments, classified according to function, were compiled for

TABLE 10.1. *Availability of directory data, 1791–1850*

Study centres	1791	1811	1822–23	1828 and 1830–31	1850
1. Llanidloes		×		×	×
2. Newtown	×	×	×	×	×
3. Welshpool	×	×	×	×	×
4. Montgomery	×	×	×	×	×
5. Rhayader		×		×	×
6. Llandrindod Wells					
7. Builth Wells		×		×	×
8. Hay-on-Wye		×		×	×
9. Presteigne		×		×	×
10. Shrewsbury	×	×	×	×	×
11. Ludlow	×		×	×	×
12. Bishop's Castle	×		×	×	×
13. Craven Arms					
14. Church Stretton	×		×	×	×
15. Hereford	×		×	×	×
16. Leominster	×	×	×	×	×
17. Kington			×	×	×
18. Knighton		×		×	×
19. Llanwrtyd Wells					
20. Caersws					
21. Llanfyllin		×		×	×

× indicates suitable directory data

each central place. Given these data, an objective measure, devised by Davies,[38] was used to assign functional index values to the study towns. A location coefficient was calculated for one outlet of all functional types, using the formula:

$$C = \frac{t}{T} \times 100$$

where C = location coefficient of function t,

    t = one outlet of function t,

    T = total number of outlets of function t in the study centres.

By multiplying the number of outlets of each functional type at each centre by the relevant location coefficient, centrality values were derived for all the functions characteristic of each centre. Addition of the centrality values scored by each settlement produced functional index values. Whereas Davies confined his analysis to retail functions, the present study includes social service and professional functions.

In order to compare the status of the study centres through time, the crude index values have been converted into percentage index values. The most striking feature to emerge from ranking the centres and

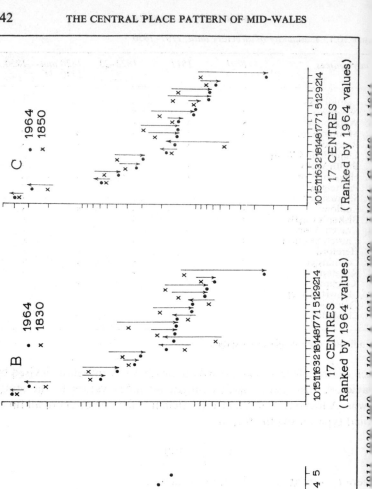

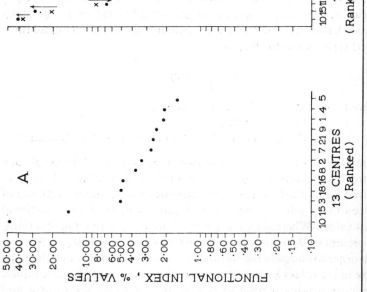

acing changes through time, is the concentration of commercial
ctivities at Shrewsbury and Hereford at the expense of central places
ι Mid-Wales. Located in the rich agricultural lowlands of the eastern
orderland, Shrewsbury and Hereford were by far the largest centres
t the beginning of the nineteenth century, with populations of 14,739
nd 6,828 respectively in 1801. The functional indices calculated for
ιirteen centres in 1811 (Fig. 10.3a) reveal the importance of these
νo towns, which stand apart at the top of the graph. Apart from this
ιe break in the distribution of indices, the values of the remaining
leven centres show no significant grades, but, rather, are aligned in
 continuum from Welshpool (centre number 3) down to Rhayader
5). This pattern can be interpreted by recalling the preceding com-
ιents on the state of transportation, which dictated a close mesh of
ιarket centres, and on the contribution of local industries to the
rosperity of the Mid Wales centres. A corroborative statement on
ιe indices calculated for 1811 is given in Powell's study of the upper
evern valley towns in the early nineteenth century, where it is noted
ιat 'there were few functional contrasts between the towns, although
Velshpool appears less dependent than the others upon industry'.[39]

For 1830 and 1850 trade information has been analysed for seven-
ɛen centres, and the index values are compared graphically with those
or 1964 in Figs 10.3b and 10.3c. Shrewsbury (10) and Hereford (15)
btain greater importance; Ludlow (11), Leominster (16), Welshpool
3) and Newtown (2) show small losses in status; and smaller centres,
xemplified by the old county towns of Presteigne (9) and Mont-
omery (4), show marked decline. The town of Church Stretton (14),
/hich functioned as a small market centre before the impetus given by
pa development at the end of the nineteenth century, assumes greater
tatus over the period. A cursory examination of directory lists for
ιe beginning of the twentieth century reveals that Llandrindod
Vells and Llanwrtyd Wells experienced similar expansion as health
ɛsorts.

The index values assigned to the twenty-one study settlements on the
ιasis of 1964 field data, are plotted in Fig. 10.4. The distribution of
ιalues is more stepped than even, and breaks of slope have been taken
s cutting points to give five grades of centres, designated A, B, C, D
nd E (Table 10.2). This classification, derived from the index values
omputed for 125 retail, service, and professional functions, has been
ccepted after testing the validity of the breaks by using various com-
inations of functions.[40] The lowest grade, comprising Llanfyllin (21),

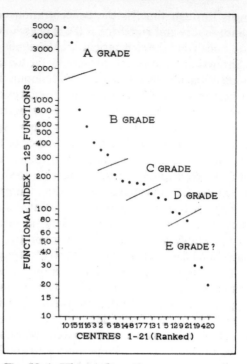

Fig. 10.4. The grading of twenty-one settlements. 1964 field data.

Llanwrtyd Wells (19), Montgomery (4), and Caersws (20), represents
'tail-off' to village settlements rather than a distinct grouping of
centres.

TABLE 10.2. *Five grades of centres, based on 1964 field data*

A	B	C	D	E
10. Shrewsbury	11. Ludlow	18. Knighton	13. Craven Arms	21. Llanfyllin
15. Hereford	16. Leominster	14. Church Stretton	1. Llanidloes	19. Llanwrtyd Wells
	3. Welshpool	8. Hay-on-Wye	5. Rhayader	4. Montgomery
	2. Newtown	17. Kington	12. Bishop's Castle	21. Caersws
	6. Llandrindod Wells	7. Builth Wells	9. Presteigne	

This hierarchical arrangement has resulted from a process of selective reorganisation in the central place pattern. In the nineteenth century local industrial and craft activities helped to maintain the status of the medieval market centres. The gradual decline of these 'basic' functions in the Mid-Wales towns meant that their future prosperity largely depended on their efficacy as agricultural service points. By the turn of the century road making was in the hands of county councils, and, with the development of the internal combustion engine, the rationalisation of the former close mesh of market centres began. A report prepared by the Ministry of Agriculture and Fisheries in the 1920s, on agricultural marketing in England and Wales, summarises the changes that were to characterise the study area:

> The increase in railway facilities, and, more recently, the enormous increase in motor traffic, has enabled the farmer to send his produce to more distant markets than formerly. As a result, some markets have grown considerably; others—notably the smaller livestock markets—are declining. In fact, a number of livestock markets have become insignificant from the point of view of supplies and some are moribund.[41]

Agricultural marketing today is centred at the A and B grade centres, with the exception of Llandrindod Wells (6), and at the C grade centres of Knighton (18), Builth Wells (7), and Hay-on-Wye (8). With the exception of Craven Arms (13), which gained importance through railway development, the lower order centres have lost regular livestock markets and possess only seasonal stock sales.

Although Fig. 10.4 illustrates the range of index values, the status of the active market centres can best be appreciated from an examination of their spatial distribution. Along the eastern lowlands the centres of Shrewsbury, Craven Arms, Ludlow, Leominster, and Hereford are foci for agricultural marketing. In Mid-Wales, markets are located at central points in the valley lowlands—at Newtown and Welshpool in the Severn valley, at Knighton in the Teme valley, and at Builth Wells and Hay-on-Wye in the Wye valley. Although Llandrindod Wells is classed as a B centre for the Wye valley, its high index derives from a concentration of professional and social service functions, occupying boarding houses vacated after the spa boom at the beginning of the century. In effect, Llandrindod Wells and Builth Wells together comprise the equivalent of a B grade centre, for the latter maintains the agricultural market.

Up to this point in the analysis, the decline of the small market centres has been related to transportation innovation and subsequent marketing centralisation. But in addition to these forces the area has experienced consistent depopulation, and thus a lowering in the demand for central place functions. It is to this that we must now turn.

POPULATION CHANGE

Rural depopulation in the study area is not confined to the uplands of Mid-Wales but is equally characteristic of the valley corridors and the agricultural lowlands of Shropshire and Herefordshire. In the upland areas of rural Wales the peak population total was reached towards the end of the nineteenth century. In certain specific areas the decline of the lead mining and woollen industries was responsible for pockets of sudden population loss, but, more generally, depopulation has been a slow process, accompanying a decrease in agricultural employment. The processes of farm amalgamation and mechanisation account for diminishing job opportunities in the area—a situation characteristic of all rural areas of Britain. Where alternative employment is not available in local urban areas, emigration is the inevitable consequence. The demographic structure of the study area, and the causes of rural depopulation, have been outlined elsewhere,[42] but it is considered necessary to describe, briefly, those features of population change which are instrumental in reorganising the settlement pattern.

If rural depopulation is viewed from an agricultural standpoint it would appear that the drift from the land is an essential step towards securing larger and more efficient farming units. In the review of the allocation of grants to hill and upland farmers, contained in an agricultural White Paper presented in 1965, official Government support was given to farm rationalisation: 'In view of the importance attached to the improvement of the structure of farming, especially in the hill and upland areas, it would not be consistent with the general aims of the Government's policy to re-introduce a hill land improvement scheme of a type which would tend to perpetuate the existing pattern of farm structure.'[43] While agricultural objectives may be reached, the population has to readjust to the changing employment situation. The contraction of local industries at the end of the last century and, more recently, the programme of railway closures, have further restricted employment possibilities, with the result that, on balance, rural districts have experienced steady out-migration. Over the last sixty

years, the area administered by the Mid-Wales Industrial Development
Association has lost 17 per cent of its population.

At the village level population loss is reflected in the declining
numbers of primary schools and in the relegation of many retail outlets from permanent businesses to sideline ventures. The small market
towns have been faced with lower demands for central place functions
from their hinterland areas. A survey of the C, D, and E grade centres

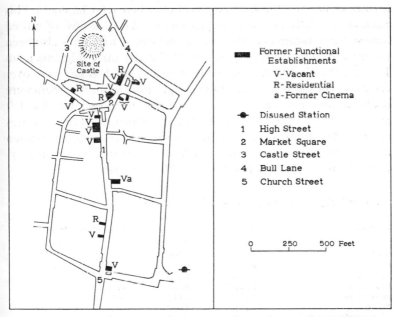

Fig. 10.5. Bishop's Castle: changes in functional use. 1964 Field Survey.

distinguished in this study reveals that the business cores of many are
fragmented by vacant shops and business premises converted into
houses. Fig. 10.5 illustrates the pattern of decay revealed in Bishop's
Castle. Given the present population trend and employment situation,
there is no prospect of the regeneration of their central place activities.

Taking the lower grade centres, their populations, as crude totals,
have decreased during the present century. For instance, the population of Llanfyllin declined from 1,652 in 1901 to 1,252 in 1961, and
that of Knighton decreased from 2,139 to 1,824 over the same period.
However, these general figures mask the internal pattern of migration

within the study area. Whilst population loss is the rule for the area, the market centres appear to act as magnets in the initial movements of rural inhabitants, or as temporary stopping-off points in the outward drift. In Jones's study of rural migration in a small area of the upper Severn valley, it was noted that Llanidloes attracted migrants from the Old Hall and Cwmbelan areas of Llangurig and Llanidloes Without parishes.[44] The contribution of this in-migration to the small centres is to leave a core of middle-aged and retired people, for the children, on leaving school, must seek employment elsewhere (cf. Chapter 8). This nucleus of elderly people is emphasised by the back-flow of retired natives from distant conurbations, a movement which has also been observed by Jones: 'Thus thirty-six of the fifty-three migrants from London, the West Midlands conurbation and South Wales were over forty years of age at the time of their migration and most of them were people returning in retirement to their native area which they had left as young people.'[45] Consequently, the age structures of these centres are weighted towards the over-forty-five age groups, and the children of these inhabitants, by moving to distant centres in search of employment, do not promote population growth in the area.

TABLE 10.3. *Population changes at A and B grade centres, 1951–1961*

Centres	1951	1961	Percentage change
Shrewsbury	44919	49566	10·3
Hereford	32501	40434	24·4
Ludlow	6456	6796	5·3
Leominster	6290	6405	1·8
Welshpool	6036	6330	4·9
Newtown	5431	5517	1·6
Llandrindod Wells	3212	3251	1·2

On the other hand, the populations of the A and B grade centres show an upward trend, particularly the two centres of Shrewsbury and Hereford. This is illustrated in Table 10.3 which compares 1951 and 1961 population levels. Unfortunately, the decennial Census does not give a detailed breakdown of migration data whereby population change can be related to specific age groups. An approximate measure has been used by House and Knight in a study of migration in north-east England.[46] Given 1951 Census population figures, recorded by quinary age groups, for rural and urban areas, the expected 1961 population can be calculated for each age group by making allowance for deaths in the intervening period. Comparison of the expected 1961 figures with the actual 1961 Census figures reveals the amount of change in each age group due to migration. This measure has been applied to population data for the urban areas of Mid-Wales and the middle Welsh Borderland. The centres of Shrewsbury and Hereford emerge as the main recipients of school-leavers, both male and female. To a lesser extent, Ludlow, Newtown, Welshpool, and Llandrindod Wells show in-migration in the younger age groups, but this movement is overshadowed by heavy immigration in the over-forty age groups. For the remaining urban areas the general pattern is one of out-migration up to about forty-five years of age, and in-migration in the older age groups (cf. Chapter 8). The former spa centres of Church Stretton and Llandrindod Wells show marked female immigration in the sixty-plus ages, which reflects their attraction as retirement towns. This analysis suggests that where a low grade centre has shown population increase in recent decades, the increase is attributable to the immigration of retired persons.

Bearing in mind these general comments on migration by age groups, an attempt can be made to classify the study centres by population characteristics. In Fig. 10.6, the four components of population change—natural increase, natural decrease, net in-migration, and net out-migration—are represented as graph axes, and eighteen centres, for which Census data are given, are located according to their population changes between 1951 and 1961. On balance, those centres lying to the right of the diagonal line show population increase, and those to the left show decrease.[47] The centres of Hereford, Shrewsbury and Ludlow display natural and migrational increases; Welshpool, Newtown, and Leominster have experienced out-migration, but the birth rate has compensated for the loss; at Church Stretton, Llanidloes, and Llandrindod Wells, in-migration is sufficiently large to compensate for natural losses; and at the remaining centres, with the exception of Montgomery (population 972 in 1961), population decline is the rule. At Knighton, Builth Wells, Hay-on-Wye, and Llanfyllin, the decrease is a function of both out-migration and natural loss.

From these observations on population change, the A and B grade centres can be isolated as local growth points within the study area. The centre of Llandrindod Wells in the Wye valley shows the least promising features, for agricultural marketing is concentrated at the neighbouring centre of Builth Wells, and its own commercial structure is a legacy of its spa development.

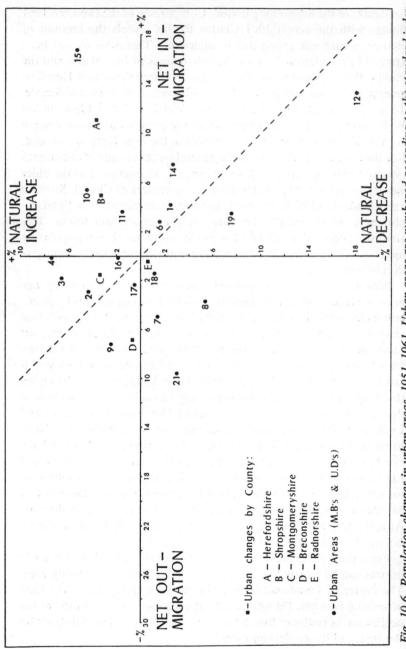

Fig. 10.6. Population changes in urban areas, 1951–1961. Urban areas are numbered according to the standard index

EMPLOYMENT

The importance of the high grade centres derives not only from their provisioning of hinterland areas but also from their status as employment nuclei. In the border towns of Shrewsbury, Ludlow, Leominster, and Hereford, factory overspill from the West Midlands conurbation has already provided new job opportunities, but in many Mid-Wales

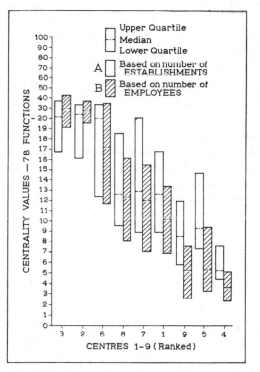

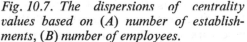

Fig. 10.7. The dispersions of centrality values based on (A) number of establishments, (B) number of employees.

centres, the retail, social service, and office outlets appear as the main employment units for the inhabitants of rural villages.

In order to measure the employment status of the Mid-Wales centres, personal interviews were carried out at 867 central place outlets, in Llanidloes, Newtown, Welshpool, Montgomery, Rhayader, Llandrindod Wells, Builth Wells, Hay-on-Wye, and Presteigne. The questionnaire sought to determine the number of employees at each establishment and their journey to work patterns. Labour figures were obtained for all commercial and office functions at the nine centres; only 2·6 per cent of the businesses refused to divulge residence details of employees.

The grading of centres derived in this study is based on functional indices calculated from the crude numbers of establishments enumerated at each settlement. Data on employment allow refinement in the computation of index values; Davies has described the calculation of centrality values by weighting establishments by the number of workers.[48] In Fig. 10.7, a comparison is given between centrality values calculated by crude numbers of establishments and centrality values weighted by numbers of employees, for the nine Mid-Wales centres; the dispersions of values for the centres are summarized by quartile deviations.

The centrality values of the B grade centres of Welshpool (3) and Newtown (2) are higher by number of employees, whereas those of the other seven centres are lower. The centralisation of marketing and commercial activities at Welshpool and Newtown has given rise to larger outlets, which stand in contrast to the small family concerns at the lower grade centres. The B centre of Llandrindod Wells (6) shows mixed characteristics, for whilst professional and office outlets are comparable in size with those at Newtown and Welshpool, retail establishments are smaller.

The incorporation of establishment size into the analysis not only refines the ranking technique but is also useful in indicating the different employment opportunities offered by central place activities in the study centres. The questionnaire schedules reveal that the low grade centres within the study area offer few jobs to rural dwellers, as shown by the journey to work patterns for Llanidloes, Rhayader, Montgomery and Presteigne in Fig. 10.8. The small influence of these settlements as employment centres can be contrasted with that of Welshpool (Fig. 10.9). These work flows relate to forty-eight retail functions, and when professional and office data are added to the picture, Welshpool, Newtown, and Llandrindod Wells clearly emerge as the dominant work centres for the upper Severn and Wye valleys. The future prosperity of the smaller settlements may lie in their development as commuter villages to the A and B grade towns (cf. the conclusions reached in Chapter 7, in which the dependence of Bow Street on Aberystwyth, in Cardiganshire, has been illustrated).

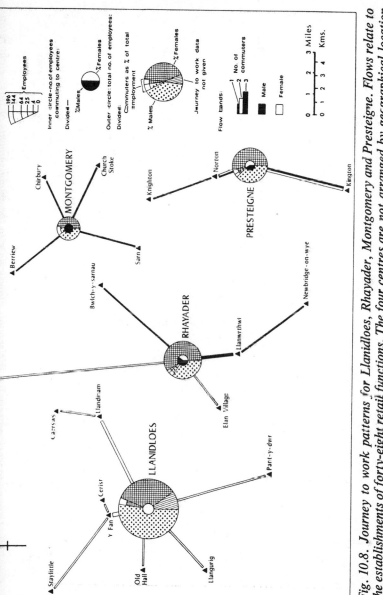

Fig. 10.8. Journey to work patterns for Llanidloes, Rhayader, Montgomery and Presteigne. Flows relate to the establishments of forty-eight retail functions. The four centres are not arranged by geographical location in the figure.

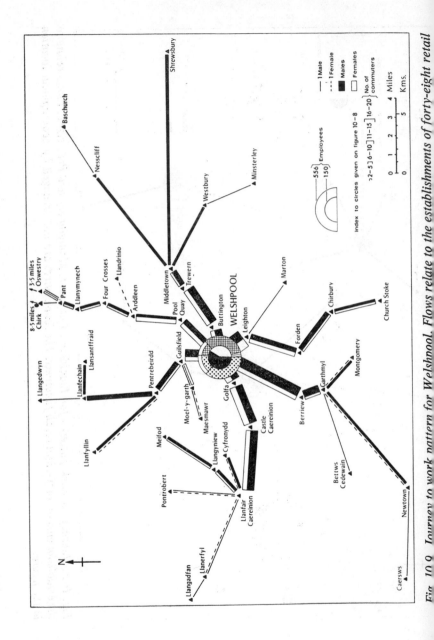

Fig. 10.9 Journey to work pattern for Welshpool. Flows relate to the establishments of forty-eight retail

No comparable detailed information is available for the remaining twelve study centres, and questionnaire survey by one person proved impracticable. A general measure of journey to work flows can be obtained from the 1951 Census (Usual Residence and Workplace tables). The high grade centres of Shrewsbury, Ludlow, and Hereford, and, to a lesser extent, Leominster, stand out as the recipients of workers from neighbouring administrative areas.

PROBLEMS IN THE MEASUREMENT OF THE STATUS OF CENTRAL PLACES

It has been demonstrated that the A and B grade centres, distinguished on the basis of 1964 field data, have increased their territorial importance in the study area. Their status as service centres has been quantified through time, and a brief examination of their population and employment structures has shown that they can be viewed as potential growth points in the urban system. But it is necessary to point out certain accepted generalisations which undermine the accuracy of the functional analysis.

Gradings have been produced by interrupting the events of evolution at selected time-points. Certainly, it is possible to locate the time-points near to major formative phases in urban growth, but in this study, as in many others, the availability of comparable directory information has determined the cross-sections through time, and the year of graduation of the author defined the timing of data on contemporary functions. Unless the arbitrary nature of these time decisions is appreciated, the most that can be hoped for are static peeps at a dynamic system.

It can be assumed that random incisions made into time for the collection of data may cut across the processes at work in promoting changes in the relative status of towns. Acceptance of this assumption must lead to a search in the data at hand for evidence of change. This point is made in Curry's study of service centres within towns.[49] Examining the locational aspects of the demand/supply balance within urban areas he anticipates change in the event of constant urban expansion:

> It is clear that if the housing area of a town is increasing there will be a tendency for service centres to be constantly moving out of equilibrium. Fringe areas will be being added to the markets of centres already adequate in size. Until other centres arise there will be 'surplus' markets too small for the normal activities to serve them.[50]

18

Realising that this transitional situation may be accompanied by response from entrepreneurs in the existing centres, in order to increase their profits, he advocates that 'such a fringe system must be an integral part of even a static analysis of an expanding town'.[51] The adoption of this approach in interurban central place analysis should enable the urban geographer to describe those functional features which characterise the period of transition (or 'fringe' period), when a small unsatisfied demand appears in an area.

This unsatisfied demand may result from two types of change. The pattern revealed by the analysis and projection of urban status through time may be either the concentration of central place activities at one or two focal points at the expense of less favourable locations, or the gradual build-up of all centres within an area, due perhaps to continued immigration of population. The evolutionary pattern identified for the central places of Mid-Wales and the middle Welsh Borderland, showing concentration at the A and B grade centres, can be placed in the first situation. Curry's attempt to anticipate the growth of shopping centres within expanding metropolitan areas is recognition of the second situation. The attainment of either situation will involve modification of the central place nets, from an old pattern to a new pattern. During the intervening period there will be imbalance between supply and demand.

On the one hand, the imbalance may derive from a very low scattered demand, in which case the operations of a businessman must extend to many settlements in order to 'accumulate the necessary volume of demand for survival'.[52] On the other hand, imbalance may be reflected in an unusually high level of demand. This can be viewed at a theoretical level. The nesting together of hexagonal nets rests on the geometrical rationalisation of threshold population. If we anticipate a wide range of threshold levels for various commodities, the non-fixed K network of Lösch is flexible enough to ensure normal profits for many of these commodities. But the network cannot incorporate all threshold requirements because of the geometrical rigours of the model. Thus, 'if sales in thirty-two settlements, say, were required to make a certain commodity profitable, area No. 13 with thirty-one settlements would be too small. But the next area is the unnecessarily large market area 14, with thirty-six settlements, so that sales must extend to thirty-six settlements'.[53] The entrepreneur selling this commodity now has the opportunity of obtaining greater profits by satisfying the demands at the four extra settlements.

In reality, because of the changing populations of centres, disequilibrium between supply and demand may be the rule. A situation of population decline exists in the Rhondda–Pontypridd area of South Wales. Davies showed that failure to incorporate the size of establishments into central place analysis led to underestimation of the degree of focality of the largest central places. Moreover, adjustment to a lower (higher) demand was met initially by a run down (increase) in the size of establishments rather than by the disappearance (creation) of establishments.[54] In the study area, depopulation has undermined businesses at the lower grade centres, leaving demands unsatisfied in their local areas. Recognition of the existence of low demands at various points poses the question as to how these can be tapped.

PART-TIME FUNCTIONS AND THE CENTRAL PLACE HIERARCHY

In formulating this study it was postulated that periodic functions should be incorporated in the analysis in order to show how demand is satisfied when the population level is insufficient to maintain full-time establishments. The part-time function may be a branch of a full-time establishment located at another central place, or the result of the enterprise of a local inhabitant, as a sideline venture to some other regular employment. In the former case, the profit available will accrue to a businessman; in the latter case, the profit will supplement a regular weekly wage.

The action of an entrepreneur from a neighbouring centre may be one of two alternatives: (*a*) to operate a part-time outlet, geared to the traditional marketing structure of the outlying town and operated on its former market day, or (*b*) to operate a mobile sales-van service (this must not be confused with a delivery service). The alternative selected would appear to depend on the type of commodity to be distributed. In the case of a professional service, the operation of a part-time establishment can be suggested, with the professional practitioner visiting the outlying offices on specified days. In the case of general consumer products, the implementation of a mobile selling unit would mean that stock-holding would not be necessary at part-time outlets for perhaps four or five non-productive days per week.

Many published studies of central place systems either make no mention of part-time establishments and sales van circuits or include them as ingredients making up a descriptive miscellany of urban functions. Few authors point to their role in maintaining the balance between supply and demand when disequilibrium is the rule in the system.[55] Palomäki, in his study of central places in South Bothnia, identified travelling shops in the rural areas, but considered that these have 'probably not grown into a formidable factor in South Bothnia'[56] and they are not given detailed analysis. Curry, dealing with an expanding metropolitan area, sees part-time outlets and travelling shops as solutions to provisioning a scattered demand.[57]

Although periodic functions are incorporated in some studies of central place patterns in the modern western world, it is necessary to turn to research carried out in developing countries for precise statements on itinerant trade. Whilst the type of trade differs markedly from that in western societies, the achievement of periodic functions is the same—to satisfy a scattered population when the demand is insufficient to support permanent entrepreneurs.

The market structure of the Yoruba country of south-western Nigeria has been studied by Hodder.[58] The travels of individuals are restricted to walking distances, and marketing and service outlets are migratory in order to satisfy the scattered demand. It is observed that female traders distribute goods from the major settlement of Ibadan by travelling around several rural markets with their wares, before returning to the central settlement to replenish stocks. Similar characteristics are noted in Belshaw's description of Haitian market systems.[59] A more penetrating study of periodic functions has been carried out by Skinner in rural China.[60] In the analysis of changes in local marketing through time, information is culled from *fang-chih* (i.e. gazetteers, prepared for *hsien* and other administrative units, which can be equated with directories used in this study); the contemporary pattern is based on field work in Szechwan, 1949–50. In this case study of rural China, as in the Nigerian study, the state of transport is regarded as the crucial factor in determining the demand area of a firm and the hinterland area of a market. When the demand contained within the dependent area is insufficient to maintain a permanent entrepreneur, periodic functions satisfy that demand. With improvements in transport, sufficient demand can be focused at fewer central places to support permanent entrepreneurs, who themselves replace the former mobile outlets.

Within the study area, depopulation and marketing centralisation have concentrated commercial activities at the A and B grade centres, leaving a scattered demand at former market towns. The emergent central place pattern is focused on the high grade centres, and periodic functions operated from these central settlements satisfy demands in the surrounding lower grade towns. In the field survey, carried out in the twenty-one study settlements, it was possible to collect data on part-time establishments operated by local inhabitants and by entrepreneurs from neighbouring centres, but the plotting of circuits followed by mobile shops proved impossible.[61] The days on which part-time establishments are open in the central places are not random; they coincide with the traditional market days still observed at the small centres.

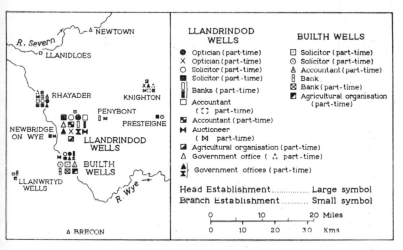

Fig. 10.10. Professional and social service branches operated from Llandrindod Wells and Builth Wells.

In the study area, part-time establishments are found at C, D, and E centres plus village communities, usually operated from parent concerns located at the A and B centres. Fig. 10.10 shows the part-time professional and social service outlets operated from Llandrindod Wells and Builth Wells at surrounding settlements.

If part-time functions are incorporated in the functional analysis described above, then the lower grade centres are upgraded. In Fig. 10.11, centrality values calculated for full-time establishments are compared with centrality values calculated for full-time and part-time establishments. The dispersions are summarised by quartile deviations. In general, the redistribution of centrality values by the incorporation of periodic functions is to the advantage of the declining towns, for on their traditional market days their functional contents are boosted.

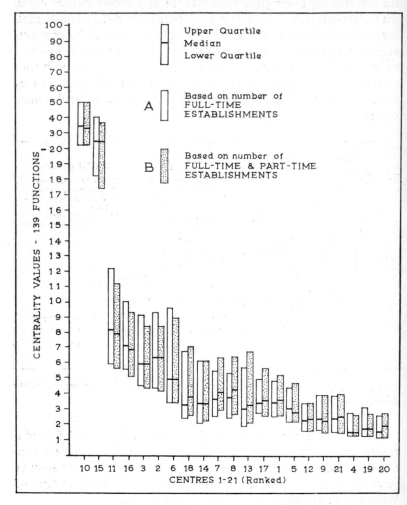

Fig. 10.11. The dispersions of centrality values based on (A) full-time establishments, (B) full-time and part-time establishments.

The A and B grade centres supply these functions, and thus their centrality dispersions are undermined by the inclusion of part-time outlets in the analysis.

The effect of periodic functions on functional indices is to reduce the disparity between centres. The index values of the A and B centres are lowered, and those of C, D, and E centres are increased. In Fig. 10.12, gradings produced by the two measures are compared. The rankings are similar by both measures (Spearman's Rank Correlation Coefficient of +0·989), but in (b) of Fig. 10.12 the grades are blurred,

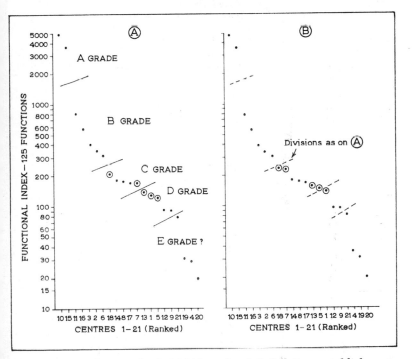

Fig. 10.12. Urban grades in 1964 based on (A) full-time establishments, (B) full-time and part-time establishments.

for Builth Wells (7) and Knighton (18) have moved upwards towards a higher grade, and Craven Arms (13), Rhayader (5), and Llanidloes (1) record values approaching those of the C grade centres.

On market days, the C, D, and E centres, with the exception of the residential town of Church Stretton, contain functions characteristic of respectively higher grade centres. The concentration of part-time outlets in the professional and office functions justifies the selection of thirty-three of these functions to illustrate the redistribution of functions to grades. These functions include solicitors, auctioneers, accountants, banks, and various national government offices, e.g. Ministry of Labour. Accepting that a function is characteristic of a

TABLE 10.4. *Redistribution of thirty-three functions to grades by inclusion of part-time establishments in the analysis*

By full-time establishments		By full-time and part-time establishments	
Functions		Functions	
	95	95 NC	
	109	109 NC	
	110	110 NC	
	116	116 NC	
	120	120 NC	
Grade	139	139 NC	Grade
A	140	140 NC	A
	141	141 NC	
	147	147 NC	
	148	148 NC	
	150	150 NC	
	154	154 NC	
	157	157 NC	
	115		
	131		
Grade	133	115 NC	Grade
B	138	131 NC	B
	114	133 NC	
	130	138 NC	
	137		
	153		
	106	106 NC	
Grade	108	108 NC	Grade
C	113	113 NC	C
	104	114 [1]	
	112	153 [1]	
	129		
		105 NC	
Grade	105	107 NC	Grade
D	107	104 [1]	D
	101	112 [1]	
		137 [2]	
		102 NC	
	102	103 NC	
Grade	103	128 NC	Grade
E	128	101 [1]	E
		129 [2]	
		130 [3]	

NC—no change   [1]—down one grade
[2]—down two grades   [3]—down three grades

particular grade even if only one outlet of that function occurs at that grade, in the allocation of full-time outlets the C, D, and E grades are characterized by 6, 3, and 3 functions, respectively, and the A and B grades by 13 and 8 functions, respectively. By the inclusion of periodic outlets the groupings of functions are altered in favour of the centres of the D and E grades—6 functions in grade E, 5 in grade D, 5 in grade C, 4 in grade B, and grade A maintains the same 13 specialised functions. The redistribution of functions is summarised in Table 10.4; the thirty-three functions are not named but numbered as on the data sheets used in the actual analysis.[62]

In the reorganisation of the central place pattern of Mid-Wales and the middle Welsh Borderland it is suggested that periodic functions characterise the decline, or transitional, period of the small market towns. Thus, the relationship between central places of different grades is not only expressed in consumer movement from low grade centres to high grade centres for the purchase of higher order goods. The centres are linked in business organisations. Many enterprises within the study area operate through regional headquarters, head offices, permanent branches, sub-branches, and part-time branches, and, in general terms, it is possible to recognise a grading of establishments. Scattered round the A and B centres are the lower grade settle ments which are the recipients of their part-time establishments. Withdrawal of these period functions may be the next stage in functional reorganization.

CONCLUSIONS

At the beginning of this essay care was taken in defining a meaningful study area. Assuming that this was achieved, it can be suggested that the analysis of central places in Mid-Wales and the middle Welsh Borderland has pinpointed those centres which have established themselves as growth points in the regional structure. Decay at the former market settlements has naturally aroused the civic leaders into action, and efforts have been made to attract industrial development. The Mid-Wales Industrial Development Association has been active in this respect.

What is needed is a constructive policy for investment at selected nodes. The present regional economy is primarily founded on agriculture, and commercial and marketing activities revolve around the centres of the A and B grades (taking the associated centres of

Llandrindod Wells and Builth Wells as the equivalent of an effective B
centre for the Wye valley). Investment at these centres will both consoli-
date the emergent pattern identified in this study and provide employment opportunities in the area. The future of declining market towns
must be seen in their development as commuter settlements.

These proposals arise from a detailed study of the central place
pattern, but, unfortunately, action is a function of political decisions
that may not take into account the contemporary structure of the
area. In recent years two proposals for development in the study area
have been put forward: the building of a new town in the upper
Severn valley[63] and the expansion of Rhayader.[64] The first proposal,
which envisaged a population of 70,000, has already been shelved in its
original form. In its place, development at Newtown is planned, with
a view to doubling its population (to about 10,000) in the next ten
years.[65] This policy is consistent with the findings of the above study.
The second proposal outlines the expansion of Rhayader from 1,250
to 2,500 within the next ten years. Rhayader, graded as a D centre in
this chapter, is a declining market town at the head of the Wye valley.
The terms of reference given to the consultants were to prepare proposals for its expansion, and this has been done. The author submits
that a hasty decision was taken in the initial selection of Rhayader, for
examination of the regional structure reveals that Llandrindod Wells
and Builth Wells can tender stronger claims for development. It must
be noted that a development survey has been undertaken at Builth
Wells by the Breconshire County Planning Department.[66]

The grading of central places, based on 1964 field data, is one cross-
section in a time continuum. The present centralisation of commercial
activities and job opportunities at the high grade centres stems from
reorganisation within the study area. Transportation innovation,
industrial decline, and population change have been described as variables effecting urban concentration. Reference to trade directories
facilitated the measurement of urban status in the nineteenth century.

Because of the arbitrary nature of the cross-sections through time an
attempt has been made to identify characteristics of change in the
central places. In this context, periodic functions have been recognised
as characteristic of towns which have experienced decline in status.
The appearance of part-time functions in central place systems is not
confined to the western world. Hodder and Skinner have illustrated
their operation in developing societies, although the type of trade is less
sophisticated. Hodder's statement that 'the principles and methods of

marketing geography as it is being developed in more advanced societies appear to have little if any relevance to local market studies in tropical underdeveloped lands'[67] would appear to be a fair comment on studies which are simply aimed at classifying centres into neat hierarchical compartments based on permanent commercial establishments. But the findings of this analysis suggest that part-time functions in an advanced society can be incorporated into central place analysis. They achieve the same end as pedlars in underdeveloped lands—the provisioning of population when permanent establishments cannot command their threshold requirements. Hence it is suggested that this organisation of space might well be a useful tool in the redevelopment of areas that are already in decline.

REFERENCES

1. SMITH, B. C., *Regionalism in England*, Acton Society Trust, London, 1964, Vol. 1.

2. SELF, P. J. O., 'Regional planning in Britain: analysis and evaluation', *Regional Studies*, 1, 1967, pp. 6–8.

3. CHRISTALLER, W., *Central places in Southern Germany*, trans. C. W. Baskin, Prentice-Hall, 1966.

4. LÖSCH, A., *The Economics of Location*, trans. W. H. Woglom and W. F. Stolper, Wiley, 1967.

5. A summary of regional subdivisions suggested by FAWCETT, C. B., GILBERT, E. W., TAYLOR, E. G. R. and DICKINSON, R. E., is given in DICKINSON, R. E., *The City Region in Western Europe*, London, 1967, Ch. 9.

6. SENIOR, D., ed., *The Regional City*, Longmans, 1966.

7. *The West Midlands: a regional study*, HMSO, London ,1965, p. 2.

8. *Report and Proposals for Wales*, Local Government Commission for Wales, HMSO, London, 1963, paras 579–85.

9. *Depopulation in Mid-Wales*, HMSO, London, 1964, p. 41.

10. BOUDEVILLE, J.-R., *Problems of Regional Economic Planning*, Edinburgh University Press, 1966, p. 10.

11. DAVIES, W. K. D., 'Some considerations of scale in central place analysis', *Tijdschr. econ. soc. Geogr.*, 56, 1965, p. 221.

12. NYSTUEN, J. D. and DACEY, M. F., 'A graph theory interpretation of nodal regions', *Proc. reg. Sci. Ass.*, 7, 1961, pp. 29–42.

13. BOUDEVILLE, *Problems of Regional Economic Planning*, p. 38.

14. PRESCOTT, J. R. V., *The Geography of Frontiers and Boundaries*, Hutchinson, London, 1965.

15. CHRISTALLER, *Central Places in Southern Germany*, p. 196.

16. LÖSCH, *The Economics of Location*, pp. 196–210.

17. THOMAS, J. G., 'A geographical study of the Eire/Northern Ireland boundary', unpublished M.A. Thesis, University of Wales, 1949.

18. PLATT, R. S., *A Geographical Study of the Dutch-German Border*, Münster Westfalen, 1958, p. 72.

19. FOX, C., *Offa's Dyke: A Field Survey of the Western Frontier-works of Mercia in the Seventh and Eighth Centuries A.D.*, British Academy, London, 1955.

20. MARSHALL, G., 'The defences of the city of Hereford', *Trans. Woolhope Nat. Field Club*, 1940, pp. 67–78.

21. STEWART, C., *A Prospect of Cities*, Longmans, 1952, p. 62.

22. PIRENNE, H., *Medieval Cities*, Princeton University Press, 1925.

23. CARTER, H., *The Towns of Wales*, University of Wales Press, 1965, p. 13.

24. HORSFALL-TURNER, E. R., *A Municipal History of Llanidloes*, Llanidloes, John Ellis, 1908, p. 24.

25. CARTER, *The Towns of Wales*, pp. 32–50.

26. *Henrici de Bracton de Legibus et Consuetudinibus Angliae*, ed. and English trans. by SIR TRAVERS TWISS, Longmans, 1880, vol. 3, pp. 583–6.

27. BIRCH, W. DE GRAY, *The Historical Charters and Constitutional Documents of the City of London*, London, Whiting, 1884, p. 50.

28. PEASE, J. G. and CHITTY, H., *A Treatise on the Law of Markets and Fairs*, London, Knight, 1899, p. 76.

29. MORGAN, F. C., 'Hereford presentments, 1611 to 1659', *Trans. Woolhope Nat. Field Club*, 1940, p. 84.

30. CARTER, *The Towns of Wales*, pp. 43–44.

31. HOWSE, W. H., *Radnorshire*, Hereford, Thurston, 1949, p. 299.

32. BOWEN, E. G., *Wales: A Physical, Historical and Regional Geography*, Methuen, 1957, p. 221.

33. *Report on Markets and Fairs in England and Wales, I: General Review*, Min. of Agr. and Fish., Econ. Ser., No. 13, HMSO, 1927, pp. 37–8.

34. MENDENHALL, T. C., *The Shrewsbury Drapers and the Welsh Wool Trade in the XVI and XVII Centuries*, Oxford University Press, 1953.

35. Details of the creation of the Urban District of Llandrindod Wells are contained in the 1901 Census.

36. DAVIES, W. K. D., GIGGS, J. A. and HERBERT, D. T., 'Rate books, directories and the commercial structure of towns', *Geography*, **53**, 1968, pp. 41–54.

37. 'Outlet' and 'establishment' are used interchangeably in this chapter.

38. DAVIES, W. K. D., 'Centrality and the central place hierarchy', *Urban Studies*, **4**, 1967, p. 63.

39. POWELL, J. M., 'An Economic Geography of Montgomeryshire in the Nineteenth Century', unpublished M.A. Thesis, University of Liverpool, 1962, p. 53.

40. The grading accepted in this Chapter is the most common grouping of centres derived from dispersions of index values. These dispersions were based on various combinations of functions within an overall total of 125 functions.

41. *Report on Markets and Fairs in England and Wales*, 1927, p. 39.

42. *Depopulation in Mid-Wales*, HMSO, London, 1964; LOMAS, G. M., 'Population changes and functional regions', *J. Tn Plann. Inst.*, **50**, 1964, pp. 21–31.

43. *The Development of Agriculture*, Cmnd 2738, HMSO, London, 1965, p. 6.

44. JONES, H. R., 'A study of rural migration in central Wales', *Trans. Inst. Br. Geogr.*, **37**, 1965, p. 41.

45. *Ibid.*, p. 42.

46. HOUSE, J. W. and KNIGHT, E. M., *Migrants of North-East England*, Papers on Migration and Mobility in North-East England, No. 2. University of Newcastle upon Tyne, 1965, p. 20.

47. WEBB, J. W., 'The natural and migrational components of population changes in England and Wales, 1921–1931', *Econ. Geogr.*, **39**, 1963, pp. 130–48.

48. DAVIES, W. K. D., *Tijdschr. econ. soc. Geogr.*, 1965, p. 224.

49. CURRY, L., 'The geography of service centres within towns: the elements of an operational approach', *Proceedings of the I.G.U. Symposium in Urban Geography*, *Lund*, 1960, pp. 31–53. Gleerup, Lund, 1962.

50. *Ibid.*, p. 52.

51. *Ibid.*, p. 53.

52. BERRY, B. J. L., *Geography of Market Centers and Retail Distribution*, Prentice-Hall, 1967, p. 91.

53. LÖSCH, *The Economics of Location*, p. 120.

54. DAVIES, W. K. D., *Tijdschr. econ. soc. Geogr.*, 1965, pp. 224–5.

55. For literature in this field see footnotes in BERRY, *Geography of Market Centres and Retail Distribution*, pp. 89–105.

56. PALOMÄKI, M., 'The functional centres and areas of South Bothnia, Finland', *Fennia*, **88**, 1964, p. 79.

57. CURRY, L., *Lund Symposium*, pp. 52–3.

58. HODDER, B. W., 'Rural periodic markets in part of Yorubaland', *Trans. Inst. Br. Geogr.*, **29**, 1961, pp. 149–59; *id.*, 'The Yoruba rural market', in P. Bohannan and G. Dalton, eds., *Markets in Africa*, Northwestern University Press, 1962, Ch. 4.

59. BELSHAW, C. S., *Traditional Exchange and Modern Markets*, Prentice-Hall, 1965, p. 55.

60. SKINNER, G. W., 'Marketing and social structure in rural China', *J. Asian Stud.*, **24**, 1964–5, pp. 3–43; 195–228; 363–99.

61. This survey comprises part of a research project by the author: 'The distribution of central places in Mid-Wales and the middle Welsh Borderland', Ph.D. thesis, University of Wales, Aberystwyth (in preparation).

62. *Ibid.*

63. *A New Town in Mid-Wales*, HMSO, London, 1966.

64. *Expansion at Rhayader*, Report to the Mid-Wales Industrial Development Association by Planning Consultants, 1967.

65. GARBETT-EDWARDS, D. P., 'The development of Mid-Wales— a new phase', *Town and Country Planning*, **35**, 1967, pp. 349–50.

66. *Mid Wales '67*, The Mid-Wales Industrial Development Association, Tenth Annual Report, p. 23.

67. HODDER, *Trans. Inst. Br. Geogr.*, 1961, p. 158.

CHAPTER 11

URBAN PROBLEMS IN WALES:

THE SPATIAL BACKGROUND

Wayne K. D. Davies and C. Roy Lewis

Throughout its history, Wales has only received attenuated and watered-down versions of urban planning movements that have attained full flower in other parts of Europe.[1] But being on the fringe of European urban civilisation has meant more than this. Ideas have usually taken rather a long time to penetrate to the region, so that the new urban forms have always been rather late in appearance. Today Wales cannot afford to remain in the backwater of planning movements. The new mobility and scale of urban life necessitates a radical rethinking of the urban pattern, and nothing is more important in this than the need to view the Welsh urban network as a system of towns, not as a series of disconnected nodes. It is the objective of this last chapter to sketch the background to the major problems of the network in the light of the evidence revealed in the preceding chapters. This does not mean that the chapter is in any sense a review of the academic problems dealt with by each of the contributors to this set of essays, or that a comprehensive plan for Welsh towns will be outlined. Given the small number of towns surveyed, and the limited academic problems dealt with, such objectives would be presumptuous. However, it has been suggested time and time again that the academic problems isolated in these chapters all have some applied value, even if it only consists of isolating the extent of a problem (e.g. substandardness in Chapter 3), defining the commercial sizes of towns (Chapters 9 and 10), or demonstrating the nature of the decisions that are involved in the creation of an urban area (Chapter 4). Given these possible applications, and the fact that the problems of Welsh towns are rarely looked at on a national scale, and are infrequently studied in spatial terms, it was felt necessary to outline a geographical interpretation of the Welsh urban network.

Regional planning is at last an accepted, if not a fully operational technique in Britain. But integrated proposals that adequately define and stress the functional role and relations of towns in regional schemes are still few and far between. Most towns in Britain still exist as administrative enclaves, cut off and frequently in dispute with their surroundings. In an increasingly urban world such a situation seems intolerable, and the prospects for change are not particularly bright if towns are continually viewed in local terms. In Wales few signs of a breakaway from this attitude can be seen in official circles, for two recent reports from the Welsh Office fail to tackle, in any fundamental sense, the problems of the Welsh urban network. Thus, *Wales: The Way Ahead*[2] is merely an emasculated economic report that fails to deal with such crucial sectors of the economy as the service industry, and makes no attempt to lay down any viable planning guidelines for future urban development or integration. Fortunately the White Paper on local government[3] recognises the need for positive integration, but its proposals perpetuate most of the existing anomalies by a policy aimed at grouping existing government units. Only lip service is paid to the contemporary pattern of society (Chapter 2) and no attempt is made to integrate the ideas with the economic plan or with such other administrative changes as the recent spatial reorganisation of the police force and judiciary. No attempt has been made to define the hierarchy of urban units in Wales, nor to interrelate individual parts of the network, adapting each unit to the needs of the region in which it is situated.

This recognition of the fundamental role of towns in modern society may present a problem in Wales. Even the pill of acceptance of Wales as an urban society may be particularly hard to swallow since Wales has traditionally been, and has been romanticised as, a rural society. Also, even the industrialisation that at first sight should have destroyed community feelings and integration, has preserved and fostered cultural cohesion, albeit in a slightly different form. How much of this can be attributed to the Welsh character or to the community of interest provided by the workplace is impossible to estimate. Yet the urban form that developed surely played some part in this retention. Industrial development often took the form of relatively small communities sprawled along the valleys of South Wales. A local awareness and identity grew up in these areas that might otherwise be lacking in a sprawling metropolis.

Now the curtain has risen on a new scene. Another set of problems threatens the historic pattern that has developed. Depopulation in rural Wales follows from the contraction of employment in primary production, particularly in agriculture, a process that is modifying the existing rural and market town structure (Chapter 10). In the industrial areas of South Wales, the employment prospects that once drew people into the narrow valleys are increasingly limited. New growth is concentrated along the coast. The valleys are declining in population, their urban structure is frequently in decay (Chapter 3). All this is accompanied by an accelerating urban sprawl along the coast and Vale of Glamorgan. Must sprawl be the concomitant of prosperity?

Solutions to these problems are still piecemeal, limited in scope and areal context. Yet it seems essential to view the problem as a whole. Certainly the background needs to be understood if rational solutions are to be *derived from*, rather than *imposed on*, Wales. But since many of the forces for change have a worldwide distribution, solutions should be tempered by an awareness of what has happened elsewhere.

RURAL WALES

Rural Wales is the repository of Welsh culture. Inevitably the continued depopulation of the area has a cultural as well as an economic significance. Yet cultural considerations should not obscure the fact that depopulation is not a peculiarity of Mid-Wales. It is present in all rural areas of the western world. The drift from the land may be inevitable in view of modern farming practices, but it is nevertheless disconcerting.

One characteristic migration pattern of a rural surplus is a movement to the local town. The population change is not a loss, but a redistribution. Today the migration from country to town can still be recognised, but it has changed in scale; the movement is focused not on all towns, but only on the largest cities. This has long been the pattern of migration from rural Wales, the local towns remain small and largely undeveloped. With one or two exceptions they have stagnated or show a very slow growth rate, a decay all the more remarkable if the absolute figures are compared with the booming towns of other parts of Britain. Indeed, it seems that the basic problem of Welsh towns stems from their size. They are not large enough to attract and sustain even small-scale growth industries. Some industrial growth has certainly occurred under the stimulus of development associations

19

and government assistance, but even this has not halted the out-migration, it has only marginally ameliorated the situation. Consequently the question must be posed as to why the towns of rural Wales are so small. What is the background to this basic problem that affects their present-day growth?

(1) The major function of the towns of rural Wales is to serve the countryside with goods and services. They act as distribution nodes. But since Wales is a relatively poorly endowed agricultural area the dependent rural population is smaller than the richer lowland areas of England or Europe. Inevitably the service centres depending on this rural support are smaller in Wales. So it is not surprising that the major regional centres of rural Wales such as Carmarthen, Aberystwyth and Brecon are smaller than their English counterparts, Worcester, Hereford and Winchester. Since initial size is now one of the determinants of growth the future prospects are not particularly good.

(2) Towns have functions other than this element of service to their immediate hinterland or service area. Most of the towns of rural Wales grew to their present size in the nineteenth century by the appearance of additional economic functions (Chapters 7, 8, 10). For instance, woollen manufacturing in the Severn valley and sea-borne trading along the coast before the railway era, added to the prosperity of centres. Others grew as a result of more specialised functions. One of the most outstanding examples is Llandrindod Wells, its rapid growth being associated with its development as an inland resort and spa town.

In this century specialisation of production and centralisation of manufacturing and distribution has removed many rural industries. The towns become only distribution points. Slate and lead mines have decayed. Inland spas are no longer fashionable. Once thriving towns are mere shadows of themselves, not so much, it is important to stress, in absolute terms, for the problem concerning us is a relative decay. Cities become larger and larger, places that stagnate lag further and further behind. They are left to serve their immediate hinterland with goods and services. In other words, the towns of rural Wales have not succeeded in accreting enough additional functions to allow expansion.

(3) Finally a set of location factors must be incorporated with these major considerations.

Most thriving rural areas of Britain are not really 'rural' at all (Chapter 7). They are the areas near prosperous cities that have been subjected to the overspill of industrial and residential growth. Distance from industrial growth points seems to be a major determinant in the prosperity of these so-called 'rural' areas. Rural Wales is outside this zone of overflow, at least at present. But it is instructive to remember that the actual distances from much of east Wales to the larger metropolitan centres would not be such a great drawback in terms of the overspill of prosperity in a North American context. The tighter spatial grouping of British industry, the lower mobility, and certainly the attitudes of industrialists towards these so-called remote areas, does seem to account for a continued isolation from what may be termed a spontaneous overflow. But if increased mobility becomes as characteristic as in North America such isolation may be broken down.

Nor should the influence of the physical background be forgotten. The central upland core is fringed by coastal plateaux and pene-trated by narrow valleys. This has produced fragmented areas of agricultural potential. Inevitably, a peripheral distribution of towns is derived. But more important than the pattern is the consequence of this distribution. The growth of any town is restricted by the size of the fragmentary region unless some overwhelming economic function provides a stimulus for growth unrelated to service for the local area. (For instance, the coal export trade provided such a stimulus for Cardiff.) Elsewhere, in rural Wales, such overwhelming stimuli were absent. The growth of towns was limited by their areal position, they were unable to dominate large regions. Industrial growth, if it was present, was small-scale or transitory. The result is that the larger towns on the English side of the border have come to serve consider-able areas of Wales (Chapters 2 and 10). Not for nothing has Shrews-bury been called the capital of Wales.

Given this situation in rural Wales it seems inevitable that the recent proposal to build a new town in Mid-Wales is an attractive solution[4]. A new start, moreover a new urban start, can be given to the area. Taken in isolation the scheme seems more than useful. Growth must, in this age, be based on a town. But when the scheme is placed within the context of Wales, rather than part of Mid-Wales, its limitations are apparent.

Will a new town between Llanidloes and Newtown help to check depopulation in Caernarvonshire or Breconshire? Are these and other areas to be left to fend for themselves simply because the same problem does not have the publicity associated with the extreme case?

The proposed location of the new town also raises many questions. Surely it is too far up the Severn Valley to serve as a regional centre? Would not a new town in the area merely accelerate the decline of the existing smaller centres and accelerate rural depopulation? Will a centre of the proposed size be large enough to attract growth industries? Even assuming that these questions are adequately answered it does seem that the limited brief given to the consultants represents a fundamental error. Must the cost of the solution to this area be at the expense of other areas?

But what is the alternative to doing nothing? Schemes have already been aired for developing Aberystwyth and creating a sub-metropolis of 250,000.[5] Superficially this scheme is also attractive. Certainly this size should be large enough to sustain growth, but again this solution has only a limited spatial relevance to one part of rural Wales. Other areas of Britain qualify just as well for such expansion, and this location does not, given the scale of the project, seem the best location in view of local site conditions. At a time of economic strain the cost of such a huge expansion would also seem to be prohibitive in any order of priorities. It is true that the problem of depopulation would be obliterated, at least in one small area, but only by annihilation of part of the Cambrian coast.

Such proposals represent partial solutions that bear limited relevance to a widespread problem. In this connection it would seem more useful to use the experience already derived from a study of the whole network of Welsh towns. If the root of the problem lies in the fact that existing towns are too small, why not enlarge them? If the towns in some areas are too small, yet are also too near each other and share regional functions, why not group them together?

Complete dependence on the land as we knew it in the past has vanished. Growth must be concentrated on urban nodes. So rather than allow towns to pursue their own attempts to attract industry and to draft their own redevelopment plans in isolation it would be better to encourage them to create some supra-administrative structure. Instead of fragmentary growth related to existing small centres, it might be more useful in some areas to look to the problems of the future and channel growth and expansion on to the linear link between them. Joint development plans for the superstructure of a future linear town could then be created with government aid. The existing older forms would make historic bastions at either end.

A linear solution could be applied in many areas of Wales. The best possibilities for such linked growth would seem to be between Bangor and Caernarvon (Menai?), Newtown and Welshpool (Powys?), and Builth Wells and Llandrindod Wells (Ffynnon?). In Pembrokeshire the piecemeal development within the middle sections of Milford Haven seems shortsighted. A magnificent site deserves a town worthy of it, given the needs and existing industrial potential of the area. A linear town embracing both shores and using all the existing settlements (outside the two stretches of National Park) as nodal points would seem to be the most attractive scheme. Perhaps it would finally remove the spectre of unemployment that continually haunts the haven.

Yet linear solutions are not feasible in all regions of Wales, for in some areas only one town is dominant. Many of the larger regional centres are already showing their superiority as employment centres, the result of forces of economic rationalisation. Detailed demographic analysis has confirmed this. The adoption of centres such as Aberystwyth, Brecon, and Carmarthen as development nodes will mean adequate provision for the farming community and at the same time provide employment opportunity in industrial and service expansion, if such tendencies are positively strengthened. Hence the necessary urban expansion should be based on linear groupings in some areas, and on isolated nodes in areas dominated by one town.

Obsession with industrial growth seems misplaced in an age of the expanding service sector. Aberystwyth has derived important growth from educational and administrative functions. It is to be hoped that any new urban area in the Severn valley would possess an important administrative sector, if it is not to become another isolated Welsh industrial town. National functions, such as the Welsh Office and educational institutions, could be relocated here, though such a proposal may be far too radical. Yet if adopted, benefits would not only flow to this town, congestion in the Cardiff area might be slightly relieved, and perhaps North and Mid-Wales would be drawn less closely into the already congested nets of Liverpool and Birmingham.

The first step is to create adequate administrative machinery to develop these centres and to plan adequate transport links to enable them to carry out their regional functions. It would be encouraging if existing authorities recognised the problems created by their size and produced expansion and twinning schemes on the lines suggested, rather than waiting for them to be imposed or for the towns to stagnate in their present independent state. Benefits would accrue to the whole area, not just to the locality.

But what is happening? Fortunately the new linear town proposal for the Upper Severn has been quietly shelved by the Welsh Office and replaced by a scheme aimed at expanding existing centres. This is in line with the ideas sketched above, but it seems to have been brought about not by the creation of a deliberate plan based upon a detailed survey of the area, but by political motivation—the need to satisfy leaders in the various communities involved. Moreover some of the towns chosen for development, for instance Rhayader, seem far too small, and will probably experience recurring crises as firms move in and out as part of general economic change. Also few comments have been made about the retirement potential of these centres, probably because the in-migration consists mainly of elderly people and this, in an age obsessed with economic growth, is largely a wasting asset (Chapter 8). Yet it does need to be catered for.

No attempt has been made to recognise the spread of suburbanisation (Chapter 7) round these small towns or to try to channel future development on to the links between existing areas and to deal with distances in motor age time, not walking time. But at least, subject to a more rational choice of centres, a start in the right direction has been made—however this policy was initiated. It remains to develop these beginnings coherently by recognising, first that the basis for viable units of 40,000 population exists (Bangor and Caernarvon are already halfway there), and secondly that the economic benefits are not restricted to the towns. Large-scale commuting already exists and spreads the benefits of future development to the villages around. Indeed if one accepts the not unreasonable half-hour driving time for the journey to work, these benefits will spread from ten to fifteen miles from the development nodes (cf. medieval market distances referred to in Chapter 10) and will effectively incorporate most of the more densely populated areas of rural Wales.

INDUSTRIAL SOUTH WALES

In rural Wales, urban and regional problems revolve around the fact that the towns are too small. In many parts of industrial South Wales the opposite is true. Many of the settlements are too large for their present and projected functions. The locally orientated mining communities are vanishing, just as the iron towns did before them. All the settlements are being drawn into a wider orbit. Economic change is upon us.

What makes this economic change so important from an urban point of view is that a locational change is taking place at the same time. Growth is increasingly concentrated in the lowland zone between the coalfield and the Bristol Channel. The major nodes in the zone, Swansea—Port Talbot, and more especially Barry—Cardiff, and Newport, have been the areas of most rapid increase, a trend that will continue and be emphasised with the development of Severnside.

It is this locational change that forms the heart of the urban problem in South Wales. Moreover, the need to accommodate the declining valley settlements in any plan makes the situation especially acute. There is no clean slate on which to work. Already the problems are obvious. The employment prospects in many valleys are far from good, many of the settlements are already dormitory settlements for the growth zone, while the urban structure badly needs renewing. Thus renewal proposals must be integrated with the growth zones.

In the rapidly growing coastal belt the problem is also one of distribution. Growth must be channelled to avoid creating the sprawl that everywhere seems to accompany the expansion of motor age cities. The alternative to adequate plans is an urban chaos in which the environment is ruined. The spoliation of the coal valleys in the last 100 years bears grim testimony to what will happen if adequate and integrated plans are not forthcoming.

Yet South Wales has been fortunate in one sense. The urban complexity and chaos of other industrial regions of equal size has been avoided so far. Basically this is due to the type of development that has occurred, and also to the physical build of the area. A linear form has developed. Local nodes exist within this framework, with the major focal points having crystallised around the ports.

To all exponents of the motor age city such an existing, though decayed, linear arrangement should be immediately attractive. Given the integration of small settlements into a wide urban region, and the increasing use of the motor car, it seems impossible to allow ease of access in all directions, unless one wants to create a miniature Los Angeles. It is increasingly recognised in the U.S.A. that the best form of growth in such circumstances is to channel it along the lines of communication from the major nodes. No wonder the Washington D.C. planners found the linear corridor so attractive when they were faced with an urban sprawl that would have joined the city to Baltimore.

But what has happened in South Wales? Depopulation of the valleys, the decay of their industrial, residential, and communication bases, have not made any of the existing valley corridors particularly attractive. Moreover many of the vital rail links have been cut in recent years. Schemes aimed at scattering light industry throughout the valleys have only slightly improved the situation. Concentrated industrial zones seem to be the most successful, though even these are snarled up at peak hour periods by inadequate transport links.

Faced with such a situation the immediate impulse is to get out and implement a holding policy. This is what has happened. Growth is expected and encouraged along the coastal belt, but fortunately the dangers of wholesale expansion are recognised. Cardiff and south-east Glamorgan are expected to experience the greatest pressure according to the recent Glamorgan Planning Report, but unfortunately the solution leaves much to be desired. A new town of 130,000 is envisaged at Llantrisant, while Barry is also to be expanded. The problem is, of course, one of scale. The centre of the new town will only be seven miles away from Cardiff. Whether one intends it or not, such proximity will create a great deal of interaction, and the eventual growth of a great urban blob in south-east Glamorgan, separated not by a green belt, but what will become in time a large urban park.

Again, these proposals do not seem to bear any relevance to the creation of a future Severnside, or to Newport. Is the expansion west of Cardiff conditioned by the position of the Monmouthshire boundary? Can we afford to plan within county boundaries that are the arbitrary results of historical accidents?

In many ways, therefore, the urban future of South Wales does not seem particularly bright. A linear framework, however much decayed, already exists, and seems the best possible adaptation to the motor age. Given adequate transport links it does not seem particularly relevant that each community is self-sufficient in industry. Already many settlements are dormitory centres. Why not channel this trend and adapt it? The nodes and primary growth zone could still be on the coast. There is no necessity for all new houses to be within shouting distance of factories. Few people walk to work today, and the distances involved in the area are small. Given transportation management on the 'tidal flow' basis for peak periods, and adequate links (whether road or rail) capable of accommodating speeds of 50–60 m.p.h., most places can be within a forty-minute journey of the major nodes of Cardiff, Newport and Swansea. Thus, it is not self-sufficiency or vast urban sprawl that are alternatives. Another alternative can be recognised once the existing framework is recreated and adapted. Linear development should be stimulated in many (though obviously not all) of the existing areas, and created elsewhere. But these developments should be focused on the already functioning nodes at Swansea, Bridgend, Cardiff, and Newport. As always, such proposals wait upon the creation of an adequate regional transport net, not only for Glamorgan but for all South Wales. Without it, chaos is increasingly likely.

CONCLUSION

The relief of Wales, valley and relatively narrow coastal plain, seems ideally suited to some form of linear development. Historically, and in a regional sense, the linear channelling of movement has always been important. Now added momentum has been given to this spatial conditioning by the rapid transit provided by motor transport. If the form is being developed out of necessity in uniform areas on the American continent it is surprising that it has not been proposed as a planning guide in an area that already possesses the framework.

Linear development would eliminate much of the unnecessary competition existing between many places in rural Wales, and would circumvent the problems of individual towns too small to act as focal points for sub-regional growth. Regional trade areas would be integrated and extended rather than split up among small centres.

Even socially the linear form has much to recommend it. Existing small towns and settlements could be preserved within this larger framework, and additional communities could be absorbed. All would contribute to the whole and would preserve their individual community life without becoming submerged in the anonymity of a large urban complex. Self-sufficient communities, work-place and residence in close proximity, have gone for ever. Why not recognise the fact and plan for it?

Most of the discussion has centred around the problems of rural Wales and industrial South Wales. There are other problem areas. The need to integrate the urban region focused upon Wrexham and to develop Deeside are probably equally pressing, while the North Wales coast presents even greater problems as well as a warning against uncoordinated linear sprawl. Even here the structure of an important regional grouping suggests itself in the integration of Colwyn Bay,

20

Llandudno and Conway. Urban sprawl has given the link. To fight for continued separation seems parochial in this metropolitan age.

The separation of town from country, and suburbs from cities, are problems that exist in all western countries. They will not be solved merely by regional planning that does not integrate towns with their regions. Historically, an urban way of life has been alien to Wales. The urban forms that developed were only faint copies of more splendid examples elsewhere. Despite industrialisation, some of the aspects of life prized by the Welsh survived in what is an urban environment. Given an inevitable urban future, not a peasant society, can we afford to repeat the mistakes of the past? Can we remain at the fringe of urban movements, accepting half-hearted and inadequate proposals of urban form? The framework exists: imaginative implementation of some alternative to rural decay or metropolitan sprawl must be forthcoming.

REFERENCES

1. CARTER, H., *The Towns of Wales*, University of Wales Press, 1965.

2. *Wales: The Way Ahead*, Welsh Office. Cmnd. 3334, HMSO, Cardiff, 1967.

3. *Local Government in Wales*, Welsh Office, Cmnd 3340, HMSO, Cardiff, 1967.

4. ECONOMIC ASSOCIATES (Consultants), *A New Town in Mid-Wales*, HMSO, London, 1966.

5. MOUNFIELD, P. R., 'Aberystwyth: growth point?' *Town and Country Planning*, **34**, 1966.

POSTSCRIPT

During the two years between the writing of these essays and the production of this book many major planning reports dealing with Welsh towns have appeared, whilst many important Government decisions have been made. Inevitably, these reports and decisions will have a significant effect on the future pattern of development of Welsh towns. Although the subject matter of the essays in this book is not dominantly concerned with planning problems it was thought necessary, for the sake of completeness, to include some reference to these reports and decisions. Naturally a complete survey of this material would form the subject of a book in itself, so only a brief but, it is thought, representative sample of the type of material available is provided. It is to be hoped that this will indicate the range of material that has appeared and will provide a starting point for further study by interested readers. A note of caution should be added, that some of the reports mentioned are not generally available to the public.

(1) *New towns, overspill and expansion schemes*
    (*a*) Completed reports are available for:
        Cardiff: *Cardiff: Development and Transportation Study.* A report to Cardiff City Council prepared by Colin Buchanan and Partners. April 1968.
        Part of the debate following from this report is given in BARR, J., 'Cardiff: divided city', *New Society*, No. 345, May 1969, pp. 701–4.
        Llantrisant: *Llantrisant: Prospects for Urban Growth.* Report prepared by Colin Buchanan and Partners. April 1969. Obtainable H.M.S.O.
        Mid-Wales: *A New Town in Mid-Wales.* A report to the Secretary of State for Wales by Economic Associates Ltd., H.M.S.O., 1966. The scheme submitted in this report was shelved in its original form; a Mid-Wales Development Corporation was set up in December 1967 with the initial task of expanding Newtown. Planning proposals were completed in November 1968.

    (*b*) Feasibility studies have been written for:
        Builth Wells: *Builth Wells Town Expansion.* A report published by Builth Wells Town Expansion Committee. May 1968.

Aberaeron: *The Aberaeron Report.* A report to Aberaeron U.D.C., prepared by the Department of Geography, University College of Wales, Aberystwyth. March 1968.

Rhayader: *Expansion of Rhayader.* A report to the Mid-Wales Industrial Development Association, prepared by Sir Percy Thomas and Son, Architects and Planning Consultants. March 1967.

Lampeter: *The Expansion of Lampeter.* A report to the Mid-Wales Industrial Development Association, prepared by the Department of Economics, University College of Wales, Aberystwyth. 1967.

Bala: *The Expansion of Bala.* A report by local authorities. 1967.

(A referendum was held on the expansion of Bala in 1968. The inhabitants of the town and surrounding area rejected the expansion proposals.)

(c) Feasibility studies are in progress for:

Deeside project: planning and engineering studies in progress by consultants. Findings to be submitted to the Welsh Office in 1970.

Severnside project: planning study in progress. Welsh Office.

(2) *Urban renewal*

(a) General:

Welsh Housing Condition Survey. Welsh Office, 1969.

(This latest survey of substandard property revealed that 90,000 unfit houses were present in Wales. This figure represents a considerable increase on previous totals, but is similar to the figure arrived at by D. W. Drakakis-Smith in Chapter 3.)

Feasibility studies are in progress for:

Rhondda Valleys. Building Design Partnership Ltd., Belfast. Due 1970/1.

Aber Valley (Caerphilly). This Urban Renewal Project is designed to act as a model for twilight area development in the industrial valleys of South Wales.

(b) Shopping Centres:

Practically all shopping centres have had some renewal schemes. Among the major developments for which planning permission has been granted are those for Port Talbot, Bridgend, Newport and Ebbw Vale.

(c) Conservation Schemes:

Although no reports on the scale of the Chester, Bath and York reports for England have been prepared, signs of interest in these problems do exist:

   (i) The Civic Trust for Wales has attempted to influence the creation of more attractive townscapes, e.g. *Llandeilo*, a report prepared by the Civic Trust for Wales and the Llandeilo Civic Trust Society. August 1967, *The Rhondda Valleys: Proposals for the transformation of an environment*. Civic Trust. April 1965

  (ii) *Llantrisant: a Welsh hill town*. A report prepared by G. Cullen and Associates, and produced by Glamorgan County Council, April 1968.

 (iii) Of wider interest, and related to urban renewal, is the study of the Lower Swansea Valley: HILTON, K. J. (ed.) *Lower Swansea Valley Project*, Longmans, London, 1967.

(3) *Transportation surveys*

   (a) Transportation surveys are currently in progress (1969) for Monmouthshire, Glamorgan and Swansea.

   (b) Individual reports have also appeared for smaller towns, e.g. Aberystwyth: *Aberystwyth Transportation Survey*. A report to Cardiganshire County Planning Committee prepared by C. H. Dobbie and Partners, Consulting Engineers. October 1968.

   (c) The Severn Bridge Project, a study undertaken by the Department of Economics, Swansea University, Newport College of Technology and Bath University (in progress).

(4) *General economic and political change*

   (a) Hunt Committee report. *The Intermediate Areas*, Cmnd. 3998, H.M.S.O., 1969.

   (b) *Roads for the Future*. Green Paper, Ministry of Transport, H.M.S.O., 1969.

   (c) Amendments to Local Government White Paper (1967). Welsh Office. November 1968.

GENERAL INDEX

INDEX OF PLACE NAMES